Lecture Notes in Computer Science 9559

Commenced Publication in 1973
Founding and Former Series Editors:
Gerhard Goos, Juris Hartmanis, and Jan van Leeuwen

More information about this series at http://www.springer.com/series/7407

Shaoying Liu · Zhenhua Duan (Eds.)

Structured Object-Oriented Formal Language and Method

5th International Workshop, SOFL+MSVL 2015
Paris, France, November 6, 2015
Revised Selected Papers

 Springer

Editors
Shaoying Liu
Hosei University
Koganei-shi, Tokyo
Japan

Zhenhua Duan
Xidian University
Xi'an, Shaanxi
China

ISSN 0302-9743   ISSN 1611-3349 (electronic)
Lecture Notes in Computer Science
ISBN 978-3-319-31219-4   ISBN 978-3-319-31220-0   (eBook)
DOI 10.1007/978-3-319-31220-0

Library of Congress Control Number: 2016933476

LNCS Sublibrary: SL1 – Theoretical Computer Science and General Issues

Printed on acid-free paper

This Springer imprint is published by Springer Nature
The registered company is Springer International Publishing AG Switzerland

Preface

Practical software development requires effective but simple development methods with efficient tool support. How to achieve such methods and support still remains a challenge for the formal methods and software engineering research communities. The development of the Structured Object-Oriented Formal Language (SOFL) over the last two decades has shown some possibilities of achieving effective integrations to build practical formal techniques and tool support for requirements analysis, specification, design, inspection, review, and testing of software systems. SOFL integrates data flow diagram, Petri nets, and VDM-SL to offer a graphical and formal notation for writing specifications; a three-step approach to requirements acquisition and system design; specification-based inspection and testing methods for detecting errors in both specifications and programs; and a set of tools to support modeling and verification. Meanwhile, the Modeling, Simulation and Verification Language (MSVL) is a parallel programming language developed over the last decade. Its supporting tool MSV has been developed to enable us to model, simulate, and verify a system formally. The two languages complement each other.

Following the success of the previous SOFL workshops, the 5th International Workshop on SOFL+MSVL (SOFL+MSVL 2015) was jointly organized in Paris by Shaoying Liu's research group at Hosei University, Japan, and Zhenhua Duan's research group at Xidian University, China, with the aim of bringing industrial, academic, and government experts and practitioners of SOFL or MSVL to communicate and to exchange ideas. The workshop attracted 22 submissions on modeling, specification, verification, model checking, testing, debugging, transformation, and algorithms. Each submission was rigorously reviewed by two or three Program Commitee members on the basis of technical quality, relevance, significance, and clarity, and 15 papers were accepted for publication in the workshop proceedings. The acceptance rate is approximately 68 %.

We would like to thank ICFEM 2015 for supporting the organization of the workshop and all of the Program Committee members for their great efforts and cooperation in reviewing and selecting papers. We would also like to thank all of the participants for attending presentation sessions and actively joining discussions at the workshop. Finally, our gratitude goes to Alfred Hofmann and Anna Kramer of Springer in their continuous support in the publication of the workshop proceedings.

November 2015

Shaoying Liu
Zhenhua Duan

Organization

Program Committee

Shaoying Liu (Co-chair)	Hosei University, Japan
Zhenhua Duan (Co-chair)	Xidian University, China
Yuting Chen	Shanghai Jiaotong University, China
Stefan Gruner	University of Pretoria, South Africa
Gihwon Kwon	Kyonggi University, Korea
Richard Lai	La Trobe University, Australia
Karl Leung	Hong Kong Institute of Vocational Education, SAR China
Mo Li	Hosei University, Japan
Xiaohong Li	Tianjin University, China
Weikai Miao	East China Normal University, China
Fumiko Nagoya	Aoyama Gakuyin University, Japan
Shin Nakajima	National Institute of Informatics (NII), Japan
Kazuhiro Ogata	JAIST, Japan
Shengchao Qin	Teesside University, UK
Fenggang Shi	Thales Canada Transportation Solutions, Canada
Wuwei Shen	Western Michigan University, USA
Jing Sun	University of Auckland, New Zealand
Kenji Taguchi	AIST, Japan
Cong Tian	Xidian University, China
Xi Wang	Shanghai University, China
Xinfeng Shu	Xi'an University of Posts and Telecommunications, China
Jinyun Xue	Jiangxi Normal University, China
Xiaobing Wang	Xidian University, China
Haitao Zhang	JAIST, Japan
Hong Zhu	Oxford Brookes University, UK

Contents

Algorithm and Transformation

Modeling and Specification

Genericity in PAR Platform

Jinyun Xue[⊠]

State International S&T Cooperation Base of Networked Supporting Software,
JiangXi Normal University, Nanchang 330022, China
jinyun@vip.sina.com

Abstract. The main purpose of genericity in high lever programming language is to increase efficiency of software development and the safety and reusability of software. Genericity is the useful tool to implement generative software development and MDA. However, few modelling language has genericity mechanism and the mechanisms in typical programming language, say C++, Java, etc., is not sufficiently and is not ease to use. The situation in PAR platform is quite different. PAR platform supports Model Driven Software Engineering (MDE) and consists of algorithm modelling language Radl, abstract program modelling language Apla, a set of rules for the model transformation and a set of automatic transformation tools of algorithm model and program model. One of the distinct features of the PAR platform is the agile genericity mechanisms. In PAR not only a value, a data type and a computing-action (including operator, method, function and procedure, etc.) can be generic parameter, an ADT can be generic parameter also. We present new concepts, say type region, action region and ADT region, which can increase the safety of generic software obviously. The paper will pay special attention to describe the syntax and semantics of the ADT parameter. The case study describes the method to develop generic program with ADT as parameter.

Keywords: PAR method · Platform · Genericity · Generic programming · Generic parameter

1 Introduction

The main purpose of genericity in high lever programming language is to increase the safety and reusability of program and efficiency of software development. Genericity is the important tool to implement generative software development. MDA can be implemented conveniently based on the genericity. However, the current genericity mechanism in typical programming language is not sufficiently and is not ease to use [1–12, 25]. For example, in C++ and Java only type can be as generic parameter; in Ada although type and subprogram can be parameter but there is no constrain mechanism on the parameters that reduces the safety of the corresponding software. This situation can be improved in PAR platform that support Model Driven Software

This research was supported by the National Natural Science Foundation of China under Grant No. 61020106009, 61272075, 61472167.

S. Liu and Z. Duan (Eds.): SOFL+MSVL 2015, LNCS 9559, pp. 3–14, 2016.
DOI: 10.1007/978-3-319-31220-0_1

Engineering (MDE). In Sect. 2. We give a brief description of the PAR Platform. PAR platform consists of PAR programming methodology, algorithm modelling language Radl, abstract program modelling language Apla, a set of rules for the model transformation and a set of automatic transformation tools of algorithm model and program model. Section 3 present some new definition and concepts about generic mechanisms In PAR not only a value, a data type and a subprogram (including method, function and procedure, etc.) is as generic parameter, but an ADT can be as generic parameter also. The instantiation of the generic program unit is described in Sect. 3. Section 4 shows you a very interesting cases study that related with semiring. The conclusion and future work are given in final Sect. 5.

2 A Brief Description of the PAR Platform

PAR method given in [14–16] is a formal method. It provides the methodology that supports formal development of algorithmic programs described using some executable language, say Ada, Java, C++ and Delphi, from their formal specification. The Forming of PAR is a long term research plan and been supported by a series of national research foundations including NNSF and 863 High-Tech program. It containsseveral key techniques for developing algorithms and programs. The first one is new definition of loop invariant and two new strategies for developing loop invariant [14]. The second one is a unified and systematic approach for designing algorithmic program that is called partition-and-recur [16]. It covers several existed algorithm design techniques including divide-and-conquer, dynamic programming, greedy, enumeration and some nameless methods. The designer of algorithms using PAR can partly avoid the difficulty in making choice among various existed design methods. For supporting formal development of efficient and correct algorithmic programs, we added a lot of formal stuff to partition-and-recur approach and rename the approach as PAR method [19–21]. Using PAR method, we have formally developed many nontrivial algorithmic programs, including graph algorithms [15], travel tree algorithms [21], sorting algorithms [16], array section algorithms and some numeric algorithms [16]. A more convincing example is formal development of Knuth's challenging program that converts a binary fraction to decimal fraction with certain conditions [17, 18]. The PAR method consists of algorithm design language Radl, rules of specification transformation, abstract programming language Apla and PAR platform that is a set of automatic program transformation tools. Recently, we add powerful generic structures to PAR and make it to support convenient generic programming.

2.1 Modeling Language Radl

Radl was designed for the description of algorithm specifications, transformation rules for deriving algorithms and algorithms itself. We presented a set of abstract notations for expressing pre-defined abstract data type, say array, set, sequence, binary tree and graph, etc. The motivation of developing these mathematics-oriented notations is aimed at making specification transformation, algorithm derivation and program proof like operating traditional mathematical formula. The most important notion in PAR method is *recurrence relation of problem solving sequence*, short for *recurrence*. Based on the recurrence the structure of an algorithm is defined as follows:

ALGORITHM:<algorithm name> [<list of type or subroutine parameter

>]

SPECIFICATION:<algorithm specification>

BEGIN: <initialization of variables and functions in the recurrences>
TERMINATION:<termination condition of recuring>

RECUR: < set of recurrences>

END

The Radl expressions have referential transparency that makes the formal derivation of algorithms possible. Radl was designed for the description of algorithm specifications, transformation rules for deriving algorithms and algorithms itself. We presented a set of abstract notations **for** expressing pre-defined data type, say array, set, list, tree, graph and database, etc. Radl provides a user-defined mechanism for abstract data type.

2.2   Rules of Specification Transformation

Most of specification transformation rules are quantifier properties and are proved in [15, 16]. Following are used in this paper. Let θ be an binary operator and big θ be the quantifier of operator θ, then

$$(\theta i : r(i) : f(i))$$

means 'the quantity of f(i) where i range over r(i)'. We write the quantifier of binary operator $+$, $\bullet$, $\wedge$, $\vee$, $\Diamond$(minimum), $\blacklozenge$(maximum), $\cap$(intersection), $\cup$(union) and $\uparrow$ as Σ, Π, $\forall$, $\exists$, $\Diamond$, $\blacklozenge$, $\cap$, $\cup$ and $\uparrow$. Obviously operator $+$, $\bullet$, $\wedge$, $\vee$, $\Diamond$, $\blacklozenge$, $\cap$, $\cup$ are associative and commutative and their quantifier θ have following properties:

(1) Multi-dummies $(\theta\ i,\ j:\ r(j) \wedge s(i,\ j) : f(i,j)) = (\theta\ i:\ r(i):\ (\theta\ j:\ s(i,\ j):\ f(i,\ j)))$
(2) Split with no overlap $(\theta\ i : r(i) : f(i)) = (\theta\ i:\ r(i) \wedge b(i) : f(i))\ \theta\ (\theta\ i:\ r(i) \wedge \neg b(i) : f(i))$
(3) *One point split* $(\theta\ i : 0 \leq i<n + 1: E(i)) = (\theta\ i : 0 \leq i<n: E(i))\ \theta\ E(n)$
(4) Split with overlap if θ is idempotent then
     $(\theta\ i : r(i) \vee s(i) : f(i)) = (\theta\ i : r(i) : f(i))\ \theta\ (\theta\ i : s(i) : f(i))$
     Obviously, binary operator $\wedge$, $\vee$, $\Diamond$, $\blacklozenge$, $\cap$, $\cup$ are idempotent.
(5) *Generalized Split with* overlap if θ is idempotent then
     $(\theta\ i : \exists(j: r(j):p(j,\ i)) : f(i)) = (\theta\ j: r(j) : (\theta\ i : p(j,\ i) : f(i)))$
(6) *Generalized Associativity and Commutativity*
     $(\theta\ i : r(i) : s(i)\ \theta\ f(i)) = (\theta\ i : r(i) : s(i))\ \theta\ (\theta\ i : r(i) : f(i))$

2.3   Modeling Language Apla

The purpose of developing Apla is to implement functional abstract and data abstract in program development perfectly so that any Apla program is simple enough and is ease for understanding, formal derivation or proof. It is also ease to transform into some OOP language programs, say C++, C#, Java, and VB, etc.

Apla is a object-based programming with convenient generics. The purpose of developing Apla is to implement functional abstract and data abstract in program development perfectly so that any Apla program is simple enough and is ease for understanding, formal derivation or proof. It is also ease to transform into some OOP language programs, say C++, Java, C# etc. Apla and Radl have same standard procedures and functions. The data types and Predefined ADTs and are also same. We borrow some control structure from Dijkstra's Guarded Command Language, but restrict the nondeterminism.

2.4   Generic Constructions

Generic programming is parameterized programming. Generic programming makes programming simpler and increases obviously the reusability, security and reliability of programs. Ada and C++ are two popular programming languages that supporting generic programming. Types and subroutines can be parameters in ada and only types can be parameters in C++. However, there is no explicit generic mechanism in Java, Delphi and VB. It is not convenient to implement generic programming using Java, Delphi and VB. There are explicit generic mechanism in Apla and Radl [13, 20, 22–24]. It allows data value, data type and subroutine as parameter of procedure, function and abstract data type. The generic Apla programs can be transformed to generic programs described in Java, C++ and VB. In PAR, one can implement generic programming using programming language that has no explicit generic mechanism [24].

2.5   The New Techniques for Generating Database Application Program

In Radl and Apla, accessing to database is an expression of relational algebra rather than SQL statements. The expression is much simpler and shorter than SQL statement. It gives us one methodology to develop the database application system with high reliability and productivity. This makes formal derivation or proof of a database application program possible.

2.6   Model Automatic Transformation Tools

Radl algorithms and Apla programs are simple enough and ease for formal derivation and proof. But, it cannot be executed in a computer. Therefore, we developed the PAR platform that consists of 5 automatic transformation tools of algorithms or programs. One of them would be able to transform a Radl algorithm into Apla program. Others may transform Apla programs to the programs of target language, says C++ and Java, etc. Based on the PAR platform, the efficiency of developing algorithmic program and reliability of the programs are increased obviously.

2.7   The Application of PAR

Using the approach, we have formally developed many nontrivial algorithmic programs, including graph algorithms [15], travel tree algorithms [21], sorting algorithms
[16], array section algorithms and some numeric algorithms [16]. The Gries' abstract
notation of binary tree [21] was implemented in PAR platform. The abstract
Hopcroft-Tarjan planarity algorithm was described in Apla. The Apla program was
transformed by PAR platform to C++ code that can correctly test the planarity and
generate planar embedding. We developed a bank account query system based on the
relational algebra in Apla. A more convincing example is formal development of Knuth
¢ s challenging program that converts a binary fraction to decimal fraction with certain
condition [17, 18].

3   Genericity Mechanisms in PAR

Currently, the generic mechanisms in typical programming language, say C++, Java,
etc., is not sufficiently and is not ease to use. In C++ and Java, only data type can be
generic formal parameter. There is no computing- action as generic formal parameter.
Few modelling language has genericity mechanism. PAR platform is an exception.
PAR platform supports Model Driven Software Engineering (MDE). One of the distinct features of the PAR platform is the agile genericity mechanisms. In PAR not only
a value, a data type and a computing-action (including operator, method, function and
procedure, etc.) can be generic parameter, but an ADT can be as generic parameter
also. We present new concepts of type region, action region and ADT region, which
can increase the safety of generic software obviously.

3.1   Definitions About Genericity

There are many different definitions about genericity. Some definitions is not precise.
According to our research and understanding about genericity, we have following
definitions about genericity:

Definition 1. Generic Programing (GP): GP is a parameterized programming, where
the parameter can be data (value), data type, action (include operator, subprogram,
function, method and procedure), abstract data type (ADT), component, service etc.;
based on the parameters, design the program with versatility. The parameters are called
as generic formal parameters.

GP is a new programming paradigm that is an extension of traditional programming
with one formal parameter, value or data. In PAR, the type, actor and ADT can be
generic formal parameters.

Definition 2. Generic program unit: Suppose class, function, method, procedure and
ADT are the unit of program. The unit that contains generic formal parameters is called
as generic unit. Therefore we have the concept of generic class, generic procedure,
generic function, generic method and generic ADT.

Definition 3. *Parameter region*: The set of generic formal parameters with common properties is called *parameter region*. Based on the definition, we have the similar definition of the type *region*, *actor region* and *ADT region*. Similar to data variable, we have the concept of *type variable*, *action variable* and *ADT variable*. We use the keyword **somrtype, someaction and someadt** denote the type region, action region and ADT region.

Examples of parameter region:

Type region: sometype = {bool, int, double, char};
Logical operator region: someaction = {∧ ⌐ ∨ ≡ =>};
Set operator region:typeaction = {∩ ∪ ∈}
Satisfying closed semiring ADT region = {(bool, ∨, ∧), (real, ◇, +), ({real, ◆, +), (real, ◆, ◇)}

The concept of the parameter region is very useful in describing the common properties of each category generic formal parameter, which can increase the safety of generic software obviously.

3.2   Type Region and Type Variable

In Radl and Apla, we define the set of types that satisfy some properties as type region and a type parameter in a program unit as type variable.The syntax of the type region declaration is as follows:

sometype = {set of types satisfied some properties};
Following is an example that defines a generic ADT stack with type variable elem:
define ADT stack(sometype elem, [size]);

function push(x:elem):stack;

function pop:elem;

procedure top;
function IsEmpty:boolean;

enddef;
implement ADT Stack(sometype elem, [size]);

......

endimp;
sometype = {integer, char, real|, boolean};
Based on the generic ADT stack, some actual stack type can be produced. Following are some examples:

Adt stack1: new stack(integer, 100) // Define a data type stack whose element type
                                    is integer //and maximal number of stack's
                                    elements is 100.
Adt stack2: new stack(char, 100) // Define a data type stack whose element type is char and
                                    maximal number of stack's elements is 100.

3.3   Action Region and Action Variable

We define the set of all action that satisfy some properties as action region and an action parameter in a program unit as action variable. The syntax of the action region declaration is similar with type region. The action can be the predefined operators of Apla and defined procedures, functions and services by users.

Action region: someaction = {set of actions satisfied some properties};

Following is an example that defines an action region someaction used in InsertSort algorithm.

```
program InsertSort;
procedure sort(someaction comp);
type list=array[0..n-1,integer];
Var a:list; j, i:integer; t:integer;
someaction ={≤, ≥};
begin
foreach(i:0≤i≤n:read(a[i]););
i:=1;
do i≤n→ t,j:=a[i],i-1;
    do (j≥0)∧ (t comp a[j])→a[j+1],j:=a[j],j-1;od;
    a[j+1]:=t;
    i:=i+1;
od;
end.
```

Where comp is action variable

Following is the instantiation statements of the procedure sort which generates sort ascending and sort descending algorithms.

```
procedure sortascending: new Sort (≥);
procedure sortdescending: new Sort (≤);
```

3.4   ADT Region and ADT Variable

The ADT consists of the set of data and the set of operations. The model of ADT can be a algebra system. We define the set of all ADT that satisfy some properties as ADT region and an ADT parameter in a program unit as ADT variable. The syntax of the action region declaration is similar with type region.

ADT region: someadt = {set of ADT satisfied some properties};

Example:

someadt ={ (<, integer), (<, real), (>, integer) }

program InsertSortProg;
procedure sort(someadt(comp, elem));
type list=array[0..n,elem];
var
a:list; j,i:integer; t:elem;
someadt ={ (<, integer), (<, real), (>, integer) }
begin
foreach(i:0≤i≤n:read(a[i]););
i:=1;
do i≤n→ t,j:=a[i],i-1;
    do (j≥0)∧ (t comp a[j])→a[j+1],j:=a[j],j-1;od;
    a[j+1]:=t;
    i:=i+1;
od;
end.

Where elem is type variable, comp is action variable. Following 3 instantiation state ments generate 3 different sorting algorithm.

procedure sortascending: new Sort (>, integer);
procedure sortdescending: new Sort (<, integer);
procedure sortdescending: new Sort (<, real);

3.5   Instantiation of the Generic Program Unit

There are 4 generic program units in Apla: that is program, procedure, function and ADT. Each generic program unit should have instantiation statement. The syntax of the instantiation statement is:

    <name of program unit class> <name of instantiation prgram>: new <name of generic program unit> (list of actual parameters). Following is the example of instantiation statements:

procedure sortascending: new Sort (≥);
procedure metrics1: new metrics (real∪{+ ∞}, ◇, +, +∞, 0);

During the executing of the instantiation statement, the transformation system will check the actual parameters of the statement, that is to test whether the actual parameters are in the region or not. The system will generate an actual program unit if the result of test is yes. If not, the error information will be output.

4 Case Study: Matrices Product

Problem: In general case, the product a·b of two n x n matrices a and b can be stored in matrix c and defined by

$$c[i, j] = (\Sigma i, k: 0 \leq i \leq n \text{ and } 0 \leq k \leq n \text{ } a[i, j] \cdot b[j, k]).$$

Let $\oplus$ be the quantifier of operation $\oplus$, $\odot$ the quantifier of operation $\odot$ and $\diamondsuit$ the quantifier of operation $\diamondsuit$(min), we have

We need a generic algorithm to compute the product a•b for abstract addition $\oplus$ and abstract multiplication $\odot$, that is to computing

$$C[i, k] = (\oplus i, k: 0 \leq i \leq n \text{ and } 0 \leq k \leq na[i, j] \odot b[j, k])$$

Then some concrete product can be generated by the generic algorithm. The concrete product as follows:

$$c[i, j] = (\Sigma i, k: 0 \leq i \leq n \text{ and } 0 \leq k \leq n \text{ } a[i, j] \cdot b[j, k]) \qquad (6.1)$$

$$c[i, j] = (\Pi i, k: 0 \leq i \leq n \text{ and } 0 \leq k \leq n \text{ } a[i, j] + b[j, k]) \qquad (6.2)$$

$$c[i, j] = (\diamondsuit i, k: 0 \leq i \leq n \text{ and } 0 \leq k \leq n \text{ } a[i, j] \cdot b[j, k]) \qquad (6.3)$$

For solving the program, following algebra and definitions are needed [26].

Definition 4. A set S with an associative binary operation # is said to be a **semigroup.**

Definition 5. A semigroup with an identity is called a **monoid.**

Definition 6. A set S with distinguished elements O and I and binary operations (abstract) addition $\oplus$ and (abstract) multiplication $\odot$ is a *semiring* if

(1) (S, $\oplus$, O) is a commutative monoid, that is for all a, b, c $\in$ S
     (a $\oplus$ b) $\oplus$ c = a $\oplus$ (b $\oplus$ c)
     a $\oplus$ b = b $\oplus$ a
     a $\oplus$ O = O $\oplus$ a = a [O is the identity under $\oplus$]
(2) (S, $\odot$, I) is a monoid, that is for all a, b, c $\in$ S
     (a $\odot$ b) $\odot$ c = a $\odot$ (b $\odot$ c)
     a $\odot$ I = I $\odot$ a = a [I is the identity under $\odot$]
(3) Multiplication $\odot$ distributes over addition $\oplus$ and O is a null-element with respect to multiplication,
     that is for all a, b, c $\in$ S
     (a $\oplus$ b) $\odot$ c = (a $\odot$ c) $\oplus$ (b $\odot$ c)
     c $\odot$ (a $\oplus$ b) = (c $\odot$ a) $\oplus$ (c $\odot$ b)
     O $\odot$ a = a $\odot$ O = O

A semiring $(S, \oplus, \odot, O, I)$ is commutative if the operation $\odot$ is commutative. Based on the definitions, we get following semirings:

$R1 = (R^+, +, \cdot, 0, 1)$ for Eq. 6.1
$R2 = (R^+, \cdot, +, 1, 0)$ for Eq. 6.2
$R3 = (R^+ \cup \{+ \infty\}, \diamondsuit, +, +\infty, 0)$ for Eq. 6.3

```
Procedure metrics( someadt(T , ⊕, ⊙, O, I, )) ;

var

a,b,c:array[0..99,array[0..99,T]];

s:T

begin

i, j:=0, 0;
someadt={(real, +,  • , 0, 1), ( real,  • , +, 1, 0), (real∪{+∞}, ◇, +, +∞, 0)}
do i <100 →
    do j<100  →  read(a[i, j]);read (b[i, j]); j:=j+1od;
    i:=i+1;
od;
i, j, k:=0, 0, 0;
do i<100  →
    do j<100  →
        begin
          s:= o
          do k<100  →  s:=s ⊕ a[i, k] ⊙b[k, j]; k:= k+1 od;
          c[i, j]:=s;
        end;
        j:=j+1;
    od;
    i:=i+1;
od
end;

procedure metrics1 : new metrics (real, +,  • , 0, 1);

procedure metrics2: new metrics (real,  • , +, 1, 0);

procedure metrics3 : new metrics (real∪{+∞}, ◇, +, +∞, 0);
end;
```

5 Conclusion and Future Work

In this Paper, we proposed a new definition of generic programming that is more precise and made all generic terms more consistent, two new generic mechanisms: action and ADT. The definition of parameter region is presented. The new generic mechanisms and new concept of parameter region made generic programming more efficiency and more safe.

We are trying to present an algorism to implement generic mechanism that made the implementation more simple and ease. Then try to implement the proof of generic program and checking of parameter region using theorem proof tool.

Acknowledgments. Thanks to Xu Wensheng, Zoo Zenkang, Zheng Yujun, Shi Haihe, Wang CJ, Hu Qimin, Yue Zen and Xie Wuping who attended the previous work of the project when they studied in JXNU.

References

1. Gregor, D., Jarvi, J., Siek, J.G., Stroustrup, B., Reis, G.D., Lumsdaine, A.: Concepts: linguistic support for generic programming in C ++. In: Proceedings of the ACM SIGPLAN Conference on Object Oriented Programming, Systems, Languages, and Applications (OOPSLA 2006), pp. 291–310. ACM Press, New York (2006)
2. Liveira, B.C.D.S., Gibbons, J.: Scala for generic programmers: Comparing Haskell and Scala support for generic programming. J. Funct. Program. **20**(3–4), 303–352 (2010)
3. Oliveira, B.C.D.S., Schrijvers, T., Choi, W., Lee, W., Yi, K.: The implicit calculus: a new foundation for generic programming. In: Proceedings of the 33rd ACM SIGPLAN Conference on Programming Language Design and Implementation (PLDI 2012), pp. 35–44. ACM Press, New York (2012)
4. Siek, J.G., Lumsdaine, A.: A language for generic programming in the large. Sci. Comput. Program. **76**(5), 423–465 (2011)
5. David, V., Haveraaen, M.: Concepts as syntactic sugar. In: Proceedings of Ninth IEEE International Working Conference on Source Code Analysis and Manipulation (SCAM 2009), pp. 147–156. IEEE Computer Society Press, California (2009)
6. Sutton, A., Maletic, J.I.: Emulating C++ 0x concepts. Sci. Comput. Program. **78**(9), 1449–1469 (2013)
7. Gibbons, J., Paterson, R.: Parametric datatype-genericity. In: Proceedings of the the 2009 ACM SIGPLAN Workshop on Generic Programming (WGP 2009), pp. 85–93. ACM Press, New York (2009)
8. Chen, L., Xu, B.W., Qian, J., Zhou, T.L., Zhou, Y.M.: Refactoring generic instantiations based on type propagation analysis. J. Softw. **20**(10), 2617–2627 (2009). (in Chinese with English abstract)
9. Chen, L.: Research on refactoring of generic program. Ph.D. thesis. Southeast University, Nanjing (2009) (in Chinese with English abstract)
10. Gregor, D., Jarvi, J., Kulkarni, M., Lumsdaine, A., Musser, D., Schupp, S.: Generic programming and high-performance libraries. Int. J. Parallel Prog. **33**(2–3), 145–164 (2005). doi:10.1007/s10766-005-3580-8

11. Jarvi, J., Gregor, D., Willcock, J., Lumsdaine, A., Siek, J.G.: Algorithm specialization in generic programming: challenges of constrained generics in C++. In: Proceedings of the 2006 ACM SIGPLAN Conference on Programming Language Design and Implementation (PLDI 2006), pp. 272–282. ACM Press, New York (2006)

12. Hinze, R., Loh, A.: Generic programming in 3D. Sci. Comput. Program. **74**(8), 590–628 (2009)

13. Xue, J.Y.: Formal derivation of a generic algorithmic program for solving general path problems. In: Proceedings of the 3rd ASCM, pp. 253–258, August 1988

14. Xue, J.Y.: Two new strategies for developing loop invariants and their applications. J. Comput. Sci Technol. **8**(2), 95–102 (1993)

15. Xue, J.Y.: Formal derivation of graph algorithmic programs using partition-and-recur. J. Comput. Sci. Technol. **13**(6), 143–151 (1998)

16. Xue, J.Y.: A unified approach for developing efficient algorithmic programs. J. Comput. Sci. Technol. **12**(4), 103–118 (1997)

17. Xue, J.Y., Davis, R.: A simple program whose Derivation and Proof Is Also. In: Proceedings of the First IEEE International Conference on Formal Engineering Method (ICFEM 1997). IEEE CS Press, November 1997

18. Xue, J.Y., Davis, R.: A derivation and proof of Knuth's binary to decimal program. Softw. Concepts Tools **18**, 149–156 (1997)

19. Xue, J.Y.: Formal derivation of graph algorithmic programs using partition and recur. J. Comput. Sci. Technol. **13**(6), 143–151 (1998)

20. Xue, J.Y.: Developing the generic path algorithmic program and its instantiations using PAR method. In: Proceedings of the Second Asia Workshop on Programming Languages and Systems, Korea (2001)

21. Xue, J.Y.: PAR method and its supporting platform. In: Proceedings of International Workshop on Formal Method for Developing Software, Annual Report, No. 348, UNU-IIST, Macao (2006)

22. Wang, C.J., Xue, J.Y.: Formal derivation of a generic algorithmic program for solving a class extremum problems. In: Proceedings of 10th ACIS International Conference on Software Engineering, Artificial Intelligences, Networking and Parallel/Distributed Computing (SNPD 2009), pp. 100–105. IEEE Computer Society Press, California (2009)

23. Wang, C.J., Xue, J.Y.: Formal Derivation of a High-Trustworthy Generic Algorithmic Program for Solving a Class of Path Problems. In: Deng, X., Hopcroft, J.E., Xue, J. (eds.) FAW 2009. LNCS, vol. 5598, pp. 27–39. Springer, Heidelberg (2009)

24. Xu, W.S., Xue, J.Y.: Research on java-based implementation of generic programming paradigm. Technique Report of Jiangxi Normal University (2003)

25. Unifying Theories od Generic Progrmming (2015). http://cs.ox.ac.uk/projects/utgp/

26. Ross, K.A., Wright, C.R.B.: Discrete Mathematics. Prentice- Hall Inc., New Jersey (1985)

Modeling and Verification of an Interrupt System in µC/OS-III with TMSVL

Jin Cui, Zhenhua Duan$^{(\boxtimes)}$, Cong Tian, and Nan Zhang

ICTT and ISN Laboratory, Xidian University,
Xi'an 710071, People's Republic of China
zhenhua_duan@126.com

Abstract. Interrupt mechanism is a useful means to ensure timely response to asynchronous events in real-time systems. Modeling and verification of the correctness of interrupt systems are important in practice. This paper proposes an efficient way to formalize the interrupt mechanism in TMSVL. We apply TMSVL to model and verify a timer interrupt application running under µC/OS-III. To do so, the real-time system is formalized in TMSVL, and properties to be verified are specified by projection temporal logic (PTL) formulas or TMSVL statements. Then a model checker built in the toolkit MSV is employed to check whether or not the model satisfies the properties automatically.

Keywords: Real-time systems · Interrupt · Schedulability · µC/OS-III · Model checking

1 Introduction

µC/OS-III is a widely used open source real-time operating system (OS) [10,13]. It is a portable, ROM-able, scalable, preemptive, and real-time deterministic multitasking kernel. It has the following features: (1) priority-based preemptive scheduling; (2) synchronization and communication between tasks, for instance, mutual exclusion semaphores with built-in priority ceiling protocol to prevent priority inversions; (3) interrupt and time management. µC/OS-III is used in a wide variety of industries such as avionics, medical equipments, industrial controls, and so on.

A real-time system using µC/OS-III which performs reliably and safely is vital. It is important to ensure the correctness, reliability and safety of such a system. At present, there are several approaches that can be used to improve these properties of real-time systems. For instance, (1) simulation and testing based approaches; (2) verification approaches such as theorem proving and model checking. However, simulation and testing try to find out bugs of a system based on enumeration of either simulation environments or test cases [9]. As Dijkstra pointed out "testing can only find the presence of errors never their

This research is supported by the NSFC Grant Nos. 61133001, 61322202, 61420106004, 91418201, and 61272117.

S. Liu and Z. Duan (Eds.): SOFL+MSVL 2015, LNCS 9559, pp. 15–28, 2016.
DOI: 10.1007/978-3-319-31220-0_2

absence" [5]. Verification is a strict mathematical approach which can be used to prove whether or not a system satisfies a property by means of theorem proving or model checking. However, theorem proving needs involvement of manual efforts while model checking suffers from so called state explosion problem [11]. In addition, the model of a system and the property to be verified are defined using different notations. This makes the verification process complicated. To overcome this problem, Timed Modeling, Simulation and Verification Language (TMSVL) [7] which can be used to model, simulate and verify real-time systems is introduced.

TMSVL [8] is a timed version of MSVL [7]. A unified model checking approach has been carried out for TMSVL, that is, a system is modeled as M and the desired property is specified as ϕ in the same formalism, thus whether $\vDash M \rightarrow \phi$ can be checked effectively. A supporting toolkit MSV is developed to model a system in terms of TMSVL programs, to simulate a system by executing of a path of the model, and to verify properties of the system by means of the unified model checking. In this paper, we utilize TMSVL to formalize the timer interrupt application running under μC/OS-III. First, we formalize a general interrupt mechanism in TMSVL with a derived structure. Then this structure is applied to formalize a timer interrupt system. At last, the correctness and timeliness properties are specified in TMSVL and verified with the unified model checker MSV. An advantage of TMSVL model checking over other model checking approaches is that the model of the system and the property to be verified are both defined in TMSVL. Further, the verification process can automatically be performed using MSV.

There are several techniques which are used to verify systems developed under similar OS. In [4], a method is presented for converting the Trampoline kernel code into formal models for the model checker SPIN and a series of experiments using an incremental verification approach has been used to improve the performance of the verification. While the formal language PROMELA as an input of SPIN does not aim at modeling real-time systems. Thus time-dependent properties may not be verified in SPIN. Timed automata [1] are extended from Büchi automata by introducing the real-valued clock variables. It is a useful formalism to model real-time systems. In [15], a distributed fault-tolerant real-time application is modeled with timed automata. In [14], timed automata are used to model a real-time operating system compliant with an OSEK/VDX standard. Timed automata are also used to model primitives of Ravenscar run-time kernel for Ada [12]. However, the variable used to measure the execution time of tasks is an integer. This violates the characteristic of continuous time. A well-known tool for model checking timed automata is UPPAAL [2]. While systems and properties are not described in the same formalism. Since the desired property is usually described in CTL, LTL [11] or TCTL [3].

The paper is organized as follows. The next section introduces TMSVL language and a formalization of the interrupt mechanism. Section 3 gives an overview on μC/OS-III. In Sect. 4, we show how a timer interrupt application running under μC/OS-III can be modeled and verified in TMSVL. Finally, conclusion and future work are drawn in Sect. 5.

2   TMSVL

MSVL is a temporal logic programming language consists of conjunction, selection, sequence, parallel, branching, loop as well as projection statements [6]. It is an executable subset of PTL (Projection Temporal Logic) [7], for the MSVL statements are defined by basic PTL formulas. A toolkit named MSV has been developed to preform simulation, modeling and verification automatically.

However, MSVL is inefficient to describe time constraints since it abstracts away from time, retaining only the sequence of states. For instance, a process p starting at time point t_1 and ending at t_2 cannot be expressed in MSVL with reals. It can be expressed by $len()$ statement in MSVL if the time increments of each two successive states are identical. However, this makes the time increment be the least one of all the successive states, which unnecessarily increases the number of states for the model and thus reduces the efficiency for model checking. To avoid this defect, we extend MSVL by making time explicit and introduce a time constraint statement in the form of $(t_1, t_2)p$ to describe the situation where a process p starts at time point t_1 and ends at t_2. The extended MSVL is named TMSVL [8] with variables T and Ts being used to describe time and time increment, respectively. Meanwhile, we have extended the toolkit MSV with TMSVL thus verification of real-time systems can automatically be performed using MSV.

2.1   Statements in TMSVL

TMSVL consists of arithmetic expressions, boolean expressions, and basic statements. The arithmetic expression e and boolean expression b are defined by the following grammar:

$$e ::= n \mid x \mid \bigcirc e \mid \ominus e \mid e_0 \ op \ e_1 (op ::= + \mid - \mid * \mid / \mid mod)$$
$$b ::= true \mid false \mid e_0 = e_1 \mid e_0 < e_1 \mid \neg b \mid b_0 \wedge b_1$$

where n is a constant, x a variable; $\bigcirc e$ and $\ominus e$ denote e at the next state and previous state over an interval, respectively.

Elementary statements of TMSVL are defined as follows:

1. MSVL statement p
2. Time constraint statment $(t_1, t_2)tp$
3. Conjunction statement $tp_1 \wedge tp_2$
4. Selection statement $tp_1 \vee tp_2$
5. Sequential statement $tp_1 \ ; \ tp_2$
6. Parallel statement $tp \parallel tq$
7. Conditional statement   if b then $\{tp\}$ else $\{tq\}$
8. While statement   while (b) $\{tp\}$
9. Projection statement $(tp_1, \ldots, tp_m)$ prj (tp)

MSVL statements are included first. Suppose t_1 and t_2 are arithmetic expressions and tp a TMSVL statement. The time constraint statement $(t_1, t_2)tp$ means that tp is executed over the time duration from t_1 to t_2. $tp_1 \wedge tp_2$ means that tp_1 and tp_2

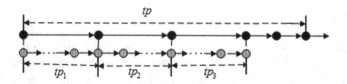

Fig. 1. An example of projection structure

are executed concurrently, and terminate at the same time. Selection statement $tp_1 \vee tp_2$ means tp_1 or tp_2 is executed. $tp_1; tp_2$ means that tp_2 is executed after tp_1 finishes. Parallel statement $tp \parallel tq$ means that tp and tq are executed in parallel, while they are not required to terminate at the same time. Conditional and while constructs are consistent with that in general programming language like C and $Java$.

Projection statement $(tp_1, \ldots, tp_m)$ prj tp means tp is executed in parallel with $tp_1; tp_2; \ldots; tp_m$ over an interval obtained by taking endpoints of the intervals over which $tp_1, \ldots, tp_m$ are executed. An endpoint denotes the first or the last state of an interval. Taken (tp_1, tp_2, tp_3) prj tp as an example. We assume tp_3 terminates before tp. The construct of (tp_1, tp_2, tp_3) prj tp is depicted in Fig. 1.

If $tp_1, \ldots, tp_m$ are identical, we usually use $((tp_1)^m)$ prj (tp) to represent $(tp_1, \ldots, tp_m)$ prj (tp) for simplicity. $((tp_1)^{\circledast})$ prj (tp) means m can be any non-negative integers, and $\circledast$ is named projection-star.

2.2   Interrupt in TMSVL

In real-time embedded applications, interrupt-driven systems are widely adopted due to strict timing requirements. Interrupt mechanism is an effect way to handle events like a request to an external device or timed detection and control. When an interrupt is triggered, the processor stops executing the current task and switches to handle the specified program, namely interrupt service routine (ISR) or interrupt handler. The process including responding to interrupt and recovering from interrupt can be modeled by a derived statement q when b do p, which is defined as follows.

$$q \text{ when } b \text{ do } p \overset{\text{def}}{=} ((\text{if } b \text{ then } p \text{ else skip})^{\circledast}, \ r \wedge \varepsilon) \text{ prj}(q \,; r \wedge \varepsilon) \wedge \text{halt}(r)$$

Here q represents the process which may be interrupted, p is the interrupt handler and b indicates that the interrupt is triggered and can be processed. The definition of interrupt is a conjunction of *projection* and *halt* statements. The *projection* statement describes the relation between the main process q and the interrupt handler p. When the interrupt is triggered, b becomes true, p is performed, and only when p is finished, q is resumed. Otherwise, q is executed. *skip* is a MSVL statement which means the length of an interval is one. An interval is a non-empty (possibly infinite) sequence of states. The length of an interval is the number of sates minus one. Interrupt is processed only when q does not terminate. This is realized by introducing the auxiliary proposition r

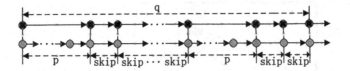

Fig. 2. The structure of interrupt in TMSVL

which neither occurs in q nor p. Whenever q is terminated, $r \wedge \varepsilon$ is attached to the end state of the execution of q. This enables statement $halt(r)$ to handle the termination since $halt(r)$ ensures when r becomes true, q is terminated. Thus, the execution of whole *projection* statement ends. An example of the interrupt structure is illustrated in Fig. 2. In addition, p can also be an interrupt structure for the case of interrupt nesting.

3   μC/OS-III Overview

3.1   Tasks Management

The functionality of a real-time application is usually achieved by a number of different priority tasks coordinated by the scheduler of the operating system. In μC/OS-III, a task has five states: sleeping, ready, running, waiting and suspended. How states of tasks change is shown in Fig. 3. Sleeping state refers to that a task resides in memory only in the form of code, and is not known by the operating system. When a task is created by a program, it is registered in the operating system and turns the sleeping state into ready state. A ready task can also be deleted by a user program, which will lead the state to change to sleeping state. If a ready task obtains the processor, it will be executed and in the running state. A running task may turn into waiting state when it waits for the occurrence of some events, or turn into ready state when it is preempted by a higher priority task, or become suspended when an interruption occurs. A task in waiting state can either become ready when the waited events occur or turn into sleeping when it is deleted. A task in suspended state turns into ready state if the interrupt handler makes a higher priority task ready, otherwise, the interrupted task is resumed.

3.2   Events Management

μC/OS-III provides events management for task synchronization and communication. An event can be a request for common resource such as hardware device and buffer, or release of the common resource. The process that a task requests or releases common resource is managed by the operating system. Furthermore, the operating system manages these events with appropriate mechanisms such as semaphore, mutex semaphores, event flag groups, mailbox and message queues according to different characteristics of common resources.

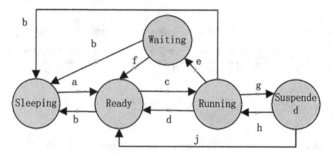

a: a task is created; b: a task is deleted; c: a ready task gets the processor; d: a task is preempted; e: a task waits for the occurrence of some events; f: the waited events have occurred; g: a task is interrupted; h: the interrupted task is resumed j: the interrupt makes a higher priority task ready

Fig. 3. State transition graph of tasks

3.3 Interrupt Management

In μC/OS-III, interrupt has higher priority than tasks. Interrupt mechanism is adopted to deal with asynchronous events timely. When an interrupt request is received, if interrupt is not disabled, the OS suspends the current running task and switches to the corresponding interrupt handler. At the end of the interrupt handler, the OS scheduler puts the highest priority ready task into running state instead of just returning to the interrupted task.

Timer interrupt is a fundamental hardware condition for tasks synchronization. It is the heart of μC/OS-III. By setting the hardware timer, the interrupt arrives every 10~200 ms. The corresponding ISR is timer tick ISR. It does the following jobs: (1) increasing the timer by one time tick; (2) traversing the task control block and decreasing the delayed tasks by one time tick. Turning the waiting tasks with the delay being zero and waiting for no event to ready state; (3) conducting task scheduling. Interrupt is enabled until the end of a single execution of the timer tick ISR. Without timer interrupt, multi-task scheduling operating systems do not exist, neither do real-time systems.

3.4 OS Kernel Service

Kernel is an important part of OS. Its primary function is task scheduling. The task scheduling function mainly does the following work: (1) finding the highest priority ready task; (2) if the highest priority ready task is not the current running task, performing a task switching, namely, making the processor available for the highest priority ready task and saving the context of the preempted task. There are two schedulers in μC/OS-III, that is, task level and interrupt level scheduler. Interrupt level scheduling occurs at the end of interrupt processing, whereas task level scheduling is triggered in the following conditions: (1) a task is added or deleted, or the priority of a task is changed; (2) a task delays itself, or the delay time is decreased to zero; (3) the event a task requests occurs.

4   Modeling and Verification of a Timer Interrupt Application

In this section, we utilize TMSVL to verify the correctness and timeliness of an abstract timer interrupt application running under μC/OS-III.

The application consists of three tasks $Task_0$, $Task_1$, and $Task_2$. We assume the priority of each task is 5, 10, and 14. The lager value is corresponding to lower priority. Therefore, $Task_0$ has the highest priority, followed by $Task_1$ and finally $Task_2$. $Task_0$ and $Task_2$ need to access the mutex semaphore sem when they are executed. The pseudo-code of the three tasks is given in Fig. 4.

$Task_0 ()$	$Task_1 ()$	$Task_2 ()$
{	{	{
$sem{=}OSMutexCreate(pri,\ err);$	$while(1)$	$while(1)$
$while(1)$	{	{
{	$Comp_1;$	$pend(sem);$
$pend(sem);$	$OSTimeDly(n_1)\ ;$	$Comp_2;$
$Comp_0;$	}	$post(sem);$
$post(sem);$	}	$OSTimeDly(n_2)\ ;$
$OSTimeDly(n_0)\ ;$		}
}		}
}		

Fig. 4. Tasks pseudo-code

$Task_0$ creates sem by invoking the system function $OSMutexCreate()$. The first parameter namely pri is the priority to use when accessing the mutex semaphore, the second parameter err indicates the error message, and the return value is the created semaphore. We should specify pri a priority that is higher than any of the tasks competing for sem to prevent the priority inversion. This is the essence of the priority ceiling protocol. Thus the value of pri is lower than 5. $Task_0$ and $Task_2$ request sem before performing $Comp_0$ or $Comp_2$ and release sem after finishing $Comp_0$ or $Comp_2$. Then the tasks invoke the system function $OSTimeDly()$ to cede the processor and turn to the waiting state. The parameter of $OSTimeDly()$ is the number of time ticks the tasks block themselves. The three tasks are loop structures. Each new execution circle of the three tasks except for the first one is preceded by a delay of n_i ($i = 0, 1, 2$) time ticks.

In order to verify the abstract application, we assume the three tasks are created at the same time ST. The correctness and timeliness properties depend both on the design of the application and hardware environment. We assume the timer interrupt is triggered every 20 ms, and the time it takes to handle the timer interrupt is 0.2 ms.

```
struct m_task{
   int rd, ex,wait,spd and
   float C,D,ac, acD,dly
};
struct m_task Task[3]
```

Fig. 5. Data type for tasks

4.1   Modeling of the Application

A new data type m_task is defined in Fig. 5 to store task information for the modeling and verification purpose. In m_task, $rd, ex, wait, spd$ are integer variables. $rd = 1$ if a delay of a task finishes, $rd = 0$ otherwise; $ex = 1$ if a task is running, $ex = 0$ otherwise; $wait = 1$ if a task is at the state of waiting, $wait = 0$ otherwise; $spd = 1$ if a task is suspended by interrupt, $spd = 0$ otherwise. C, D, ac, acD, dly, d are float variables. C denotes the time it takes to perform a computation. D is the deadline of each computation of a task. ac stores the accumulated running time of a task in the current period. acD denotes the accumulated delay time of a task in the current period. dly is the time a task delays each time.

$Task[3]$ is an array of m_task type, and $Task[i]$ is corresponding to $Task_i$. Other notions and their meanings are given below (i is an integer and $i = 0, 1, 2$, N is a constant and $N = 2$):

- $d[i]$: a real variable, with a non-negative value denoting the remainder of the delay time if $Task_i$ is delayed; otherwise, $d[i]$ is an infinity.
- $d[N + 1]$: a real variable, if the interrupt has been triggered at the current state, $d[N + 1]$ represents the time needed for finishing the interrupt handler; otherwise, it indicates the time needed for the next arrival of an interrupt.
- $d[N+2]$: a non-negative real variable indicating the time required for finishing the remaining part of a running task. If there is no running task at the current state, it is an infinity.
- inp: a boolean variable. $inp = 1$ indicates that the current request of the interrupt is still standing while $inp = 0$ indicates that the current request of the interrupt is fulfilled.
- $runTaskNum$: an integer variable, with a non-negative value indicating the highest ready task's subscript. That is, $runTaskNum = i$ if $Task_i$ is running, $runTaskNum = -1$ otherwise.
- ST and ET: non-negative real variables indicating the start and end time of the tasks.

The TMSVL model of the above application is defined as follows:

$$M \stackrel{\text{def}}{=} clock(e_T, e_{Ts}) \wedge TsSet \wedge (\mathtt{while}(T < ET)\{Q\} \wedge P)\mathtt{when}(b)\mathtt{do}(ISR)$$

Each TMSVL program is a conjunction of $clock(e_T, e_{Ts})$ and statements. $clock(e_T, e_{Ts})$ initializes T and Ts, the current time and time increment, with the evaluations of arithmetic expressions e_T and e_{Ts}, and enables T to increase with the increment Ts. Meanwhile, Ts can be set in the TMSVL program.

The module $TsSet$ sets the time step Ts to eliminate states without events to reduce the state space for model checking. Events including the occurrence of the interrupt, the start and end of interrupt processing, the completion of a computation, and the start and finish of a task delay. At every state, the time needed for the occurrences of those events are calculated and they are stored in the array d. Ts is always set to the minimum element of d.

$(\text{while}(T < ET)\{Q\} \wedge P)\text{when}(b)\text{do}(ISR)$ is the TMSVL interrupt structure. It is used to describe the relation between the tasks scheduling and the hardware interrupt. Q denotes a task scheduling. $\text{while}(T < ET)\{Q\}$ means Q is executed repeatedly and terminated at time point ET. P denotes the tasks module, and ISR denotes the interrupt handler. The notion b is a boolean condition here, which means that the timer interrupt is triggered and the system does not disable the interrupt.

The TMSVL model of the scheduler is shown in Fig. 6. Lines 8 to 11 show the scheduling of $Task_2$ which has the lowest priority. If $Task_2$ is ready and $Task_0$ and $Task_1$ are not ready or executing, $Task_2$ can be executed and it cannot be preempted, which is realized by the $while$ statement at Line 10. As long as $Task_2$ does not finish computation, namely $Task[2].ac < Task[2].C$, the scheduler will not schedule other tasks. The scheduler makes $Task_0$ be the running task by setting $runTaskNum$ to 0 if $Task_0$ is ready, which is shown in Lines 2 to 3; if $Task_0$ is not ready but $Task_1$ is ready, $Task_1$ will be scheduled. When none of the three tasks is ready, $runTaskNum$ is set to -1.

$Q \overset{\text{def}}{=}$
```
1.  //Selecting the ready task with the highest priority
2.     if(Task[0].rd=1)
3.        then{runTaskNum=0}
4.     and
5.     if(Task[0].rd=0 and Task[1].rd=1)
6.        then{ runTaskNum=1}
7.     and
8.     if(Task[0].rd=0 and Task[1].rd=0 and Task[2].rd=1)
9.        then{runTaskNum=2 and skip;
10.           while(Task[2].ac<Task[2].C){ runTaskNum=2 and skip }
11.        }
12.     else { skip }
13.     and
14.     if( Task[0].rd=0 and Task[1].rd=0 and Task[2].rd=0)
15.        then{runTaskNum=-1 }
```

Fig. 6. TMSVL model of the scheduler

$P_i \stackrel{\text{def}}{=}$

1. while(T<ET)
2. { await(runTaskNum=i);
3.   Task[i].ac=0 and
4.   while(Task[i].ac<Task[i].C)
5.   { if(inp=0 and runTaskNum=i)
6.   then{Task[i].ac:=Task[i].ac+Ts and Task[i].ex=1 and Task[i].wait=0}
7.   else{ Task[i].ex=0 and skip} };
8.   if(Task[i].ac=Task[i].C)
9.   then{(T,T+Task[i].dly)keep(next Task[i].acD=Task[i].acD+Ts and
10.   Task[i].rd=0 and Task[i].ex=0 and Task[i].wait=1);
11.   if(i=2)then{await(runTaskNum!=0)};
12.   Task[i].acD=0 and Task[i].rd=1 and empty }
13. }

Fig. 7. TMSVL model of each task

The task module is a parallel of tasks. P can be expressed with the parallel statement below:

$$P \stackrel{\text{def}}{=} ||_{i=1}^{N} P_i$$

where P_i is the TMSVL model of $Task_i$ and it is defined in Fig. 7. The structure of P_i is a *while* loop. In the loop body, the task is waiting for its opportunity to run which is shown in Line 2. If $Task_i$ gets the opportunity to run, namely $runTaskNum = i$, the *await* statement terminates and the statement following starts work, wherein $Task[i].ac$ is set to zero at Line 3. Otherwise, the *await* statement will not terminate and the statement after it cannot work. The value of $runTaskNum$ is determined in the scheduler Q. If $Task_i$ runs, the accumulated execution time of $Task_i$ at the next state is the sum of $Task[i].ac$ and Ts at the current state. When $Task_i$ starts a new circle, $Task[i].ac$ is set to zero. If $Task_i$ finishes an execution of a circle, that is, $Task[i].ac = Task[i].C$, it will delay $Task[i].dly$ time units, during which the task is at the waiting state. For $Task_0$ and $Task_1$, they will be ready again and repeat the above steps after delaying $Task[0].dly$ and $Task[1].dly$ time units. While for $Task_2$, after delaying $Task[2].dly$ time units, only when *sem* is released by $Task_0$ can it be in ready state, which is shown in Line 11.

The TMSVL model of ISR is given in Fig. 8. When the OS begins to handle interrupt, the running task turns to the suspended state and this is shown in Lines 1 to 4. The interrupt handler takes 0.0002 s, during this period, the running task is suspended by setting $Task[runTaskNum].ex$ to 0 and $Task[runTaskNum].spd$ to 1. When the interrupt processing is finished, the interrupted task leaves the suspended state and a task scheduling is triggered which is shown in Lines 5 to 7.

$ISR \overset{\text{def}}{=}$

1. (T,T+0.0002) (temp=runTaskNum and
2.   keep(if(temp!=-1)
3.   then{ Task[temp].spd=1 and Task[temp].ex=0}
4.   ));
5.   Q and
6.   if(temp!=-1)
7.   then{ Task[temp].spd=0}

Fig. 8. TMSVL model of the ISR

4.2 Verification of the Application

Verification is based on constructing Normal Form Graph (NFG) [6]. Given a TMSVL program p, we can construct a graph named NFG that explicitly illustrates the state space of the program. An NFG is a directed graph, denoted as G=<V,E>, with a node in the set V of nodes representing a program in TMSVL and an edge in the set E of edges representing a state. In fact, NFG determines the execution paths of the corresponding TMSVL program.

Suppose the TMSVL model of a system is p and the property to be verified is ϕ. To check whether or not ϕ is valid on p amounts to deciding whether $p \to \phi$ is valid. Further, whether $p \to \phi$ is valid is equivalent to check whether $p \wedge \neg\phi$ is unsatisfiable. This can be achieved by constructing NFG of $p \wedge \neg\phi$ and then checking whether no paths in the NFG are acceptable. Otherwise, an acceptable path presents a counterexample in the program that violates the property. We have developed a prototyping tool based on the toolkit MSV for supporting verification of TMSVL programs. The following properties are verified in MSV.

(1) Safety: when the lowest priority task, namely $Task_2$ is running, it should not be preempted by $Task_0$ or $Task_1$.

This can be expressed by p_1 as follows:

$$\Box(Task[2].ac < Task[2].C \wedge Task[2].ac > 0 \to (inp = 1 \vee Task[2].ex = 1))$$

p_1 means that once $Task_2$ starts executing, namely, $Task[2].ac > 0$ and $Task[2].ac < Task[2].C$, it is either suspended by the interrupt $(inp = 1)$ or at the executing state $(Task[2].ex = 1)$. $inp = 1 \vee Task[2].ex = 1$ indicates that $Task_0$ and $Task_1$ are not executed. Since at each state, at most one task is executing($\Box(Task[0].ex + Task[1].ex + Task[2].ex \leq 1)$), which can be verified first. When interrupt occurs, none of the three tasks can execute, this can be expressed as $\Box(inp = 1 \to Task[0].ex + Task[1].ex + Task[2].ex = 0)$ and has been verified using MSV.

(2) Timeliness property: the three tasks can always finish in their deadline periodically.

This can be expressed by p_2 below:

$$(0, ST)true; \wedge_{i=0}^{2}(Task[i].rd = 1 \wedge Task[i].ac = 0 \to$$
$$\{0, Task[i].D\}true; Task[i].ac = Task[i].C)^{+}$$

p_2 means that from the time point ST, once $Task_i$ is ready implies $Task_i$ finishes in $Task[i].D$ time units. $\{0, Task[i].D\}$ is the delay operation, and is derived from time constraint statement. $\{0, Task[i].D\}true$; p means p holds in $Task[i].D$ time units from the current time point. $+$ is the $chop - plus$ operator, and is derived from the sequential operator (;). $(p)^+$ means p repeats for any positive number of times.

Verification Results and Analysis. In order to verify the two properties, we set the computation time for the three tasks with $Task[0].C = 0.4$, $Task[1].C = 0.6$ and $Task[2].C = 0.8$, and the delay time with $Task[0].dly = 0.8$, $Task[1].dly = 0.6$ and $Task[2].dly = 0.4$. Meanwhile, we set the deadline for the three tasks with $Task[0].D = 1.2$, $Task[1].D = 1.5$ and $Task[2].D = 1.8$. We assume the start time of the application is at $T = 0$, that is, $ST = 0$.

The verification process with the extended toolkit MSV is conducted. With the system model and desired properties as input, we can eventually know whether or not the property is valid on the system model. The correctness property is verified and there is no path in the NFG, which indicates the property is valid.

Figure 9 is the verification result of the timeliness property. There are 3521 nodes and 3521 edges on the counterexample. Each node represents a program

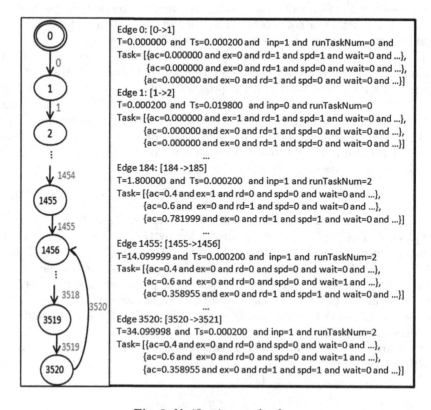

Fig. 9. Verification result of p_2

while each edge represents a state which shows the executing of the application at different time. The root node is a double circle, it represents the TMSVL program of the application. By executing the program that a node represents, two part can be obtained: the current part and future part where the current part is an outgoing edge of that node and points to the node which represents the future part. For example, edge 0 and node 1 are the executing results of node 0. The edges are state formulas while the nodes are temporal formulas which need to be further executed. In Fig. 9, we can see that edge 0 represents the state that $T = 0$, and all the three tasks are not delayed since $rd = 1$ for the three tasks. While $Task_0$ is the ready task with the highest priority, therefore $runTaskNum = 0$. $inp = 1$ indicates that the interrupt request occurs and at the second state, namely edge 2, the interrupt request is fulfilled. Then $Task_0$ starts executing. We can see that the time interval Ts is changeable and the time is measured in seconds.

In Fig. 9, edge 18 shows that when $T = 1.8$ s, the accumulated execution time of $Task_2$ is not equal to $Task[2].C$, that is, $Task_2$ does not finish in the given deadline $Task[2].D = 1.8$. Thus the timeliness property is violated in this case.

The three tasks start at the same time $T = 0$. $Task_0$ executes first, which is finished at $T = 0.4042$ s. Then it waits 0.8 s, during this duration, $Task_1$ is executing. It finishes after 0.6006 s, namely at $T = 1.0102$. Then $Task_1$ waits 0.6 s and $Task_2$ gets the opportunity to run. Once $Task_2$ starts running, it is suspended by the interrupt but it cannot be preempted, for $Task_2$ needs to access the mutex semaphore, which makes its priority raise and be higher than other tasks. After 0.8016 s, it is finished and its priority is recovered. Then it turns to waiting state at $T = 1.8182$. Therefore, $Task_2$ finishes after starting for 1.8182 time units, which is greater than the given deadline. This is consistent with the verification result of our toolkit.

5   Conclusion

We present a unified model checking approach to verify real-time systems running under μC/OS-III. The timer interrupt mechanism of μCOS-III is formalized in TMSVL. As a case study, a multi-task application with timer interrupt is provided and verified in TMSVL. With the toolkit MSV, the TMSVL program can be executed and the desired property of the system can be verified automatically. The mechanism that time intervals are adjustable for modeling improves the efficiency of verification. In the near future, we will further investigate modeling and verification techniques of time delay, timeout and other aspects of μC/OS-III applications on the basis of TMSVL.

References

1. Alur, R., Dill, D.L.: A theory of timed automata. Theor. Comput. Sci. **126**(2), 183–235 (1994)
2. Behrmann, G., David, A., Larsen, K.G.: A tutorial on uppaal. Lect. Notes Comput. Sci. **4**(12), 200–236 (2004)
3. Bozga, M., Daws, C., Maler, O., Olivero, A., Tripakis, S., Yovine, S.: KRONOS: a model-checking tool for real-time systems (Tool-presentation for FTRTFT 1998). In: Ravn, A.P., Rischel, H. (eds.) FTRTFT 1998. LNCS, vol. 1486, pp. 298–302. Springer, Heidelberg (1998)
4. Choi, Y.: Model checking trampoline OS: a case study on safety analysis for automotive software. Softw. Test. Verif. Reliab. **24**(1), 38–60 (2014)
5. Dijkstra, E.W.: Notes on structured programming. Structured Programming, pp. 1–82. Academic Press Ltd., New York (1972)
6. Duan, Z., Tian, C.: A unified model checking approach with projection temporal logic. In: Liu, S., Maibaum, T., Araki, K. (eds.) ICFEM 2008. LNCS, vol. 5256, pp. 167–186. Springer, Heidelberg (2008)
7. Duan, Z., Yang, X., Koutny, M.: Framed temporal logic programming. Sci. Comput. Program. **70**(1), 31–61 (2008)
8. Han, M., Duan, Z., Wang, X.: Time constraints with temporal logic programming. In: Aoki, T., Taguchi, K. (eds.) ICFEM 2012. LNCS, vol. 7635, pp. 266–282. Springer, Heidelberg (2012)
9. Huang, J.C.: An approach to program testing. ACM Comput. Surv. (CSUR) **7**(3), 113–128 (1975)
10. Labrosse, J.J.: uC/OS-III. The Real-Time Kernel. Micrium Press, Weston (2009)
11. Baier, C., Katoen, J.-P.: Principles of Model Checking. The MIT Press, Cambridge (2008)
12. Lundqvist, K., Asplund, L.: A ravenscar-compliant run-time kernel for safety-critical systems. Real-Time Syst. **24**(1), 29–54 (2003)
13. Lv, M., Guan, N., Deng, Q., Ge, Y., Wang, Y.: Static worst-case execution time analysis of the μC/OS-II real-time kernel. Front. Comput. Sci. China **4**(1), 17–27 (2010)
14. Waszniowski, L., Hanzlek, Z.: Formal verification of multitasking applications based on timed automata model. Real-Time Syst. **38**(1), 39–65 (2008)
15. Waszniowski, L., Krákora, J., Hanzálek, Z.: Case study on distributed and fault tolerant system modeling based on timed automata. J. Syst. Softw. **82**(10), 1678–1694 (2009)

The Interchange Format of Tabular Expressions Using XML

Mao Huang[1,2], Yihai Chen[1,2(✉)], Ridha Khedri[1,3], and Huaikou Miao[1,2]

[1] School of Computer Engineering and Science, Shanghai University,
Shanghai, China
yhchen@staff.shu.edu.cn

[2] Shanghai Key Laboratory of Computer Software Evaluating and Testing,
Shanghai, China

[3] Department of Computing and Software, McMaster University,
Hamilton, ON, Canada

Abstract. Tabular expressions, also called *tables*, are formal notations using tables to organize mathematical functions and relations. They have been widely used in documenting and analyzing software specification. Different tools are developed to support tabular expressions. To further enhance tables' usage, a convention on storing and parsing tables is required. This paper presents a canonical interchange format for tabular expressions based on XML. This format captures four aspects of tables: the constituent, dynamic, representation and additional information. Our proposal builds on syntax definition of tables and is tailored to provide flexibility in manipulation of table content. It is suitable for existing and emerging kinds of tables. This study facilitates the interchange between different tools for tabular expressions, which would prevent developer's repetitive work.

Keywords: Tabular expressions · Interchange format · Formal methods · XML

1 Introduction

The failure of safety-critical systems may jeopardize human life, introduce considerable negative financial losses. It is well known that most software errors can be traced back to the requirement stage, and the cost of fixing is rather expensive. Requirements are often stated informally using natural languages, which tend to be imprecise and incomplete. Tabular expressions are formal notation used to organize mathematical expressions based on tabular form. They were proposed by Parnas in 1970s and successfully used in the requirements of A-7 aircraft's Operational Flight Program (OFP) [1]. Writing mathematical expressions in tabular form makes specifications more readable, modifiable and no less

---

This work is supported by National Natural Science Foundation of China (NSFC) under grant 61572306.

S. Liu and Z. Duan (Eds.): SOFL+MSVL 2015, LNCS 9559, pp. 29–43, 2016.
DOI: 10.1007/978-3-319-31220-0_3

Table 1. Normal function table

	$x < 0$	$x = 0$	$x > 0$
$y < 0$	$x^2 - y^2$	$x^2 + y^2$	$x^2 - y^2$
$y = 0$	$x + y$	$x^2 - y^2$	$x^2 + y^2$
$y > 0$	$x^2 + y^2$	$x + y$	$x^2 + y^2$

precise. These qualities are of great values for specifiers and facilitate software testing and verification.

In the early stage of the work on tabular expressions, the tables' meaning was intuitive. With tables become more widely used, some complex tables become to have ambiguous interpretations. Those practical difficulties motivated efforts to define precise syntax and semantics for tables. Parnas [2] proposed ten kinds of tables and gave them formal semantics. Furthermore Parnas termed these tables as *tabular expressions*. Janicki and Abraham [3,4] proposed a semantics for tabular expressions as J-A Model, which provided a relatively general definition based on Parnas tables. Different from others, Kahl [5] defined a compositional syntax and semantics for tabular expressions. Tabular expressions were established by combining one table to other tables or adding headers to a existing table. Because new kinds of tables are continuously emerging, Parnas and Jin [6] defined a general semantics for tabular expressions. The general semantics has considerable flexibility to define existing and emerging types of tables.

The following is a traditional mathematical expression that can be represented as a tabular expression as illustrated in Table 1.

$$f(x) = \begin{cases} x^2 - y^2, & ((y < 0) \wedge (x < 0)) \vee ((y < 0) \wedge (x > 0)) \vee ((y = 0) \wedge (x = 0)) \\ x + y, & ((y = 0) \wedge (x < 0)) \vee ((y = 0) \wedge (x > 0)) \vee ((y > 0) \wedge (x = 0)) \\ x^2 + y^2, & ((y < 0) \wedge (x = 0)) \vee ((y > 0) \wedge (x < 0)) \vee ((y > 0) \wedge (x > 0)) \end{cases}$$

Table 1 is an example of the most commonly used form of tables named *normal function table*. Its corresponding traditional expression is difficult to understand for stakeholders and hard to validate its correctness for specifiers. While the tabular expression makes it very clear what the conditions and cases are, it also gives all the considered conditions. So it is pretty easy to detect the completeness and consistency of mathematical expressions using tables. Mathematical relations of industrial specifications could be much more complicated. It shows more obvious advantages to use tabular expressions to replace traditional expressions.

The rest of this paper is organized as follows: Section 2 introduces three representative tools and theirs' interchange formats and also analyzes the limitations of existing formats. Then we represent the features of XML and demonstrate our contributions compared to previous work. Section 3 describes the structure of table format from four aspects: constituent, additional information, dynamic and representation in details. The grammar of this format is defined by Backus-Naur Form (BNF). Section 4 concludes and gives directions of further work.

2   Related Work and Motivation

2.1   Previous Work and Limitations

Tabular expressions make significant contributions to software formal specifications. Many developers made great efforts to develop supporting tools for tabular expressions. For safety-critical software, tabular expressions have been successfully used in the shutdown system of Ontario Power Generation Project (OPG) [7]. A tool set was developed for the OPG project. Figure 1 provides a overview of the relationship between the documents and tools employed in the project. The requirements saved in Doc files are processed by Microsoft Word then stored in Rich Text Format (RTF) files. The Software Engineering Standards and Methods (SESM) tool are a macro program based on MS Word. Then the (Systematic Design Verification) SDV tool imported the processed specification and transformed it to Prototype Verification System (PVS) input files. Thus, the tables included in the specification could be verified using the theorem prover PVS. Then they are corrected as needed in a feedback process. Although the methodology of OPG is a motivating example, the exchange medium between the tools of OPG project is based on RTF. The RTF specifications lack some of the semantic definitions necessary to read, write and modify documents. The tabular expressions included in RTF files are hard to parse, which leads to spending significant efforts to develop support tools.

Peters et al. [7] proposed to develop an Eclipse plugin to process formal software specification including tabular expressions. Then use PVS to verify the coverage and disjointness of tabular expressions. Figure 2 provides an overview of the Peters' tool architecture. This tool was developed as an Eclipse plugin. A specification was edited by this tool according to the form of OMDoc. Then XSLT was used to translate the specification to PVS input files and verified it using PVS. OMDoc is an open markup language for mathematical documents, which attempts to provide an infrastructure for the communication and storage of mathematical knowledge [8]. OMDoc provides straightforward support for tabular expressions, which greatly facilitates tool developers to parse tabular expressions. Furthermore, OMDoc is proposed based on XML. It can be translated to PVS file easily.

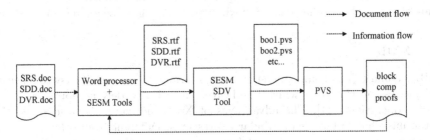

Fig. 1. The relationship between the documents and tools employed in OPG project

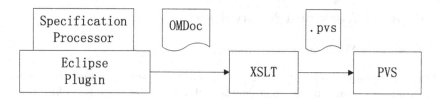

Fig. 2. The process of Peters' proposal

However, OMDoc is proposed to address the communication of specification with theories, symbols and diagrams, which is too complex for tabular expressions. Furthermore, OMDoc dose not support the general semantics of tabular expressions proposed by Jin and Parnas [6].

Wu [9,10] developed a tool to check the inconsistency of requirement specification expressed by tables called SCENATOR. SCENATOR designed TabML (Tabular Markup Language) as their interchange format. TabML is a sublanguage of XML. von Mohrenschildt [11] proposed a standard for software specification called OpenSpec, which provided communication format for tabular expressions. Wu [9] continued von Mohrenschildt's work and defined complete grammar for the interchange format of tabular expressions. This format is termed TabML. The limitation of TabML is that it is proposed according to the early Parnas tables [2]. It is not appropriate for new kinds of tabular expressions.

Interchange format is very important to develop support tools for tabular expressions. A suitable interchange format should not only store information correctly but also ease its writing and parsing. However there is no standard interchange format for tabular expressions nowadays. Developers choose or design different storage formats on their own. One tool can hardly integrate with another tool developed by others, which causes lots of repetitive work for developers. On the other hand, the existing communication formats have respective limitations. Since the early tables have no rigorous definition, the existing formats are casual and have little consideration of the semantics of tabular expressions. This paper makes efforts to propose a more general interchange format for tabular expressions. The semantics of tabular expressions have been generalized to allow more precise definition of a broader range of tabular expression types. The generality and rich features make this format appropriate to store and parse the known kinds of tables. It also has enough flexibility for emerging new kinds of tables.

2.2   XML

XML is a markup language that structures information to make it easy to receive and process on the Web, which is relatively new but widely accepted by software cooperations [11]. The advantages of XML motivate us to adopt XML as the interchange format of tabular expressions. Different from other markup languages, XML allows users to define data type by themselves, which gives semantic meaning to XML document. The relations of elements with attributes in XML can be used to represent the mathematical relations of tables. Thus tabular expressions can be easily stored into XML. Some advantages of using XML to exchange tabular expressions between tools:

- XML is a well defined international standard. all programming languages provide libraries for loading and saving XML files, so multiple-language toolsets are easier.
- XML has clear syntactic rules. Document Type Definition (DTD) or XML Schema can be used to define the structure of the interchange format.
- There are many analysis and transformation tools for XML, such as the XSLT language, which makes it easy to transform XML files into other formats.

2.3 Main Contribution

This paper provides a standard interchange format for tabular expressions. The aim is to facilitate communicating among different tools as well as storing and parsing tabular expressions. The objective is to make tabular expressions more accessible to software specifications. XML is a reasonable choice for transfer format and has extensive applications in information exchange.This paper makes four distinct contributions:

- The proposed interchange format for tabular expressions can serve as a standardized storage exchange format for different tables supporting tools.
- Our interchange format is based on the generalized semantics of tables proposed by Jin and Parnas [6] and considers Kahl's [5] work, which allows more precise definition of existing and emerging table types.
- Considering the practical application, our proposed format supports developers attach additional information to every element and record dynamic information of tables,which will be explained in Sects. 3.2 and 3.3, respectively. Furthermore, visual information is added to describe how tables show and provides the way to make parts of table special. For example, set colors to emphasize some cells.

Based on the interchange format proposed by this paper, developers do not need to develop whole tool set on their own. The universal interchange format can integrate their single tools as a powerful tool set, which releases lots of work for developers. Figure 3 shows the interoperability of a set of tools exchanging information. The editing tool of a developer B can edit tabular expressions then store them to XML files. The presentation tool of a developer A can import an XML file and parse it. Because based on the common interchange format, those tools are compatible with each other, which prevents repetitive work. Choosing XML as a transfer language makes it convenient to transform tabular expressions to the language used by PVS or any other theorem provers and verify them.

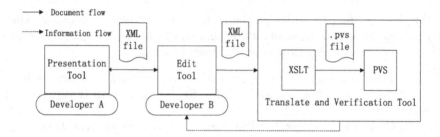

Fig. 3. Interoperability of different tools

3   The Components of Tables Format

3.1   Constituents Information

As there are various types of tabular expressions and new types continuously emerging, Jin and Parnas [6] proposed a general mathematical model for the syntax and semantics of tabular expressions. Different from the other tables' semantics, the general mathematical model does not restrict the layout of tables. Specifiers can choose different representations, according to their own cases. In addition, the general mathematical model has good flexibility. It is not only applicable to existing tables but also appropriate for emerging tables. The key points of the general mathematical model definition of tabular expressions are the following:

- A tabular expression is defined as an indexed set of grids, which is represented as a triple *(Gs, I, f)*. *Gs* denotes the grids, *I* is a set of indices and *f* is the function that maps *I* with *Gs*.
- Each grid is defined as an indexed set of expressions. It can also be represented as a triple *(Es, I, g)*. *Es* is the set of expressions, *I* is a set of indices and *g* is the function with domain *I* and range *Es*.
- The expressions in grids are either traditional expressions or tabular expressions.
- Every tabular expression has a restriction schema to give the condition that the table must satisfy and an evaluation schema to define the meaning of this table.

The interchange format based on the general mathematical model is more flexible than others. We conjecture that it is easier to be accepted by tool developers and has potential to be a standard interchange format of tabular expressions. Our proposal is based on the definition of general mathematical model table. In our format we ignore the restriction and evaluation of general model definition and extract the constituents information as Fig. 4. Each *<expression>* could be an embedded tabular expression. That means there are more than one table. The tag *<Table>* needs the attribute *level* to indicate it is a main table or embedded table. Figure 4 shows a table consisting of indexed grids, where each

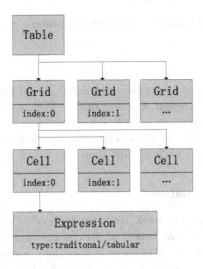

Fig. 4. The constituents of tables

grid consists of indexed cells. The indexes of $<Grid>$ and $<Cell>$ are strings, we do not restrict them must be numbers. Letters or other symbols can be chosen as index if necessary. The content of a cell can be a traditional expression or tabular expression already defined. The attribute type indicates what kind of its content. There are five values for type of $<Expressions>$: term, predicate, label, equation, table. The following segment of XML shows the constituents information of a simple tabular expression with embedded table.

```
<Document>
    <Table level=0 tabType=NorFunTab tabName=MainTable>
        <Grid index="0">
            ...
            <Cell index="0">
                <Expression exType=term>
                    x*x
                </Expression>
            </Cell>
            <Cell index="1">
                <Expression exType =table>
                    EmbeddedTable
                </Expression>
            </Cell>
            ...
        </Grid>
        <Grid index="1">
            ...
        </Grid>
        ...
    </Table>
```

```
<Table Table level=1 tabType =NorFunTab tabName =EmbeddedTable>
    ...
    </Table>
</Document>
```

In the above XML we have two tables, The attribute *tabType* of *<Table>* shows the two tables are both *normal function table*, which is one of the ten kinds of Parnas tables. The *tabName* of *<Table>* is required to help differentiate tables when they have same value of *level*. The *level* is a nonnegative integer, which increases from 0. Having a higher value than 0 means it is an embedded table.

3.2 Additional Information

In practice, especially in team work, different parts of a table may be created by different specifiers at different time. Additional information may be useful for stakeholders. Our format has attributes *author, date* for several main elements to record additional information. Furthermore, we allow users to add any other information using the tag *<Comment>*. The corresponding XML code is below.

```
<Document author=Mao date=2015.5.8>
    <Table level=0 tabType=NorFunTab tabName=Table1>
        <Grid index=0>
            <Cell index=0 author=Doctor Chen>
                <Expression exType=term>
                    x*x
                </Expression>
                <Comment>
                    This cell was made by Doctor Chen!
                </Comment>
            </Cell>
            ......
        </Grid>
        ......
        <Comment>
            this is the top level table !
        </Comment>
    </Table>
    <Comment>
        this table is used to explain our proposal !
    </Comment>
</Document>
```

The attributes *author* and *date* of element may not specify its value. In that case they have the same values as their father element in default. If all the related elements in hierarchy do not show those attributes, that means there is no need to save these information. This example shows the cell with index 0 is create by another writer. While the rest of the cells are created by the *<Document>* author. Both the table and the document have their own comment information.

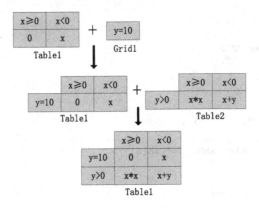

Fig. 5. The process of creating tables

3.3 Action Information

As the specification could always be changed, the tables would be frequently modified. These requirements should be met in interchange format. Kahl [5] proposed a method to create tables by merging tables and adding headers (grids). The following is the process of creating a table in Kahl's work. Our method lays good support for Kahl's compositional definition of tabular expressions. Detailed information is given in [5]. The dynamic information can be saved in $<Action>$. The *order* attribute indicates the sequence of modification. There are four values for *behavior* attribute: Merge, Split, Add, Remove. The tag $<Target>$ specifies the objects of operation. It contains at least one $<exsitTable>$ to locate the element need to be changed. Also $<Table>$, $<Grid>$ and $<Cell>$ could be included in $<Target>$ to define new elements. Note that $<existTable>$ denotes the whole table when it is an empty element. It locates specified grids by containing some empty $<existGrid>$. Cells can be located by adding $<existCell>$ to $<existGrid>$. The following is the corresponding XML representation of the table shown in Fig. 5:

```
<Document >
    <Table level="0" tabType="NorFunTab" tabName="Table1">
        <Grid index="2">
            <Cell index="0">
                <Expression exType="predicate">
                    x>=0
                </Expression>
            </Cell>
            <Cell index="1">
                <Expression exType="predicate">
                    x&lt;0
                </Expression>
```

```
            </Cell>
        </Grid>
        <Grid index="0">
            ......
        </Grid>
    </Table>

    <Action order="1" behavior="Add">
        <Target>
            <existTable tabName="Table1"/>
        </Target>
        <Target>
            <Grid index="1">
                    <Cell index="0">
                    <Expression exType="predicate">
                            y=10
                        </Expression>
                    </Cell>
                </Grid>
        </Target>
    </Action>

    <Action order="2" behavior="Merge">
        <Target>
            <existTable tableName="Table1"/>
        </Target>
        <Target name="Table2">
            <Table level="0" tableType="NorFunTab" tabName="Table2">
                    ......
                </Table>
        </Target>
    </Action>
</Document>
```

This segment of code contains a table and two actions. The first action adds a new grid to Table 1 making it two-dimensional. Then the second action merges Table 1 with Table 2. Note that the two actions $<existTable>$ was empty element, which denotes a whole table. The hierarchy of $<exsitTable>$, $<existGrid>$ and $<existCell>$ can easily locate any objects need to operate.

3.4 Visual Information

The visual properties have two functions. The attributes *width* and *length* describe the layout of the table. Writer can set the value to present tables according their own way. It is not necessary to set layout information for every grid and cell. Usually they have default values. In addition, *color* and *hide* are introduced to make special effects. For example, we can set color for a cell to emphasize its content. The attribute *hide* can help viewers ignore some unrelated parts of table. Especially the table is colossal, it increases lots of conveniences. The following is the example:

```
<Document>
    <Table level="0" tabType="NorFunTab" TabName="MainTable">
        <Grid index="1">
            <Cell index="0">
                <Expression exType="predicate">
                    x&lt;0
                </Expression>
            </Cell>
            <Cell index="1" hide="true">
                <Expression exType ="predicate">
                    x=0
                </Expression>
            </Cell>
            ......
        </Grid>
        <Grid index="0">
            ......
            <Cell index="1" color="red" width="1" height="2">
                <Expression exType ="table">
                    EmbeddedTable
                </Expression>
            </Cell>
            ......
        </Grid>
    </Table>
    <Table level="1" tabType ="NorFunTab" TabName ="EmbeddedTable" color
        ="blue">
        ......
    </Table>
</Document>
```

This code shows two tables, the second one is set as blue to indicate it is an embedded table. In main table, the cell containing tabular expression is different from other cells by changing the value of *width* and *height*. The cell with attribute *hide* means its content is not relevant and ignored by viewers. One of the advantages of tabular expressions is its great readability. Our proposal supports readability very well. The corresponding tables of above code are as Fig. 6. The cell with index 1 is set to red and its width and height is different from other cells. The default color is black. Note that the value of width and height is relative, not the exact size. The default value of width and height is 1, the cell containing table has twice the height and the same width as the normal cell. In this case, the unimportant cell's content is hidden to save readers attention. And the embedded table is marked as blue, which makes it easy to differentiate with the main table.

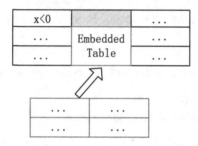

Fig. 6. Visulization of tables (Color figure online)

4   Structure of Tables Format

This format is constructed from four parts integrated together. The first provides information on the constituents. The second gives additional information such as comments to document the table. And the dynamic information of changing table is recorded in third part. Furthermore the visualization information is represented in the last part. This section gives the complete structure of the interchange format. The following is the grammar of this format written by BNF (Backus-Naur Form). In this grammar, nonterminals are typeset in bold letters. And the attributes of elements are typeset Italic.

Document ::= $<$ Document$[\boldsymbol{docName}]_0^1[\boldsymbol{author}]_0^1[\boldsymbol{date}]_0^1 >$
$\qquad$ $[\textbf{Table}]_1^n[\textbf{Action}]_0^n[\textbf{Comment}]_0^n$
$\qquad$ $< /$Document $>$

docName ::= **String**

Table ::= $<$ Table *level tabName tabType*$[\boldsymbol{author}]_0^1[\boldsymbol{date}]_0^1[\boldsymbol{color}]_0^1[\boldsymbol{length}]_0^1$
$\qquad$ $[\boldsymbol{width}]_0^1 >$
$\qquad$ $[\textbf{Grid}]_1^n[\textbf{Comment}]_0^n$
$\qquad$ $< /$Table $>$

tabName ::= **String**

level ::= **integer**

tabType ::= $NorFunTab|InvTab|VecFunTab|CirTab|LocTab|...$

Grid ::= $<$ Grid *index*$[\boldsymbol{author}]_0^1[\boldsymbol{date}]_0^1[\boldsymbol{hide}]_0^1[\boldsymbol{color}]_0^1[\boldsymbol{length}]_0^1[\boldsymbol{width}]_0^1 >$
$\qquad$ $[\textbf{Cell}]_1^n[\textbf{Comment}]_0^n$
$\qquad$ $< /$Grid $>$

Cell ::= $<$ Cell *index*$[\boldsymbol{author}]_0^1[\boldsymbol{date}]_0^1[\boldsymbol{hide}]_0^1[\boldsymbol{color}]_0^1[\boldsymbol{length}]_0^1[\boldsymbol{width}]_0^1 >$
$\qquad$ **Expression**
$\qquad$ $< /$Cell $>$

index ::= **String**

author ::= **String**

$date ::= [0...9]_4^4 - [0...9]_2^2 - [0...9]_2^2$

$hide ::= true|false$

$color ::= red|green|blue|yellow|...$

$length ::=$ **integer**

$width ::=$ **integer**

Expression $::= <$ Expression **exType** $>$

String

$< /textExpression$

$exType ::= term|predicate|lable|equation|table$

Action $::= <$ Action **order behavior** $[\textbf{author}]_0^1[\textbf{date}]_0^1 >$

$[\textbf{Target}]_1^n[\textbf{Comment}]_0^n$

$< /$Action $>$

$behavior ::= Merge|Split|Add|Remove$

$order ::=$ **integer**

Target $::= <$ Target $>$

$[\textbf{Table}]_0^n[\textbf{Grid}]_0^n[\textbf{Cell}]_0^n[\textbf{existTable}]_0^n$

$< /$Target $>$

existTable $::= <$ existTable **tabName** $>$

$[\textbf{existGrid}]_0^n$

$< /$existTable $>$

existGrid $::= <$ existGrid **index** $>$

$[\textbf{existCell}]_0^n$

$< /$existGrid $>$

existCell $::= <$ existCell **index**$/ >$

Comment $::= <$ Comment $[\textbf{author}]_0^1[\textbf{date}]_0^1 >$

String

$< /$Comment $>$

The **String** and **integer** have common meanings, they do not need special definitions. The *tabType* can be assigned those early table types proposed by Parnas or the emerging tables such as circle table, locator table. The attribute *color* can be assigned common color words or the value of RGB. For the *exType*, the value *term* means polynomial. the *predicate* and *equation* are literal sense. *label* means markup symbol. *table* means embedded table. For the *behavior*, the *Merge* and *Split* are opposite operations. So as the *Add* and *Remove*. For detail procedure of those operations, we refer the reader to [5].

The above shows the grammar of the interchange format. The Fig. 7 represents the structure of this format. The arrow means the inclusion relationship. The origination includes the destination. The top of each block diagram is the element, and below are their attributes. The document contains tables, actions

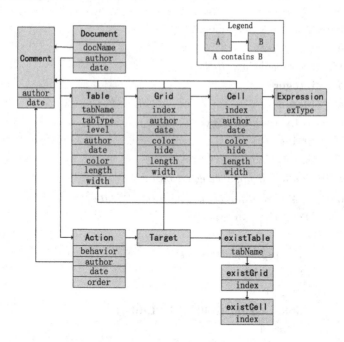

Fig. 7. The structure of tables interchange format

and comments. A table consists of grids while grid consists of cells. Every cell has a specifical expression. Comments can be added to table, grid and cell. Action contains targets and comments. It could include table, grid and cell to define new elements and has the hierarchy of $<existTable>$, $<existGrid>$ and $<exsitCell>$ to locate the objects need to be changed.

5   Discussion and Conclusion

This paper proposes a standard interchange format for tabular expressions in order to communicate tabular expressions between different tools. This format is explained from four points of view: constituents information, additional information, action information and visual information. The constituents in this format is based on the definition of general semantics proposed by Parnas [6]. The action information can easily describe the process of creating a table in Kahl's proposal [5]. The additional information allows writers store some relative information. And the visual information provides flexibility to represent different tables. The existing transfer formats have little consideration of the semantics of tabular expressions. Their limitations make them hard to be accepted by tool developers. Our proposed format considers the existing table definitions and has great flexibility for emerging tables. It has potential to be the universal interchange format of tabular expressions, which would expand the more wider usage of tabular expressions.

In future, many efforts should be made to develop tools to consolidate our achievements. Different tools respectively have the function of editing, representation and verification should be developed. That will show the collaboration between tools based on our general format.

References

1. Heninger, K.L., Kallander, J., Parnas, D.L., Shore, J.E.: Software requirements for the A-7E aircraft. NRL Memorandum Report 3876, United States Naval Research Laboratory, Washington, DC, November 1978
2. Parnas, D.L.: Tabular representation of relations. CRL Report 260, Telecomunications Research Institute of Ontario (TRIO), McMaster University, Hamilton (1992)
3. Janicki, R.: Towards a formal semantics of Parnas tables. In: Proceedings of the 17th International Conference on Software Engineering, pp. 231–240. ACM Press, April 1995
4. Abraham, R.F.: Evaluating generalized tabular expressions in software documentation. Master's thesis, McMaster University, Hamilton (1997)
5. Kahl, W.: Compositional syntax and semantics of tables. SQRL Report 15, McMaster University, Hamilton (2003)
6. Jin, Y., Parnas, D.L.: Defining the meaning of tabular mathematical expressions. Sci. Comput. Program. **75**(11), 980–1000 (2010)
7. Peters, D.K., Lawford, M., Widemann, B.T.: An IDE for software development using tabular expressions. In: Proceedings of the 2007 Conference of the Centre for Advanced Studies on Collaborative Research, Richmond Hill, IBM, pp. 248–251, October 2007
8. Kohlhase, M.: OMDoc - An Open Markup Format for Mathematical Documents. LNAI, vol. 4180. Springer, Heidelberg (2006)
9. Wu, R.: A tool for consistency verification and for integration of formal relational requirements scenarios. Master's thesis, School of Graduate Studies, McMaster University, Hamilton, November 2001
10. Khedri, R., Wu, R., Sanga, B.: Scenator: a prototype tool for requirements inconsistency detection. In: Farn, W., Insup, L. (eds.) Proceedings of the 1st International Workshop on Automated Technology for Verification and Analysis, pp. 75–86. National Taiwan University, Taiwan, December 2003
11. von Mohrenschildt, M.: Communicating software specifications using XML: OpenSpec. CRL Report 373, Department of Computing and Software, McMaster University (1999)

A GUI-Aided Approach to Formal Specification Construction

Shaoying Liu[(✉)]

Department of Computer Science, Hosei University, Tokyo, Japan
sliu@hosei.ac.jp

Abstract. To facilitate writing formal specifications in practice, we put forward a new GUI-aided approach to formal specification construction for software design. By this approach, a GUI prototyping for the system is first carried out based on an informal requirements specification with the aim of improving the informal specification and then a formal design specification is constructed to precisely define the system architecture and functionality. We describe how a prototype GUI can be derived systematically based on the informal specification and discuss how the improved informal specification can be taken into account in constructing the formal design specification.

1 Introduction

Design for a software system can be carried out by constructing a formal specification in which the architecture of the system is represented by diagrams while the functionality of components are precisely defined using a textual formal notation [1,2]. However, our experiences in collaboration with industry suggest that without exploring the structure of the potential graphical user interface (GUI) for the system before writing the formal specification, the cost-effectiveness of formal specification techniques can be seriously damaged. Lacking the understanding of the GUI usually affects the designer's decisions on the parameters for operations to be specified in the formal specification. The user may also feel difficult to communicate with the designer and to tell his or her precise ideas on requirements without GUI.

In this paper, we put forward a new *GUI-aided approach* to constructing formal specifications for software design. The essential idea of the approach is first to derive a prototype GUI for the system based on a structured informal requirements specification and to improve the informal specification by means of a technique called *GUI animation*, and then proceed to construct the formal specification for design on the basis of the improved informal specification. The overall structure of the GUI can be rather systematically derived from the structure of the informal specification, and the structure of the formal design specification can benefit from the details of the improved informal specification.

This work was supported by JSPS KAKENHI Grant Number 26240008.

S. Liu and Z. Duan (Eds.): SOFL+MSVL 2015, LNCS 9559, pp. 44–56, 2016.
DOI: 10.1007/978-3-319-31220-0_4

Note that *the proposed approach is in principle applicable universally to all of the model-based formal notations*, although our discussion in this paper uses the Structured Object-Oriented Formal Language (SOFL) as the specification language [1,3]. SOFL is one of the practical formal notations with a strong expressive capability for industrial software development and offers well-defined guidelines for structuring the informal requirements specification and the formal design specification [4,5]. A SOFL informal specification consists of three sections: *functions*, *data resources*, and *constraints*. The section of functions briefly describes the desired behaviors to be implemented by the system; the section of data resources presents the data items to be used by the functions in the specification; and the section of constraints gives possible restrictions on either functions or data resources, such as those on safety, security, availability, efficiency, or business policies. Our experiences in numerous projects over the last twenty five years suggest that such an informal specification is necessary in paving the way for writing a formal specification from the real world. A SOFL formal specification is a hierarchy of *condition data flow diagrams* (CDFDs) together with an associated hierarchy of modules. A CDFD at one level describes how processes (or operations in general) are connected based on data flows and data stores, while its associated unique module defines all of the components involved in the CDFD, such as processes, data flows, and data stores.

The rest of the paper is arranged as follows. Section 2 briefly introduces SOFL informal specification. Section 3 discusses GUI prototyping. Section 4 describes how a formal specification is constructed. Section 5 reviews related work. Finally, in Sect. 6 we conclude the paper and point out future research directions.

2   SOFL Informal Specification

As mentioned above, an informal specification in SOFL consists of three sections: *functions*, *data resources*, and *constraints*. Figure 1 shows a simplified informal specification for an ATM software. The section of functions includes six top level functions, marked by the numbers from 1.1 to 1.6. Each of the top level functions may be decomposed into several sub-functions. For example, the function 1.2, *withdraw from the bank account*, is decomposed into a set of sub-functions marked by the numbers 1.2.1, 1.2.2, and 1.2.3. The section of data resources contains three top level data items, which are marked by the numbers 2.1, 2.2, and 2.3. If necessary, any of them can be decomposed into several sub-data items. For instance, The first data item 2.1, *Bank account*, is decomposed into six sub-data items marked by the numbers from 2.1.2 to 2.1.6. Further, if a data item is used for a function, a reference from the data item to the function can be written in a parenthesis after the data item. For instance, (F1.2, F1.3, F1.4, F1.5) after data item 2.1 indicates that the data item is used by functions 1.2, 1.3, 1.4, and 1.5. The section of constraints shows four specific constraints, marked by the numbers 3.1, 3.2, 3.3, and 3.4, and each of them sets a restriction on some aspect of the system functionality, usually requiring the system cannot carry out certain actions or violate certain conditions. An example as shown in the figure is

Informal specification for a simplified ATM software:

1.Functions
  1.1 Register a customer
  1.2 Withdraw from the bank account
    1.2.1 Check the card id and password
    1.2.2 Check the amount for withdrawal
    1.2.3 Update the account balance after withdrawal
  1.3 Deposit to the bank account
  1.4 Transfer from one bank account to another
  1.5 Inquire about the balance of the bank account
  1.6 Finish operations

2. Data resources
  2.1 Bank account (F1.2, F1.3, F1.4, F1.5)
    2.1.2 Account name
    2.1.2 Account number
    2.1.3 Account password
    2.1.4 Account balance
    2.1.5 Bank name
    2.1.6 Bank branch code
  2.2 Accounts file (F1.2, F1.3, F1.4, F1.5) /*containing a set of bank accounts*/
  2.3 Customer information(F1.1)

3. Constraints
  3.1 Each withdrawal from a bank account must not exceed 200,000 JPY.
  3.2 The account balance cannot be less than 0.
  3.3 The amount of each transfer cannot exceed 1,000,000 JPY.
  3.4 The amount of each deposit cannot exceed 500,000 JPY

Fig. 1. Informal specification of a simplified ATM software

constraint 3.1, which requires that each withdrawal from a bank account cannot be over 200,000 Japanese Yen (JPY).

Since such an informal specification is usually described abstractly and its meaning is ambiguous, there is a need of an effective technique to help the user conceive the potential behavior of the desired system. Rapid GUI prototyping, as advocated in the literature [6,7], is an effective means for this purpose, which we also adopt in our approach. The problem is how to utilize the informal specification to systematically carry out the GUI prototyping and to improve the informal specification. We discuss this issue next.

3   Principle of GUI Prototyping

The essential idea of our technique for GUI prototyping includes three steps. The first step is to derive the structure of a *preliminary GUI* based on the informal specification; the second step is to refine the preliminary GUI into a *satisfactory GUI structure* by means of a dynamic technique known as *GUI animation*; and the final step is to improve the informal specification by adding necessary detailed information on input and output data resulted from the GUI animation.

3.1   Step 1: Derivation of Preliminary GUI

The prototype GUI structure can be systematically derived from that of the informal specification. Specifically, for each function in the informal specification, we build a *button* in the GUI to allow the user of the system to choose the corresponding function for its operational service, as Fig. 2 illustrates. All of the buttons corresponding to the top level functions in the informal specification constitute the top level page of the GUI. For each function that is decomposed

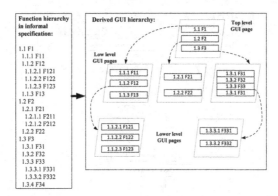

Fig. 2. Relation between the function hierarchy in the informal specification and the derived GUI hierarchy

into several low level functions, we build a low level GUI page with the buttons corresponding to the decomposed functions and link the button of the high level function to the low level GUI page. Thus, in a GUI animation (see the detailed explanation in **Step 3**), once the high level function button is clicked, the corresponding low level GUI page is expected to appear. Applying the same principle to every level function in the function hierarchy, we can systematically derive a hierarchy of GUI pages consistent with the corresponding hierarchical structure of the functions in the informal specification.

Consider the informal specification of the simplified ATM software given in Fig. 1 as example. Applying the GUI derivation principle described above, we obtain a preliminary GUI hierarchy as shown in Fig. 3. The top level GUI page contains six buttons corresponding to the six top level functions in the specification. Since only the second function, 1.2 *Withdraw from the bank account*, is decomposed into three sub-functions, the second button in the top level GUI page is connected to the low level GUI page in the figure.

Note that *using button in the GUI to represent the corresponding function is not necessarily the only choice when building the GUI*. Other options, such as menu bar or menu items, can also be the candidate for the graphical representation of the functions for the same purpose. For different applications in different domains, appropriate GUI items should be considered for effective human-machine interaction. Specific decisions should be made based on engineering judgement in practice. The most important thing to bear in mind is that GUI prototyping is *not* constructing the very final GUI for the envisaged system, but provide a graphical environment to facilitate communication between the user and the designer. Therefore, the detail of the GUI items should not be significant for the design of the overall GUI structure at this stage.

3.2   Step 2: Refinement of GUI

The goal of the second step is to obtain a consensus of the GUI structure and related information between the designer and the user through a comprehensible

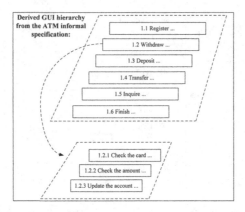

Fig. 3. The derived preliminary GUI hierarchy from the simplified ATM informal specification

communication. Achieving this goal is relatively more challenging than **Step 1** because such a consensus can hardly be precisely defined since the notion of "satisfactory GUI" is undecidable in practice. We propose to use a technique called *GUI animation* to dynamically demonstrate the potential behavior of the GUI. To this end, the designer needs to work together with the user on the following three things:

- Designing the input and output data items for each button-related function.
- Animating the GUI to demonstrate dynamically the potential behavior of each button and its related function.
- Improving the informal specification by updating functions or adding input and output data details to functions.

We discuss how each of these three tasks can be carried out through combination of GUI item design and animation below, respectively.

3.2.1 Design of Input and Output

For the design of the input and output data, a GUI page is created to represent all of the input and output data items for each button-related function. The focus here should be put on the identification of the input and output data items *only* from the user's point of view, *not* from the system's point of view. As a development strategy, obtaining all of the necessary input and output data for each function from the system's point of view will be done during the writing of the formal specification later.

The study of the input and output data can be realized by means of button isolation from the current GUI, as Fig. 4 illustrates. That is, each button, such as 1.2 *Withdraw* ... in the figure, is examined in isolation, but text fields are provided to allow the conceivable input and output data items to be represented properly. For example, the *Withdraw* function takes *amount* as input and produces one of the two possible outputs: *withdrawal cash* and *error message*. As a

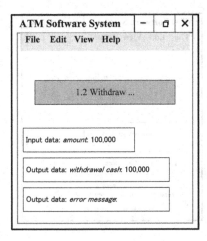

Fig. 4. Animation of a successful withdrawal

specific technique, the data items for the button-related function can be derived by considering the data items in the data resource section in the informal specification (but not always). Note that the figure only shows an abstract idea of the potential situation; the real picture or layout of the GUI page can be flexibly designed in practice to fit the application context.

3.2.2 Animation of Button-Related Functions

To confirm whether the current proposal of the input and output data items are exactly what the user wants for each button-related function, a GUI animation can be performed. By animation we mean that potential behavior of the GUI is only *demonstrated* or *displayed* with only a few data items prepared in advance by human; *not* by executing the *real corresponding program*. The purpose of the animation here is *not* to explore all of the aspects of the potential behavior of each function; *rather*, it aims to help the user learn the intended behavior of the function by exhibiting what input needs to be taken to produce what output. This can be easily realized by taking advantage of existing tool support for GUI prototyping, such as *Microsoft Visual Studio* or *Eclipse*.

In fact, the button-related functions with and without a decomposition are animated slightly differently. Specifically, one conceivable possibility is described below for the two kinds of functions, respectively.

Function without Decompostion: For each input parameter, at least one specific value is proposed and prepared in the corresponding GUI event handling "program" (executable code with artificially arranged content, *not* the real program). The same thing should also be done for each designed output parameter. Then, compile and execute the "program", the potential input-output relation of the corresponding button-related function can be demonstrated. If necessary, more sample input and output parameters can be proposed and

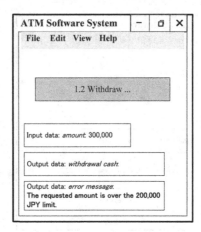

Fig. 5. Animation of an unsuccessful withdrawal

prepared for more demonstrations. For instance, Fig. 4 shows one case of animating the function *Withdraw* for a successful withdrawal, where the input parameter *amount* is assigned the value 100,000 (JPY) and the produced value for the output parameter *withdrawal cash* is 100,000, the same as the input, while Fig. 5 shows an unsuccessful case of withdrawal.

Function with Decomposition: If the function requires specific input data and produces specific output data, the same strategy for the function without decomposition must be applied. In addition, we also need to demonstrate the connection between the current button-related function and the GUI page for its decomposition. This can also be easily realized by preparing the event handling "program" properly with the existing supporting tools. Since this is rather straightforward, we do not continue the discussion here for brevity.

3.2.3   Improvement of Informal Specification

As a result of the GUI animation, the current informal specification may need to be improved by eliminating existing functions, adding additional functions, or adding input and output data items to functions. Either eliminating or adding additional functions can be carried out straightforwardly, but adding input and output data items usually needs a little more careful arrangement. Each input-output pattern with multiple input and output parameters can be clearly described with the sample values used in the GUI animation in the following format:

(Input data: *input parameter name*$_1^1$: sample value$_1^1$,

input parameter name$_1^2$: sample value$_1^2$,

...

input parameter name$_1^a$: sample value$_1^a$,

Output data: *output parameter name*$_1^1$: sample value$_1^1$,

output parameter name $_1^2$: sample value$_1^2$,

...

output parameter name $_1^b$: sample value$_1^b$)

Informal specification for a simplified ATM software:

1.Functions
  1.1 Register a customer
  1.2 Withdraw from the bank account
     (Input data: amount: 100,000 JPY,
       Output data: withdrawal cash: 100,000 JPY) |
     (Input data: amount: 300,000 JPY,
       Output data: error message: The requested amount is over the 200,000
            JPY limit.)

   ...
2. Data resources
   ...
3. Constraints
   ...

Fig. 6. An improved ATM informal specification

If there are several different input-output patterns, they must be separated by a short vertical bar. For example, Fig. 6 shows a simplified improved informal specification of the ATM system in which the two input-output patterns for the function *1.2 Withdraw from the bank account* are presented and all the rest parts are omitted for the sake of space.

4 Formal Specification Construction

A formal design specification can be systematically constructed based on the improved informal specification. Our approach focuses on three aspects of the specification: (1) hierarchical structure, (2) condition data flow diagram (CDFD) at each level in the hierarchy, and (3) module for each CDFD.

4.1 Hierarchical Structure

As briefly mentioned in the Introduction section, a SOFL formal specification is generally organized as a hierarchical structure of CDFDs together with their associated modules. Such a hierarchy usually results from decomposing high level processes into low level CDFDs. A process models a transformation from input to output, possibly including the updating of data stores (which are represented by *external variables*). A CDFD describes how processes are connected based on data flows to form a system. The semantic details of processes in the CDFD are precisely specified in the associated module.

Basically, the hierarchical structure of the specification is derived from the hierarchical structure of the function section in the informal specification. Specifically, for each function in the function section, a process is created in the formal specification. If a function is decomposed into sub-functions, its corresponding process in the formal specification will also be decomposed into a low level CDFD including all of the processes modeling the sub-functions. For each CDFD, a module for defining the semantics of the CDFD components, such as processes, data flows, and data stores, will be constructed. All of the top level functions in the function section will constitute the top level CDFD and its module in the formal specification. Figure 7 illustrates the relation between the informal specification and the formal specification at an abstract level, and Fig. 8 shows the resultant

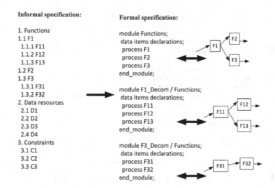

Fig. 7. Relation between informal and formal specification structures

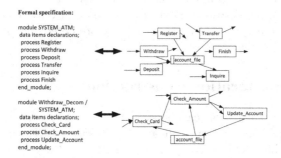

Fig. 8. The structure of the formal specification of the ATM system

formal specification at an abstract level by applying this relation to the ATM system introduced in Fig. 1.

4.2   Drawing CDFD

Drawing a CDFD for each module in the formal specification involves the idea of designing the system architecture, which is absent in the informal specification. The processes, which correspond to the functions in the informal specification or additional functions necessary to the system, are connected based on data flows, focusing on the input and output of each process. Such a CDFD is suitable for describing what to be done by the system at the architecture level rather than how it is done as a control flow diagram indicates. A high level process can be decomposed into low level CDFD, but it is important to retain the consistency between the high level process and the decomposed CDFD based on the following rules:

– All of the input, output, and store variables of a high level process must appear in its decomposed CDFD and used in the same manner (i.e., retaining their name, type, and the way of being used in the process).

- For the same inputs and data stores used in the high level process and the decomposed CDFD, if they satisfy the pre-condition of the high level process, they must also satisfy the pre-conditions of the related processes in the decomposed CDFD. For the same outputs and data stores used in the high level process and the CDFD, if they satisfy the post-conditions of the related processes in the CDFD, they must also satisfy the post-condition of the high level process. This rule actually defines a practical refinement relation between the high level process and its decomposition.

Verifying such a refinement relation can be done by means of existing techniques, such as rigorous inspection [8], specification animation [9], and/or formal proof (which is rarely used in practice).

4.3 Module Construction

For each CDFD, a module needs to be constructed in which all of the components of the CDFD must be specified or declared properly. In general, a module consists of four major parts: *data declarations, invariants, process specifications,* and *function definitions.* The data declarations include *constant declarations, type declarations,* and *data store variable declarations.* The invariants are a list of predicate expressions each of which defines a property either on some data types or on some store variables that must be sustained throughout the entire system. The part of process specifications presents a set of process specifications each of which is represented using pre- and post-conditions. The function definitions are a set of mathematical functions defined explicitly or implicitly that may be applied in some process specifications. The key question here is how the construction of such a module can benefit from the informal specification.

In our approach, we adopt the following guidelines to complete the module:

- The input and output parameters for each process specification mainly come from the input-output details of the corresponding function in the informal specification. However, additional data items to meet the demand of design may also be used and represented by appropriate variables.
- The pre- and post-conditions for each process specification are usually written based on the designer's understanding of the corresponding requirements described in the informal specification.
- The mathematical functions are defined whenever they need to be applied in the process specifications.
- The constant identifier declarations, type declarations, and data store variable declarations are made based on demands from defining the signature of the process specifications, but how they should be declared (e.g., format, structure, and scope of values for basic type variables) need to be determined on the basis of the data item descriptions given in the section of data resources of the informal specification. In principle, every data item in the informal specification must be properly represented or defined in the formal specification, but the data items declared in the formal specification are not limited to representing only the described data items in the informal specification.

– The invariants are usually defined by considering the constraints described in the informal specification. In general, a constraint can be formalized by one or more invariants in the formal specification, but it can also be possible to be formalized in some process specifications. Therefore, it usually needs the designer's engineering judgement in determining whether a constraint should be formalized by invariants or process specifications.

Let us take the ATM system for example. The module known as *Withdraw_Decom* is presented below. **For the sake of the page limit**, we only present the necessary information of the module that helps explain the idea described above and omit all of the other information.

> **module** *Withdraw_Decom* / *SYSTEM_ATM*;
> **const**
> > *max_withdrawal_amount* = 200,000;
>
> **type**
> > *Account* = **composed of**
> > > *acc_name*: **string**
> > > *acc_number*: **nat0**
> > > *acc_password*: **seq of nat0**
> > > *acc_balance*: **nat0**
> > > **end**;

var
> *account_file*: **set of** *Account*;

inv
> **forall**[*acc1*, *acc2*: *account_file*] |
> > *acc1* < > *acc2* = >
> > *acc1.acc_number* < > *acc2.acc_number*
>
> /*Every account in the data store
> account_file has a unique account number. */

process   *Check_Amount*(*customer_account*: *Account*,
> > > > *withdrawal_amount*: **nat0**)
> > > > *cash*: **nat0**, *customer_account*: *Account* |
> > > > *err_message*: **string**

ext   **rd** *account_file*: **set of** *Account*
pre   *exists*[*acc*: *account_file*] | *acc* = *customer_account*
post   **if** *customer_account.balance* > = *withdrawal_amount* **and**
> > *withdrawal_amount* < = *max_withdrawal_amount*
> **then** *cash* = *withdrawal_amount* **and**
> > *customer_account* = ˜*customer_account*
> **else** *err_message* = "The requested amount is over the
> > 200,000 JPY limit."

end_process;

end_module

The module *Withdraw_Decom* is associated with the CDFD resulting from decomposing the process *Withdraw* defined in the upper level module called *SYSTEM_ATM*. It defines all of the components occurring in the CDFD, including the three processes *Check_Amount*, *Check_Card* (omitted), and *Update_Account* (omitted), and the data store *account_file* as well as all of the data flows attached to the processes.

5   Related Work

The essential idea of our GUI-aided approach is a result of applying the idea of traditional prototyping for software development [7]. To the best of our knowledge, there is no report of other similar research in the literature. There are some studies that use formal specifications for prototyping [10] or animation [11,12], but their purpose is to validate the specification rather than construct the specification. We can therefore only give a brief review of the studies on GUI prototyping that have somehow impacted our work.

The paper [13] presents the basic notions behind user interface prototyping, a review of several tools supporting it, and a case study of nine major industrial projects. The most interesting observation pointed out in the paper is that none of the nine projects studied applied a traditional life-cycle approach and user interface prototyping is increasingly used as a vehicle for developing and demonstrating visions of innovative systems. Smith discussed the language issues in prototyping user interface and pointed out that a prototype-based language known as NewtonScript is more suitable for implementing object-oriented user interface frameworks than a class-based language in [14]. Memmel *et al.* proposed ways of agile high-fidelity prototyping as visual specifications for corporate user interface design to facilitate the collaborative design by the designer and the stakeholders [15] . Reza describes a GUI driven software development platform known as CodeMonkey-GA in his thesis [16]. By using CodeMonkey-GA, non-experts and experts alike can relatively easily turn an evolutionary algorithm design into a working Java program, with a minimum amount of manual coding.

6   Conclusion

To enhance communication between the designer and the user and therefore facilitate the construction of formal specifications for software design, we have put forward a systematic GUI-aided approach to formal specification construction. The approach offers a precise guideline for deriving a prototype GUI from an informal requirements specification and a technique known as GUI animation to help identify input and output data items from the user's point of view for functions to improve the original informal specification. The construction of a formal specification can then be systematically carried out on the basis of the informal specification. Our future research along this line will focuse on the tool development for and empirical studies of our approach.

References

1. Liu, S., Offutt, A.J., Ho-Stuart, C., Sun, Y., Ohba, M.: SOFL: a formal engineering methodology for industrial applications. IEEE Trans. Softw. Eng. **24**(1), 337–344 (1998). Special Issue on Formal Methods
2. Snook, C., Butler, M.: UML-B: formal modelling and design aided by UML. ACM Trans. Softw. Eng. Methodol. (TOSEM) **15**(1), 92–122 (2006)
3. Liu, S.: Formal engineering for industrial software development – an introduction to the SOFL specification language and method. In: Davies, J., Schulte, W., Barnett, M. (eds.) ICFEM 2004. LNCS, vol. 3308, pp. 7–8. Springer, Heidelberg (2004)
4. Liu, S., Asuka, M., Komaya, K., Nakamura, Y.: An approach to specifying and verifying safety-critical systems with practical formal method SOFL. In: Proceedings of the Fourth IEEE International Conference on Engineering of Complex Computer Systems (ICECCS 1998), pp. 100–114, Monterey, California, USA, 10–14 August 1998. IEEE Computer Society Press (1998)
5. Shen, Y., Chen, H.: Extending SOFL features for AOP modeling. In: Proceedings of 10th IEEE International Conference on Engineering of Complex Computer Systems (ICECCS), Presented at the Workshop on SOFL, pp. 14–15. IEEE Computer Society Press, Shanghai (2005)
6. Tanik, M.M., Yehissi, R.T.: Rapid prototyping in software development. The Computer **22**(5), 9–11 (1989)
7. Lim, Y.K., Erik, S., Josh, T.: The anatomy of prototypes: prototypes as filters, prototypes as manifestations of design ideas. ACM Trans. Comput. Human Interact. **15**(2), 7–33 (2008)
8. Liu, S., McDermid, J.A., Chen, Y.: A rigorous method for inspection of model-based formal specifications. IEEE Trans. Reliab. **59**(4), 667–684 (2010)
9. Liu, S., Wang, H.: An automated approach to specification animation for validation. J. Syst. Softw. **80**, 1271–1285 (2007)
10. Abdallah, A.E., Bowen, J.P., Barros, A., Barros, J.B.: A provably correct functional programming approach to the prototyping of formal Z specifications. In: Proceedings of ACS/IEEE International Conference on Computer Systems and Applications (AICCSA 2003), Tunis, Tunisia, 14–18 July 2003. IEEE Computer Society Press (2003)
11. Najafi, M., Haghighi, H.: An animation approach to develop c++ code from object-Z specifications. In: CSI International Symposium on Computer Science and Software Engineering (CSSE 2011), pp. 9–16. IEEE (2011)
12. Miller, T., Strooper, P.: Combining the animation and testing of abstract data types. In: Proceedings of Second Asia-Pacific Conference on Quality Software (APAQS 2001), pp. 249–258. IEEE CS Press (2001)
13. Baumer, D., Bischofberger, W.R., Lichter, H., Zullighoven, H.: User interface prototyping - concepts, tools, and experience. In: 18th International Conference on Software Engineering (ICSE 1996), pp. 532–541, Berlin, 25–30 March 1996
14. Smith, W.R.: Using a prototype-based language for user interface: the Newton project's experience. In: ACM Conference on Object-Oriented Programming Systems, Languages, and Applications, pp. 61–72, Austin, 15–19 October 1995
15. Memmel, T., Gundelsweiler, F., Reiterer, H., Interfaces, prototyping corporate user : towards a visual specification of interactive systems. In: Second IASTED International Conference on Human Computer Interaction (IASTED-HCI 2007), pp. 177–182, Chamonix, 14–16 March 2007
16. Reza, E.: A GUI Driven Platform for Implementing Evolutionary Algorithms in Java. PhD thesis, Concordia University, 12 September 2014

Testing and Debugging

Automatic Generation of Specification-Based Test Cases by Applying Genetic Algorithms in Reinforcement Learning

Yuji Sato$^{(\boxtimes)}$ and Taku Sugihara

Department of Computer and Information Sciences, Hosei University, Tokyo, Japan
`yuji@hosei.ac.jp`

Abstract. Automatic test pattern generation by applying genetic algorithms in reinforcement learning is proposed and the results of evaluation with an ATM system which assuming the existence of a bug related to a global variable are reported. For software development based on formal specifications, a number of methods for the automatic generation of test cases have previously been proposed. However, most of those methods are for testing whether or not the specifications are correctly implemented, and the problem of automatically generating test cases for which all of the paths can be traversed, including paths that were not anticipated, remains unsolved. We have previously demonstrated the feasibility of using genetic algorithms as an effective approach to that problem by evaluation with a simple test problem that assumes a single-variable input and evaluation assuming that the total number of paths is known. Here, we use a genetic algorithm in which the test cases are used as the gene locus values in the chromosome with redundant gene length and the difference vector is used for performing mutation. We compare this approach to the pairwise method and the vibration method, which are leading research areas, in a more realistic testing environment such as evaluation of ATM system programs. We show that the proposed method can provide higher program path coverage than the previous methods and effectively generates test cases for a bug related to a global variable.

Keywords: Formal specification · Genetic algorithm · Reinforcement learning

1 Introduction

Formal specifications eliminate vagueness by using mathematical description, making it possible to determine strictly whether or not the program runs correctly according to the specification. It is also possible to detect inconsistencies when the specifications are being written, thus averting problems due to specification issues discovered for the first time in later stages of development such as the implementation process. It is accordingly effective for developing highly trustful programs in a short time.

© Springer International Publishing Switzerland 2016
S. Liu and Z. Duan (Eds.): SOFL+MSVL 2015, LNCS 9559, pp. 59–71, 2016.
DOI: 10.1007/978-3-319-31220-0_5

Actually, even programs that have been developed on the basis of formal specifications and have passed inspection can fail during operation. That is because formal specifications that abstract actual informal problems in the process of converting informal required specifications to semi-formal or formal specifications are not necessarily guaranteed to provide a correct description, there are multiple possible implementations when the code is actually written according to formal specifications, and unanticipated paths that may result from bugs, etc. in the program.

To solve the above problems, a research for the automatic specification-based testing (ASBT) [13] has begun. The essential idea of ASBT is to generate a test set that covers every scenario by satisfying its test condition at least once. Generally, this problem may be handled by generating more test cases, but what test cases should be generated is still a big challenge. Liu has proposed the "Vibration method [12]" which tries to change the "distance" between the variables to find more test cases to cover all corresponding program paths. For example, if there are two expressions E1 and E2, the "distance" ($|E1 - E2|$) between E1 and E2 will be changed as the values of variables in two expressions changed. A test case is created to satisfy the relation when the distance is small; another new test case will be created when the distance is greater. Repeating this process by increasing and decreasing the distance between E1 and E2 until the terminated decision is made. Although this method improved path coverage rate dramatically, however it still can't ensure to cover all paths in the representative program. There is also a large body of research on specification-based testing. Many projects automated test cases generation from specifications, such as Z specification [1,2], UML statecharts [3,4], or ADL specifications [5,6]. The Korat which is one of the novel frameworks for automated testing of Java Programs, is based on Java predicates [7]. Given a predicate and a bound on the size of its inputs, Korat generates all inputs for which the predicate returns true. Marisa A.S'anchez has examined algebraic-specification based testing with particular attention to the approach reported by Gilles Bernot, Marise Claude Gaudel and Bruno Marre [8]. It did not only focus on the generation of test cases from the initial specification but also the additions and revisions during the development. D.Marinov and S. Khurshid presented a framework for automated testing of Java programs called TestEra [9]. TestEra uses the Alloy Analyzer (AA) [10] to automatically generate method inputs and check correctness of outputs, but it requires programmers to learn a specification language much different than Java. Cheon and Leavens have proposed an automatic translation of JML specifications into test oracles for JUnit [11]. But the programmers have to provide sets of possibilities for all method parameters, which add a burden of test cases generation for programmers.

In this paper, genetic algorithms (GA) has been used to address the problem by studying how to ensure the paths in the related program can be traversed completely [19]. Roy P. Pargas, Mary J. Harrold, and Robert R. Peck [18] have already applied standard genetic algorithms to generate a test data for a specific path. On the other hand, we propose improved genetic algorithms to generate test patterns that traverse all of the paths within the program, including unanticipated paths. A large number of test cases are generated as the gene locus values in the chromosome with redundant gene length, and the appropriate test cases have been discovered using GA based reinforcement learning to cover all paths in the related program.

The remainder of this paper is organized as follows. Section 2 gives a brief introduction to the automatic specification-based test cases generation. In Sect. 3, we present how to apply GA to solve this issue. Section 4 presents and discusses the experimental results and is followed by the conclusion.

2 Specification-Based Test Cases Generation and Reinforcement Learning

In this section, we formalize the problem of automatic generation of test cases that involve unanticipated paths and propose a method based on reinforcement learning in which genetic algorithms are used as an efficient stochastic search for the automatic generation of test cases.

2.1 Formalization of the Problem of Generating Test Patterns for Traversing Unanticipated Paths

Denoting the number of input variables as m, the input variables as $x_i(i = 1, ..., m)$, the test case as $t = [x_1, x_2, ..., x_m]$ the set of test cases as X, the path (permutation of execution steps in a program from input to output) as y, and the set of paths in a program as Y, consider a program f for which there is a one-to-one mapping of any element t of X to element y (path in the program) of Y. That is to say,

$f : X \to Y, f(t) = y$

Although there is only one y in Y for any t of X, generally, the elements in X that map to y are not necessarily limited to a single element. Accordingly, y is surjective but not injective. Thus, for $y \in Y$ the inverse image of y from f, $f^{-1}(y) = \{t | f(t) \in y\}$, is the set of test cases in X that transferred to path y by f.

Then, given

$X = X_1 \cup X_2 \cup ... \cup X_N, X_i \cap X_j = \phi(i \neq j)$

$X_i(X_i \subset X)(i = 1, ..., N)$

here both of X_i and N are defined as an unknown quantity. the problem of generating a test pattern that traverses all unknown paths is defined as the problem of finding

$T = [t_1, t_2, ..., t_N], t_i \in X_i(i = 1, ..., N)$

$t_i = [x_{i1}, x_{i2}, ..., x_{im}], m$: the number of input variables.

2.2 Test Pattern Generation Based on Reinforcement Learning

Because X_i, N, and y are all unknown, it is difficult to solve this problem analytically. We therefore investigate an approach that uses stochastic search

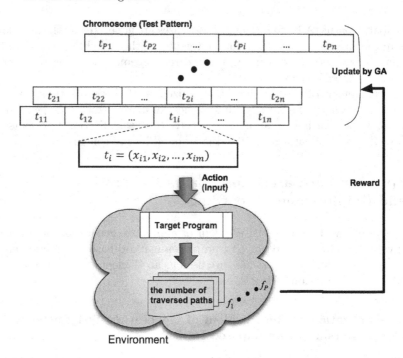

Fig. 1. The configuration of a system for generating test patterns by using GA based reinforcement learning

and reinforcement learning. The configuration of a system for generating test patterns by using reinforcement learning is illustrated in Fig. 1. In practice, we do not know how many paths in the target program, but noting that there is an open source software [17] on the internet which can check out the number of paths in the program, or there is commercially available software for showing (identifying) the execution steps in a program and that any path in the program is a permutation of the execution steps from input to output, the number of traversed paths within a program can be counted in principle. Here, we consider reinforcement learning in which the number of types of paths that are traversed when the set of test patterns is input to the program serves as the reward value. Also, test patterns composed from a set of test cases can be regarded as one type of gene, so we propose reinforcement learning that is updated by genetic calculation of the set of test patterns.

3   Applying GA to Automatic Test Case Generation

In this section, we propose applying GA to automatic test case generation based on formal specification. By utilizing GA, the process of choosing test cases will be more effective. Initially, GA generates a population based on the specification, in which each individual is a set of test cases. The individual who has high

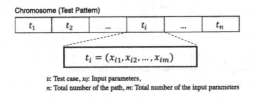

t: Test case, x_{ij}: Input parameters,
n: Total number of the path, m: Total number of the input parameters

Fig. 2. Chromosome definition for test cases generation

path coverage rate will be selected to produce next generation. After the GA manipulation, the population in the next generation will be better and have a higher path coverage rate. The evolution will continue until all the paths in the program have been traversed.

3.1   Definition of Chromosome for Automatic Test Case Generation

The first step of GA is to randomly generate population of chromosomes [16]. Each member in the population is called individual. In our work, an individual is a test set consisting of one or more test cases. The test cases are generated based on the formal specification. If the chromosome is defined as a test case, it is difficult to judge whether the chromosome is good enough to be used to generate next generation. Because every chromosome will be in only two states:one is covered a path; the other is not cover a path. If the chromosome is defined a set of test cases, there will be a path coverage rate for every chromosome, and then we can judge which one is appropriate to be selected to generate the next generation. Figure 2 shows an example of a chromosome definition for a set of test cases. Every genetic locus in each chromosome corresponds to a test case, which satisfies the precondition. For example, the input variables are numeric type from 1 to 100, and then genetic locus will be defined as a number from 1 to 100 randomly. The length of the chromosomes (how many test cases in a chromosome) equals to the number of the paths. Thus, in the Fig. 2, t_i represents a test case, and n denotes the number of the paths. By generating a large scale of chromosomes in a population, we can generate a lot of test cases satisfied the precondition.

Figure 3 shows an example of the initial population when we don't have any previous test patterns or knowledge to generate test patterns from corresponding paths map. In this example, input parameters are generated randomly in a feasible region. Figure 4 shows an example of the initial population when we have some previous test patterns or knowledge to generate test patterns from corresponding paths map. In this example, we use these test patterns as a part of chromosomes and generate other input parameters randomly.

3.2   Evaluation Function

In a genetic operation, the evaluation function is a fitness function which is devised for each problem to be solved. Given a particular chromosome, the fit-

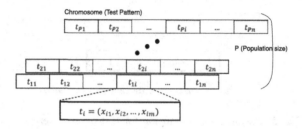

Fig. 3. An example of initial populations when we don't have any previous test patterns

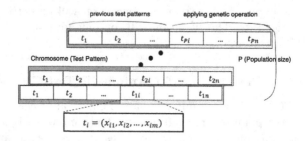

Fig. 4. An example of initial populations when we have some previous test patterns

ness function returns a single numerical "fitness", or "figure of merit", which is supposed to be proportional to the "utility" or "ability" of the individual which that chromosome represents. In this case, the fitness function is defined as the path coverage rate, when the chromosome covered more paths, its evaluation value will be higher. In this study, we assume that the number of all paths in the related program is known and define the fitness function in Equation (1) below, which is normalized to values between 0 to 1.

$$f = \frac{k}{n} \tag{1}$$

In Equation (1), f is the evaluation function, k is the number of the paths that chromosome has covered; n is the number of all paths in the corresponding programs. The individual who achieves an evaluation value $f=1$ means that the individual has covered all paths in the corresponding programs, and it is the optimal solution to the problems.

3.3 Genetic Manipulation

Selection. Selection is the stage in which individual generates for next generations from a population based on fitness values. There are many kinds of selection methods in GA, and we apply tournament selection [16] in this study. Tournament selection has a simple rule and can guarantee that the better one will be chosen and the worse one will be eliminated. Tournament selection involves randomly picking several individuals from the population and staging a tournament to determine which one is finally selected. It generates a random value between zero and one and comparing it to a pre-determined selection probability. If the random value is less than or equal to the selection probability, the fitter candidates is selected; otherwise, it select other candidates again. The probability parameter provides a convenient mechanism for adjusting the selection pressure. The tournament size is 3, selecting the highest fitness one to be parent for next generation by comparing the three individuals. The individuals selected by tournament selection as parents to do crossover.

Crossover. Crossover is a genetic operator used to vary the programming of chromosomes from one generation to the next. In this paper we choose uniform crossover [16]. This operator exchanges approximately half the genes. That is, at each gene position in parent A and parent B, a random decision is made whether that gene should go into offspring A or offspring B. Even though the uniform crossover is a poor method, empirical evidence suggest that it is a more exploratory approach to crossover than the traditional exploitative approach that maintains longer schemata. This results in a more complete search of the design space with maintaining the exchange of good information.

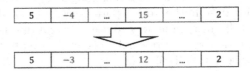

Fig. 5. An example of a simple mutation

Mutation. Mutation is a genetic operator used to maintain genetic diversity. When a number of the input parameter is 1, we can apply a simple mutation. An example of a simple mutation is shown in Fig. 5. Mutation is applied to each child individually after selection and crossover. It randomly alters each gene with a small probability. If the variable t which is generated randomly is bigger than mutation rate, the mutation manipulation will be executed. Mutation provides a small amount of random search, and helps ensure that no point in the search space has a zero probability of being examined. On the other hand, in many cases, a test case is consisted of multiple input parameters and we can't apply a simple mutation. In this case, we regard a test case $t = [x_1, x_2, ..., x_m]$ as a m-dimensional vector, and a mutation is defined as a different vector mutation.

$$\vec{t'} = \vec{t} + \Delta \vec{t} \tag{2}$$

where $\vec{t}$ is an original test case vector, $\Delta \vec{t}$ is different vector and $\vec{t}$' is a vector after mutation. An example for the two input parameters is shown in Fig. 6.

Repeat the above steps until the individuals whose fitness is 1 have been found or if the maximum evaluation value is not updated after a certain number of generations [14–16].

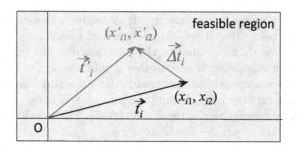

Fig. 6. An example of a different vector mutation for the two input parameters

4   Evaluation Tests

To evaluate the proposed method of generating test cases, we performed preliminary tests using a simple program, which demonstrated the validity of the method [19]. The vibration method and pairwise method that were mentioned above, on the other hand, used an ATM system that was designed on the basis of SOFL (Structured Object-oriented Formal Language) for testing, but the program was not published, so in the work reported here, we also designed an ATM system based on SOFL in the same way to use a system that is similar for comparative testing with that related research. The evaluation testing environment specifications are presented in Table 1.

Table 1. Experiment environment

OS	Windows 7
Processor	Intel Core i7 CPU 3.20 GHz
Memory(RAM)	12 GB
Operating system type	64-bit system
Tools	Eclipse Standard / SDK
	Version: Kepler Service Release 2

4.1   ATM System Overview

The six main ATM system operations (services) are 'open account', 'withdraw', 'transfer', 'deposit', 'show balance', and 'change password'. The registered customer information (CustomerAccountInfo) is managed as a map (account_file) with the account number (AccountNo) serving as the key. When the system accepts an operation, it produces an output according to the input. When the input is incorrect, such as when the account number or password is invalid, an error message that explains the problem is output.

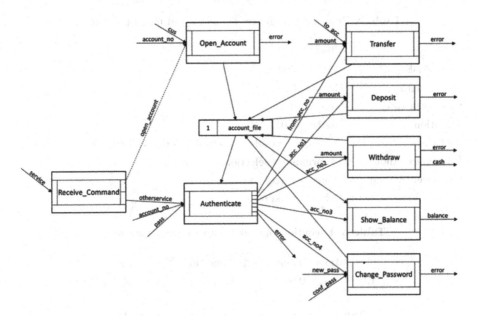

Fig. 7. ATM system CDFD

A condition data flow diagram (CDFD) that shows the overall configuration of the ATM system is presented in Fig. 7. This system comprises eight processes, including the six services described above, and one data store. The account_file contains customer information. The Receive_Command process accepts the service that the user wants to use as input. It determines whether the accepted service is Open_account or another service, and outputs to a different process accordingly. The Authenticate process verifies the account number and password. If the input account number and password combination matches what is stored in account_file, it outputs to the service process according to the service that was received from the Receive_Command process. If the input does not match, an error is output.

4.2   Test Method

We performed two types of tests. Test 1 assumed that the total number of paths is known and test 2 assumed operation that differs from the specifications or insertion of a bug that produces operation that differs from the specifications so that the total number of paths is not known. The bug inserted in test 2 was the value of a global variable used in the ATM system that resulted in operation not specified in the specifications. In addition, the gene length of the chromosome in test 2 is made twice the total number of paths before the bug was introduced, because the total number of paths is unknown. That the number of unanticipated paths can exceed the number of paths from the specifications probably goes against common sense. Furthermore, because the total number of paths is

Table 2. Program parameters for test 1 and test 2 program

	Test 1	Test 2
Individuals	250	500
Gene length	32	64
Cross-over rate	0.9	0.8
Mutation rate	0.016	0.011
Test cases	t_i (service,number of suitable input variables for the service)	
Selection method	Tournament selection	
Crossover method	Uniform crossover	
Total number of paths	32	Unknown

Table 3. Execution time and path coverage for test 1

Generations	Time (avg.)	Time (max.)	Coverage
124.56	0.98 s	1.56 s	100.0 %

Table 4. Execution time and path coverage 2

Generations	Time (avg.)	Time (max.)	Coverage
156.9	4.18 s	6.15 s	100.0 %

unknown in test 2, the number of traversed paths is used as the evaluation value, and if the maximum evaluation value is not updated after a certain number of generations, that evaluation value is judged to be the total number of paths and the processing is ended. The parameters of the test programs are listed in Table 2.

4.3 Test Results

For both test 1 and test 2, the test was repeated 50 times and the number of generations, the run time, and the average path coverage were calculated. The results are presented in Table 3 for test 1 and in Table 4 for test 2. The genetic algorithm learning curve, with the path coverage on the vertical axis and the number of generations on the horizontal axis is presented in Fig. 8 for test 1 and in Fig. 9 for test 2. For test 1, which assumes that the total number of paths is known, test patterns for which all of the 32 paths are traversed were generated, for the coverage of 100 %. For test 2, which assumes that the total number of paths is not known, the search was ended when the evaluation values, which indicate the number of paths traversed, were 40 for all of the 50 trials. The number of paths for the ATM system after introduction of the bug was confirmed to be 40, so the generation of test patterns with 100 % coverage succeeded for test 2 as well.

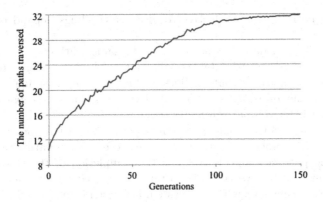

Fig. 8. Relationship of number of generations and path coverage for test 1

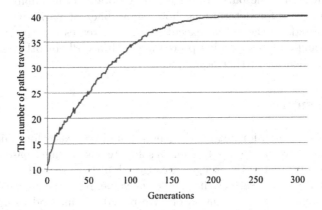

Fig. 9. Relationship of number of generations and path coverage for test 2

5 Discussion

Test patterns with 100 % coverage were successfully generated for both test 1, which assumes the total number of paths is known, and test 2, which assumes the total number of paths is not known. In test 2, however, there were cases in which test patterns for which the path coverage is 100 % were not discovered if the values for the number of individuals, the cut-off number of generations, the crossover rate, and the mutation rate were not suitable. Investigation of the reason for that result showed that the bug inserted in test 2 was the value of a global variable that resulted in operation not specified in the specifications and many generations are needed to discover those paths, and the cut-off number of generations was reached before the test patterns for which all of the paths are traversed could be discovered. The proposed method never ensures to discover all program paths for a bug related to a global variable. But the chromosome with redundant gene length generates several types of test cases corresponding to a specific path and it is effective to discover the bugs depend on a global variable.

Although the test data was not entirely the same, path coverage of 53 % by the pairwise method and 92 % by the vibration method has been reported [13]. Considering a comparison that involves evaluation using a similar system, we conclude that the proposed method effectively generates test patterns, even though the basis for comparison is not strict.

With the proposed method, program testing is essentially done in the test pattern generation process. That is to say, the success in generating test patterns for which the path coverage is 100 % is the completion of the testing of that program. Thus, we believe the test patterns generated by our method can be reused as prior knowledge when the system is revised or upgraded.

Furthermore, because these tests use a program that we wrote, the specifications are such that the path coverage can be obtained immediately. Actually, a separate program for determining how many different paths have been traversed is required, so the actual execution time increases greatly. Accordingly, faster processing through parallel processing with a GPU or other such means is probably needed for further development.

6   Conclusion

We proposed a method for automatic generation of test cases for which all program paths are traversed for application in software development based on formal specifications. Our method uses a genetic algorithm that uses a chromosome definition that has the test case as the gene locus value, redundant gene length and uses the difference vector for mutation. We tested the method using an ATM system designed on the basis of formal specifications, assuming the existence of a bug related to a global variable. The tests demonstrated the generation of test patterns that have the coverage 100 %, both in tests that assume the total number of paths is known and in tests that assume that the number of paths is not known. That is to say, comparison with previous methods by tests performed using a similar system showed the possibility of greatly improved path coverage. The proposed method is also effective to discover the bugs depend on the value of a global variable.

Acknowledgements. We would like to show my deepest gratitude to Prof. Shaoying Liu of the Department of Computer and Information Sciences in Hosei University for their valuable comments and discussions on experimental results.

References

1. Horcher, H.-M.: Improving software tests using Z specifications. In: Proceeding 9th International Conference of Z Users, The Z Formal specification Notation (1995)
2. Spivey, J.M.: The Z notation: A Reference Manual, 2nd edn. Prentice Hall (1992)

3. Offutt, J., Abdurazik, A.: Generating tests from UML specifications. In: France, R.B. (ed.) UML 1999. LNCS, vol. 1723, pp. 416–429. Springer, Heidelberg (1999)
4. Rumbaugh, J., Jacobson, I., Booch, G.: The Unified Modeling Language Reference Manual. Addison-Wesley Object Technology Series (1998)
5. Chang, J., Richardson, D.J.: Structural specification-based testing: automated support and experimental evaluation. In: Proceeding 7th ACM SIGSOFT Symposium on the Foundations of Software Engineering, pp. 285–302, September 1999
6. Sanker, S., Hayes, R.: Specifying and testing software components using ADL. Technical Report SMLI TR-94-23, Cun Microsystems Laboratories, Inc., Mountain View, CA, April 1994
7. Boyapati, C., Khurshid, S., Marinov, D.: Korat: automatically testing based on java predicates. ISSTA 2002 Proceedings of the ACM SIGSOFT International Symposium on Software testing and analysis, pp. 123–133 (2002)
8. Sánchez, M.A.: Specification-based Testing, pp. 12–47 (1997)
9. Marinov, D., Khurshid, S.: TestEra: a novel framework for automated testing of Java programs. In: Proceeding 16th IEEE International Conference on Automated Software Engineering, San Diego, November 2001
10. Jackson, D., Schechter, I., Shlyakhter, I.: ALCOA: the alloy constraint analyzer. In: Proceeding 22nd international Conference on Software Engineering(ICSE), Limerick, June 2000
11. Cheon, Y., Leavens, G.T.: A simple and practical approach to unit testing: the JML and JUnit way. Technical Report 01–12, Department of Computer Science, Iowa State University, November 2001
12. Liu, S., Nakajima, S.: A "Vibration" method for automatically generating test cases based on formal specifications. In: Software Engineering Conference, 2011 18th Asia Pacific, pp. 73–80, 5–8 December 2011
13. Liu, S., Nakajima, S.: A decompositional approach to automatic test cases generation based on formal specification. In 4th IEEE International Conference on Secure Software Integration and Reliability Improvement, pp. 147–155. IEEE CS Press, Singapore, 9–11 June 2010
14. Reeves, C.R.: Modern Heuristic Techniques for Combinatorial Problems. Blackwell Scientific, Oxford (1993)
15. Beasley, J.E.: A genetic algorithm for the set covering problem. Eur. J. Oper. Res. **94**, 392–404 (1996)
16. Beasley, D., Bull, D.R., Martin, R.R.: An overview of genetic algorithms: Part I, fundamentals. Univ. Comput. **15**(2), 58–59 (1993)
17. http://www.kailesoft.cn (cited 7 July 2014)
18. Pargas, R.P., Harrold, M.J., Peck, R.R.: Test-data generation using genetic algorithms. J. Softw. Testing Verification Reliab. **9**(4), 263–282 (1999)
19. Zhou, Y., Sugihara, T., Sato, Y.: Applying GA with Tabu list for automatically generating test cases based on formal specification. In: Liu, S., Duan, Z. (eds.) SOFL+MSVL 2014. LNCS, vol. 8979, pp. 17–31. Springer, Heidelberg (2015)

Fault Localization of Timed Automata Using Maximum Satisfiability

Shin Nakajima[1,2(✉)] and Si-Mohamed Lamraoui[1,2]

[1] National Institute of Informatics, Tokyo, Japan
nkjm@nii.ac.jp
[2] SOKENDAI, Tokyo, Japan

Abstract. Timed automata are formal models for systems whose real-time behavior is a major concern, and practical model checking tools are available for them. Although these tools are effective to detect faulty behavior, localizing root causes of faulty timed automata requires a costly manual task of studying counter-examples. This paper presents an automatic fault localization problem. The proposed approach follows the Reiter's model-based diagnosis theory to employ the consistency-based method, and details the method to show how the Reiter's general theory is applicable to timed automata. In particular, the proposed method introduces a modest assumption on the failure. The paper discusses how the failure model and properties to be checked affect the formula used in the consistency-based fault localization method.

1 Introduction

Timed or hybrid systems are employed as a *modeling* tool for a wide variety of non-functional concerns such as real-time timing properties or energy consumption [16]. Their formal models, especially linear hybrid systems [2] including timed automata [1], are well studied and industrial-strength verification tools for the timed automata are developed (e.g. [10]). These tools check the behavioral aspects automatically, but require a costly manual study of generated counter-example traces to identify root causes of the failure.

Automatic fault localization methods are successful for the case of VLSI circuit designs [19,21] or imperative programs [5,7–9]. These consistency-based approaches adapt the model-based diagnosis (MBD) theory [18] and use Boolean satisfiablity [4] as in the bounded model checking (BMC) [3], or specifically the maximum satisfiability (MaxSAT). In the MBD theory, an artifact and its property or an assertion are encoded in a logic formula. The whole formula is unsatisfiable if the artifact is faulty in that it violates the property. The fault localization problem is finding a subset of clauses in the formula to make it satisfiable if they are removed. This subset of clauses is a minimal correction subset (MCS) of the unsatisfiable formula [12].

This paper proposes a consistency-based fault localization method for timed automata using the MaxSAT. The method adopts the Boolean encoding of timed automata proposed in [20]. The contributions of this paper are as follows.

© Springer International Publishing Switzerland 2016
S. Liu and Z. Duan (Eds.): SOFL+MSVL 2015, LNCS 9559, pp. 72–85, 2016.
DOI: 10.1007/978-3-319-31220-0_6

(1) We introduce a framework of fault localization methods that details the MBD theory [18], which constitutes the main body of Sect. 4. The framework makes explicit the relationship between the failure model, the trace formula, and the property to be checked. (2) For timed automata, an important class of fault localization problems is reduced to solving a set of clock constraints. Since the constraints are expressed in linear real arithmetic theory [1], the problem is decidable. (3) This paper demonstrates the feasibility of the proposed method with experiments on small example cases using the Yices-1 [6], a partial MaxSAT solver.

Although the work is still at a feasibility study stage, it is, as far as we know, the first report on the automatic fault localization of timed automata using the maximum satisfiability.

2   Preliminaries

This section introduces the basic concepts. We use the term SAT to refer to both pure Boolean satisfiability and satisfiability modulo theories (SMT) methods.

Scope-Bounded Analysis. The SAT method is a basis of various automatic analysis methods such as bounded model checking (BMC) [3]. Given a system, we encode potential execution paths of the system in a logic formula φ_{TF}. We let φ_{AS} be a formula of the property to be checked. Because $\neg(\varphi_{TF} \Rightarrow \varphi_{AS}) = \varphi_{TF} \wedge \neg\varphi_{AS}$, a BMC problem is to see whether $\varphi_{TF} \wedge \neg\varphi_{AS}$ is satisfiable. The formula is satisfied if the system (φ_{TF}) violates the given property (φ_{AS}). The obtained assignments constitute counter-examples to demonstrate this failure. In the following, φ_{CE} refers to a formula encoding these counter-example assignments.

Fault Localization Problem. Let a formula φ_{FL} be $\varphi_{EI} \wedge \varphi_{TF} \wedge \varphi_{AS}$ for the above mentioned φ_{TF} and φ_{AS}, and φ_{EI} that encodes error-inducing formula; $\varphi_{FL} = \varphi_{EI} \wedge \varphi_{TF} \wedge \varphi_{AS}$. We construct φ_{EI} as a sub-formula of φ_{CE} so that φ_{EI} provides necessary comditions for the failing situation. From these, φ_{FL} is unsatisfiable.

If the system fails for a particular set of input data values, φ_{CE} includes a sub-formula to encode such a set of data values. In this case, φ_{EI} is simple enough to represent that the specific variables take particular values that lead the system to such a failing execution. In the fault localization of an imperative program [5,7–9], φ_{EI} encodes a set of input data values that make the program violating φ_{AS}. However, φ_{EI} may have further information that reflects the characteristics of the target system. Finding appropriate φ_{EI} for TAs will be discussed in Sect. 4.2.

The fault localization problem is finding clauses in φ_{TF} that are responsible for the unsatisfiability of φ_{FL}. These clauses, if found, constitute a *conflict*, which is an erroneous situation containing root causes of the failure. By definition, φ_{EI} and φ_{AS} are supposed to be satisfiable. Therefore, it is exactly the problem in which we search for root causes of the faulty system.

In what follows, C refers to a set of clauses that constitute a given formula φ in conjunctive normal form (CNF). We use C and φ interchangeably. For details about the basic concepts, we refer to the standard literature (e.g. [4]).

Minimal Unsatisfiable Subset. A set of clauses M, $M \subseteq C$, is a minimal unsatisfiable subset (MUS) *iff* M is unsatisfiable and $\forall c \in M : M \backslash \{c\}$ is satisfiable.

Maximal Satisfiable Subset. A set of clauses M, $M \subseteq C$, is a maximal satisfiable subset (MSS) *iff* M is satisfiable and $\forall c \in (C \backslash M) : M \cup \{c\}$ is unsatisfiable.

Minimal Correction Subset. A set of clauses M, $M \subseteq C$, is a minimal correction subset (MCS) *iff* $C \backslash M$ is satisfiable and $\forall c \in M : (C \backslash M) \cup \{c\}$ is unsatisfiable. By definition, an MCS is a complement of an MSS. MCS is sometimes called coMSS.

Hitting Set. Let Ω be a set of sets from some finite domain D. A hitting set of Ω, H, is a set of elements from D that covers every set in Ω by having at least one element in common with it. Formally, H is a hitting set of Ω *iff* $H \subseteq D$ and $\forall S \in \Omega : H \cap S \neq \emptyset$. A minimal hitting set is a hitting set from which no element can be removed without losing the hitting set property.

Partial Maximum Satisfiability. A maximum satisfiability (MaxSAT) problem for a CNF formula is finding an assignment that maximizes the number of satisfied clauses. Partial MaxSAT (pMaxSAT) is a variant of the MaxSAT, in which some clauses are marked *soft* or relaxable, and the others are marked *hard* or non-relaxable. A pMaxSAT problem is finding an assignment that satisfies all the hard clauses and maximizes the number of satisfied soft clauses.

An Example. Here is a simple example to illustrate the basic concepts [11].

$$
\begin{array}{cccc}
C_1 & C_2 & C_3 & C_4 \\
\end{array}
$$
$$
\varphi = (a) \wedge (\neg a) \wedge (\neg a \vee b) \wedge (\neg b)
$$

Its MUSes, MCSes, and MSSes are the following.

$$
\begin{aligned}
\text{MUSes}(\varphi) &= \{\ \{C_1, C_2\},\ \{C_1, C_3, C_4\}\ \} \\
\text{MCSes}(\varphi) &= \{\ \{C_1\}, \qquad\quad \{C_2, C_3\},\ \{C_2, C_4\}\ \} \\
\text{MSSes}(\varphi) &= \{\ \{C_2, C_3, C_4\},\ \{C_1, C_4\},\ \{C_1, C_3\}\ \}
\end{aligned}
$$

$\text{MUSes}(\varphi)$ and $\text{MCSes}(\varphi)$ are related by a hitting set relationship.

Next, if we mark C_3 as *hard* and all the rest to be *soft*, a set of two MCS elements, $\{\ \{C_1\},\ \{C_2, C_4\}\ \}$, is obtained as MCSes. This illustrates that there are two possible repairs to make the formula φ satisfiable under the assumption that C_3 is believed to be correct. We may remove either C_1 or both C_2 and C_4. Note that we must decide which candidate we choose to repair. This decision requires a piece of information beyond the fault localization method. The repair is not the focus of this paper.

Model-Based Diagnosis. Fault localization is finding a subset of clauses, called *diagnosis*, in the unsatisfiable formula φ_{FL} to make it satisfiable if they are removed. The model-based diagnosis framework [18] presents a way to calculate diagnoses from conflicts. Note that a *conflict* is an erroneous situation and a *diagnosis* refers to root causes. Formally, diagnoses are MCSes, a set of MCS elements, while conflicts are MUSes, a set of MUS elements. MCSes are calculated from MUSes by a hitting set relationship [12]. The consistency-based approach [7,8,19], adopted in this paper, calculates an MSS to obtain an MCS by complementing the MSS, and repeats this process to collect MCSes. Any solution to MaxSAT problem is also an MSS, although every MSS is not always a solution to MaxSAT [15]. We use MaxSAT to obtain MCSes (e.g. [13]).

The fault localization problem needs a method to represent the fact that φ_{EI} and φ_{AS} are to be satisfiable and that some clauses in φ_{TF} are suspicious. The pMaxSAT approach fits well this requirement [7–9,21]. The clauses in φ_{EI} and φ_{AS} are marked *hard*. Suspicious clauses in φ_{TF} are *soft*. The other clauses in φ_{TF} that are assumed to be bug-free are *hard*. This decision, in which clauses are marked soft, is dependent on the adopted failure model (see Sect. 4.2).

3   Scope-Bounded Analysis

3.1   Timed Automata

Timed automata are finite state transition systems that have a finite number of non-negative real-valued clocks [1]. We follow the standard definitions.

Formal Model. A timed automaton $\mathcal{A}$ is a tuple $\langle\ Loc, \ell_0, X, Edg, Inv\ \rangle$.

1. *Loc* is a non-empty finite set of locations.
2. ℓ_0 is the initial location, $\ell_0 \in Loc$.
3. X is a finite set of clock variables. For a positive natural number $n(\in \mathcal{N})$ and an operator $\bowtie\ \in \{<, \leq, =, \geq, >\}$, constraints of the form $x \bowtie n$ and $x_1 - x_2 \bowtie n$ constitute a set of primitive clock constraints. We denote $Z(X)$ to be a set of formulas constructing from these primitive constraints possibly using logical connectives of $\wedge$, $\vee$ and $\neg$.
4. *Edg* represents a set of transitions. It is a finite set $Loc \times Z(X) \times 2^X \times Loc$. An element of Edg, (l, g, r, l'), is written as $l \xrightarrow{g,r} l'$, where g is a guard condition in $Z(X)$ and r refers to a set of clock variables $(\in 2^X)$ to reset.
5. *Inv* is a mapping from *Loc* to clock constraints, $Inv : Loc \rightarrow Z(X)$.

Parallel Composition of Timed Automata. We represent a complex system as a parallel composition of timed automata, where two timed automata are synchronized on a same event. The definition of timed automata now contains a finite set of events Σ and an empty symbol ϵ, $\langle\ Loc, \ell_0, X, \Sigma \cup \{\epsilon\}, Edg, Inv\ \rangle$.

Particularly, Edg is $Loc \times (\Sigma \cup \{\epsilon\}) \times Z(X) \times 2^X \times Loc$, and its element (l, a, g, r, l') is written as $l \xrightarrow{a,g,r} l'$.

Parallel composition is defined for given two timed automata $\mathcal{A}^{(1)}$ and $\mathcal{A}^{(2)}$, where $\Sigma^{(1)} \cap \Sigma^{(2)} \neq \emptyset$. Locations of the composed automaton are pairs of locations, $\langle l^{(1)}, l^{(2)} \rangle \in Loc^{(1)} \times Loc^{(2)}$. Its invariant at each location is a conjunction, $Inv^{(1)}(l^{(1)}) \wedge Inv^{(2)}(l^{(2)})$. Symbols common to both alphabets ($a \in \Sigma^{(1)} \cap \Sigma^{(2)}$) synchronize two automata. $\mathcal{A}^{(1)}$ and $\mathcal{A}^{(2)}$ take transitions simultaneously. The parallel composition can be extended to cases where more than two automata are involved.

3.2 Boolean Encoding

Fault localization as well as bounded model checking needs Boolean encoding of a trace formula φ_{TF}. We follow the encoding method presented in [20].

Trace Formula. A state of a timed automaton $\mathcal{A}$ is characterized by a location variable (at) and clock variables ($x_1, \ldots, x_n$). Below, we use an abbreviation such as $\hat{x}$ to refer to a vector of variables ($x_1, \ldots, x_n$) $\in X^n$. We introduce a set $V = \{at, \hat{x}\}$. A timed automaton $\mathcal{A}$ is defined as $\langle I, T \rangle$ over V. We use j-indexed state variable such that $V_j = \{at_j, \hat{x}_j\}$.

1. Initial State : I is defined on V.

$$I = (at = \ell_0 \wedge \hat{x} = 0)$$

2. Discrete Transition Step : $T(e)$ is a relation on V and V' where $e = l \xrightarrow{g,r} l'$ and $z_i = 0$ if $x_i \in r$, $z_i = x_i$ otherwise.
$$T(e) = (at = l \wedge at' = l' \wedge g \wedge \hat{x}' = \hat{z} \wedge Inv(l')(\hat{x}'))$$

3. Delay Transition Step :
   D is a relation on V and V'. $Inv(S)$ is the set of locations that have an invariant different from $true$. Clock variables are updated by an amount of δ.

$$D = \exists\, \delta > 0 .\ ((\bigwedge_{l \in Inv(S)} (at = l) \Rightarrow Inv(l)(\hat{x}')) \wedge at' = at \wedge \hat{x}' = \hat{x} + \delta)$$

4. Transition Relation : T is a relation on V and V'. $T = (\bigvee_{e \in Edg} T(e)) \vee D$

5. K-step Unfolding of Timed Automaton : φ_{TF}^K is a trace formula to encode potential K-step execution paths. Let V_j be a set of j-indexed variables $\{at_j, \hat{x}_j\}$. V in I is V_0. V and V' in T_j are V_{j-1} and V_j respectively.

$$\varphi_{TF}^K = I \wedge (\bigwedge_{j=1..K} T_j)$$

Now, we consider parallel composition cases. In order to define a delay transition step, we introduce a special symbol $delay$ to represent that the automaton takes a delay transition. The input alphabet is $\Sigma \cup \{\epsilon, delay\}$. The set V is extended to include a variable act referring to an input symbol ($\{at, \hat{x}\} \cup \{act\}$).

1. Inactivity Transition : $F=(at' = at \land (\bigwedge_{x \in X} x' = x) \land (\bigwedge_{\alpha \in \Sigma \cup \{delay\}} act \neq \alpha))$

2. Discrete Transition Step for $e = l \xrightarrow{a,g,r} l'$: A discrete transition of a single timed automaton for $e = l \xrightarrow{g,r} l'$ is a special case of a being ϵ.

$$T(e) = (at = l \land at' = l' \land act = a \land g \land \hat{x}' = \hat{z} \land Inv(l')(\hat{x}'))$$

3. Delay Transition Step :
   $D= \exists\, \delta > 0$.
   $$((\bigwedge_{l \in Inv(S)} (at = l) \Rightarrow Inv(l)(\hat{x}')) \land at' = at \land \hat{x}' = \hat{x} + \delta \land act = delay)$$

4. Transition Relation : $T= (\bigvee_{e \in Edg} T(e)) \lor D \lor F$

5. K-step Unfolding of N number of Timed Automata : There are N number of timed automata $A^{(1)} \dots A^{(N)}$ composed, where $A^{(i)}$ is $\langle I^{(i)}, T^{(i)} \rangle$. $I^{(i)}$ and $T^{(i)}$ are the initial state and transition relation for the i-th automaton respectively. $T_j^{(i)}$ is j-th transition of i-th automaton.

$\varphi_{TF}^K = \bigwedge_{i=1..N}(I^{(i)} \land (\bigwedge_{j=1..K} T_j^{(i)}))$, which is rewritten as $I \land (\bigwedge_{j=1..K} T_j)$ where $I = \bigwedge_{i=1..N} I^{(i)}$ and $T_j = \bigwedge_{i=1..N} T_j^{(i)}$.

Bounded Model Checking. We introduce a labeling function Lab from each location to a set of atomic propositions, $Lab : Loc \rightarrow 2^{Prop}$. $Prop$ is defined over state variables of a timed automaton, $\{at, \hat{x}\}$. $Lab(\ell)$ is a set of propositions that are *true* at the location ℓ.

Specifically, p ($p \in Prop$) takes a form of equality or dis-equality on the location variable (at), and of primitive clock constraints for clock variables (x_j). Clock constraints are represented in linear real arithmetic (LRA). We do not consider propositions involving act ($act \in \Sigma$) because the event symbol is concerned with transition synchronization.

Although a BMC problem is usually defined for arbitrary formulas of linear temporal logic (LTL) [20], we restrict to consider only two cases, safety properties and guarantee [14]. Let $\psi(\hat{v})$ be a propositional formula constructed from $Prop$. Each $\hat{v}_j$ stands for a vector of state variables in V_j. A safety property is expressed in LTL as $\Box\psi$, and a guarantee property is $\Diamond\psi$. Recall a BMC problem is checking the satisfiability of $\varphi_{TF} \land \neg\varphi_{AS}$. As a negation of $\Box\psi$ is $\Diamond\neg\psi$ and a negation of $\Diamond\psi$ is $\Box\neg\psi$ respectively, a whole formula for the K-unfolded case is

$\varphi_{safety} = I(\hat{v}_0) \land (\bigwedge_{j=1..K} T_j(\hat{v}_{j-1}, \hat{v}_j)) \land (\bigvee_{j=1..K} \neg\psi(\hat{v}_j))$,

or

$\varphi_{guarantee} = I(\hat{v}_0) \land (\bigwedge_{j=1..K} T_j(\hat{v}_{j-1}, \hat{v}_j)) \land (\bigwedge_{j=1..K} \neg\psi(\hat{v}_j))$
$\land (\bigvee_{j=0..K-1}(\hat{v}_k = \hat{v}_j))$.

The formula $\varphi_{guarantee}$ has an auxiliary constraint that we check $\neg\psi$ against the paths to contain loops [4]. Since the check is done in a bounded scope, $\Box\neg\psi$ can be satisfied only when loops exist.

4   Fault-Localization of Timed Automata

4.1   The Framework

The problem of fault localization using the pMaxSAT is formulated as finding MCSes for an unsatisfiable formula φ_{FL} of the form $\varphi_{EI} \wedge \varphi_{TF} \wedge \varphi_{AS}$. Recall that φ_{EI} expresses a failing situation, φ_{TF} encodes all potential execution paths, and φ_{AS} is a property to be checked. We need to determine the following three aspects so as to define the fault localization problem precisely.

The first aspect concerns with the property to be checked, which is common to BMC problems. We, indeed, conduct the BMC to see if the system is correct or not with respect to a given property. As discussed in Sect. 3.2, we adopt *Prop* defined over state variables of a timed automaton, $\{at, \hat{x}\}$. Specifically, p ($p{\in}Prop$) takes a form of equality or dis-equality on the location variable (at), and of primitive clock constraints for clock variables (x_j).

The second is the failure model we assume. The formula φ_{TF} is a Boolean encoding of operational semantics of timed automata and expresses all potential execution paths. Although all the elements can, in principle, be suspicious, we look for some particular clauses in φ_{TF} to account for the failure. We will introduce a modest assumption on the failure model, which Sect. 4.2 will explain in detail.

The third aspect is what to encode in φ_{EI}. Basically, the formula demonstrates a failing situation. A conjunction $\varphi_{EI} \wedge \varphi_{TF}$ encodes a subset of all potential execution paths. φ_{EI} acts as a *filter* to extract appropriate paths from those represented by φ_{TF}. The encoding of these paths has impact on the efficiency and precision of identifying MCS elements. Therefore, φ_{EI} is sensitive to the fault localization problem, and is related to the property formula φ_{AS}. We will explain in details in Sect. 4.2.

4.2   Fault Localization Method

Failure Model. Timed automata are finite state transition systems that have non-negative real-valued clocks. Now we assume that a given set of timed automata can be composed, which means that they are not deadlocked due to inappropriate parallel compositions. Then, faulty behavior in timed automata is originated from some bugs in using clock variables. Since timed automata refer to clocks in invariants, transition guards, and resets, we consider that potential root causes are in them; invariants $Inv(l)$, and g and r on an edge of $l \xrightarrow{a,g,r} l$. These are suspicious elements in faulty systems consisting of timed automata. The fault localization problem is now checking a conjunction of clock constraints that are collected from a failing trace with respect to a given property φ_{AS}.

In the fault localization problem using the pMaxSAT method, those suspicious elements are marked *soft* or relaxable. Because an initial state is usually definite, all elements in the formula I are *hard* or non-relaxable. The inactivity transition F, for the case of composing automata, is also definite because it encodes situations that a constituent automaton does not take any transition.

We will look at the discrete transition $T(e)$ and delay transition D in detail. The elements concerning with invariants, guards and resets are marked *soft*. Below p^H shows that p is *hard* while p^S is p marked *soft*.

1. Discrete Transition Step :
$$T(e) = (\ (at = l)^H \wedge (at' = l')^H \wedge (act = a)^H \wedge (g)^S$$
$$\wedge\ (\hat{x}' = \hat{z})^S \wedge (Inv(l')(\hat{x}'))^S\ )$$

2. Delay Transition Step :
$$D = \exists\ \delta > 0\ .\ ((\textstyle\bigwedge_{l \in Inv(S)} at = l \Rightarrow (Inv(l)(\hat{x}'))^S)$$
$$\wedge\ (at' = at)^H \wedge (\hat{x}' = \hat{x} + \delta)^H \wedge (act = delay)^H)$$

In addition, we mark discrete transition steps themselves *soft*, $(T(e))^S$. Relaxing a clause that corresponds to a discrete transition step is a situation in which we identify a particular transition to be a potential root cause. Contrarily, delay transition steps must be hard $(D)^H$, because the notion of the time elapse is essential in timed automata. If they are relaxed, the automaton looses time-dependent behavior.

Multiple Transitions. A timed automaton usually has multiple edges e_i that share a common source location l_s; $e_i = l_s \xrightarrow{a_i, g_i, r_i} l_i$. They include an empty transition[1] as a special case; $e_\epsilon = l_s \xrightarrow{\epsilon} l_i$. Furthermore, a timed automaton has a delay transition D at the same source location l_s. Some of these transitions are non-deterministic that are competing to fire at the same time. For a given location l_s, we introduce a set $E(l_s)$ to include all the edges, either discrete, delay, or empty transitions, that share the location l_s as their source.

Multiple transitions make the fault localization method complicated. The consistency-based fault localization method relies on the fact that MCSes can be calculated from the unsatisfiability of φ_{FL} where φ_{EI} induces erroneous situations. However, if a system has multiple transitions, especially non-deterministic transitions, it can take transitions other than the one in the failing execution, and some of the paths may be successful. Consequently, φ_{FL} can be satisfiable for these alternative transitions. We are unable to calculate MCSes.

The above observation implies that we cannot use full flow-sensitive trace formula, which is succeeded in the case of imperative programs [8]. Such a trace formula faithfully represents all potential execution paths and thus contains non-deterministic transitions if a similar encoding method is used for timed automata. Note that imperative programs are deterministic, and that this issue does not appear.

---

[1] An inactivity transition is an empty transition.

Sliced Transition Sequence. Given a property formula φ_{AS}, we first conduct a K-scoped BMC to obtain a counter-example, c.e. $\models \varphi_{TF} \wedge \neg\varphi_{AS}$. The counter-example[2] contains a transition sequence leading to the violation of φ_{AS} $(\langle\ I,\ T(e^1),\ \ldots,\ T(e^K)\ \rangle)$ and the other information involving a set of delay values $(\delta^i = d^i)$. $T(e^j)$ is a j-th executed instance of a transition e ($e \in Edg$).

For a safety property (φ_{safety}), there is an index L ($L \leq K$) such that L is a state at which $\psi(\hat{v}_j)$ violates for the first time, a minimum of such indices. For a guarantee property ($\varphi_{guarantee}$), a counter-example takes a form of the *lasso* structure [3]. A lasso consists of a prefix sequence followed by a loop. At all the states on a lasso, the property $\neg\psi(\hat{v}_j)$ is *true*. Therefore, L is chosen to be the length of the prefix plus the circumference of the loop part. Now, the transition sequence up to L contains enough information leading to the violation of the condition. We construct a truncated sequence up to the L state, $I \wedge (\bigwedge_{j=1..L} T(e^j))$. This formula faithfully represents an executed path to the violation, which indeed defines a failing situation.

We encode the situation in the error inducing formula φ_{EI} as follows. For a source location l_s^j of each transition instance $T(e^j)$ appearing in a counter-example trace, we obtain $E(l_s^j)$ representing a set of transitions that share a common source location l_s^j. For each element $e^i \in E(l_s^j)/\{T(e^j)\}$, we introduce its Boolean encoding of transition step $\tau(e^i)$; $\tau(e^i)$ is either a discrete, delay or inactivity transition step whose source location is l_s^j. If we let $T(l_s^j)$ be a transition step fired at l_s^j, then $T(l_s^j) = T(e^j) \vee (\bigvee_{e^i \in E(l_s^j)} \tau(e^i))$. Since there is exactly one transition step at each l_s^j (actually $T(e^j)$), $T(l_s^j)$ is *true* and $\bigvee_{e^i \in E(l_s^j)} \tau(e^i)$ is *false*. Therefore, $T(e^j)$ being true is equal to $\bigwedge_{e^i \in E(l_s^j)} \neg\tau(e^i)$ being true because $\neg(\bigvee \tau(e^i)) = \bigwedge \neg\tau(e^i)$.

We use an abbreviation such that $T(e^j)^{co} = \bigwedge_{e^i \in E(l_s^j)} \neg\tau(e^i)$ in order to represent the conjunction mentioned above. $T(e^j)^{co}$ is a transition step in the obtained counter-example path, but is represented in terms of steps that are *not* taken. We use $T(e^j)^{co}$ to represent φ_{EI};

$$\varphi_{EI} = \bigwedge_{j=1..L} T(e^j)^{co} = \bigwedge_{j=1..L} \bigwedge_{e^i \in E(l_s^j)} \neg\tau(e^i).$$

Furthermore, a set of delay values in the counter-example is a kind of input data value to induce a failing situation. We augment φ_{EI} with $\bigwedge_{j=1..L}(\delta^j = d^j)$. Therefore, the formula is that

$$\varphi_{EI} = \left(\bigwedge_{j=1..L} \bigwedge_{e^i \in E(l_s^j)} \neg\tau(e^i)\right) \wedge \left(\bigwedge_{j=1..L}(\delta^j = d^j)\right)$$

A whole formula $\varphi_{EI} \wedge \varphi_{TF}$ encodes the execution paths in the failing situation, which we call a sliced transition sequence. The sliced transition sequence is similar to the flow-insensitive trace formula for imperative programs [7]. The flow-insensitive trace formula is essentially constructed from $T(e^j)$, but we use $T(e^j)^{co}$. We will discuss the difference in Sect. 5 in regard to the second example case.

---

[2] For simplicity, we assume here a case of a single TA.

Fault Localization Steps. Below is whole fault localization steps.

1. Execute K-scope bounded model checking of $\varphi_{TF} \wedge \neg \varphi_{AS}$.
2. Decide the minimum index L leading to the violation.
3. Construct φ_{EI} from the counter-example.
4. Use pMaxSAT for $\varphi_{EI} \wedge \varphi_{TF} \wedge \varphi_{AS}$ to enumerate MCSes.

Recall that φ_{EI} and φ_{AS} are hard or non-relaxable by definition, and that some clauses in φ_{TF} are soft or relaxable according to the assumed failure model.

5   Example Cases

As initial studies, we conducted experiments, under MacO/S 10.9.5 on 1.3 GHz Intel Core i5, using the Yices-1 solver [6], a pMaxSAT solver supporting LRA.

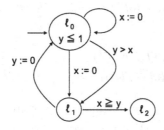

Fig. 1. A single timed automaton (reproduced [20])

Single Timed Automaton. Figure 1 is a simple timed automaton presented in [20]. Although it is not significant, we check a safety property $\Box(y \leq 2)$.

1. We execute nine-scoped BMC of $\varphi_{TF} \wedge \neg\Box(y \leq 2)$. The number of unfolding, nine, is just an initial guess. Note that $\neg\Box(y \leq 2) = \Diamond(y > 2)$. The formula is $I \wedge (\bigwedge_{j=1..9} T_j) \wedge (\bigvee_{j=1..9} (y_j > 2))$.
2. The obtained counter-example contains a transition sequence of its length five leading to the violation. $\ell_0 \xrightarrow{\delta} \ell_0 \xrightarrow{x:=0} \ell_0 \xrightarrow{\delta} \ell_0 \xrightarrow{x:=0} \ell_1 \xrightarrow{\delta} \ell_1$.
3. The property refers to a clock variable y. The formula φ_{EI} is chosen to include the encoding of delay values. Since the first, third, and fifth steps are delay transitions, a formula referring to these three $((\delta_1 = 1/2) \wedge (\delta_3 = 1/2) \wedge (\delta_5 = 3/2))$ is meaningful. The property φ_{AS} is violated in that $y_5 = 5/2$, which is $y_5 > 2$.
4. We obtain MCSes $\{\{\ell_0 \xrightarrow{x:=0} \ell_0\}, \{\ell_0 \xrightarrow{x:=0} \ell_1\}\}$, which shows that there are two possible root causes, either $\ell_0 \xrightarrow{x:=0} \ell_0$ or $\ell_0 \xrightarrow{x:=0} \ell_1$. By using this information, we manually add, for example, a reset of clock y to the edge of the second MCS, $\ell_0 \xrightarrow{x:=0; \, y:=0} \ell_1$. The first MCS is considered as a spurious root cause. Note that the repair is not automatic, but is up to the user.

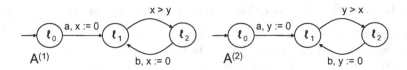

Fig. 2. Inconsistent guards

Inconsistent Guards in Two Timed Automata. Our second example, in Fig. 2, consists of two timed automata. It is easy to see that both automata are unable to go to the state l_2. The system is *stuck* at the location pair of $\langle l_1, l_1 \rangle$ $\in \mathrm{Loc}^{(1)} \times \mathrm{Loc}^{(2)}$ because two guard conditions are not satisfiable simultaneously. Imagine a guarantee property that $\varphi_{AS} = \Diamond((at^{(1)} = l_2) \vee (at^{(2)} = l_2))$.

1. We execute nine-scoped BMC of $\varphi_{TF} \wedge \neg\varphi_{AS}$. Since
   $\neg\varphi_{AS} = \neg(\Diamond((at^{(1)} = l_2) \vee (at^{(2)} = l_2))) = \Box((at^{(1)} \neq l_2) \wedge (at^{(2)} \neq l_2))$,
   the formula is actually

   $$(I^{(1)} \wedge I^{(2)}) \wedge \bigwedge\nolimits_{j=1..9} (T_j^{(1)} \wedge T_j^{(2)})$$
   $$\wedge (\bigwedge\nolimits_{j=1..9} ((at_j^{(1)} \neq l_2) \wedge (at_j^{(2)} \neq l_2))) \wedge (\bigvee\nolimits_{j=0..8} ((\hat{v}_9^{(1)} = \hat{v}_j^{(1)}) \wedge (\hat{v}_9^{(2)} = \hat{v}_j^{(2)}))).$$

   where the equality $\hat{v}_9^{(1)} = \hat{v}_j^{(1)}$ stands for a conjunction of two clauses to involve the location or clock, $(at_9^{(1)} = at_j^{(1)}) \wedge (x_9^{(1)} = x_j^{(1)})$, and $\hat{v}_9^{(2)} = \hat{v}_j^{(2)}$ is defined similarly.

2. The obtained counter-example contains a transition sequence of its length three leading to the violation. The loop part consists of consecutive occurrences of ϵ on $\langle l_1, l_1 \rangle$.
   $$\langle l_0, l_0 \rangle \xrightarrow{a} \langle l_1, l_1 \rangle \xrightarrow{\delta} \langle l_1, l_1 \rangle \xrightarrow{\epsilon} \langle l_1, l_1 \rangle.$$

3. The second transition step in the counter-example was delay, and its value was one. A sub-formula referring to the delay value is that $\delta_2 = 1$. The property to check (φ_{AS}) is not dependent on clock variables, and thus this sub-formula ($\delta_2 = 1$) is supposed to have no effect on the fault localization method.

4. We obtained MCSes consisting of one MCS element. The element consists of two transition edges, which shows that two must be repaired together. The MCSes is $\{\{l_1^{(1)} \xrightarrow{x>y} l_2^{(1)}, l_1^{(2)} \xrightarrow{y>x} l_2^{(2)}\}\}$. By using this information, we modify manually two guards, $x > y$ in the automaton $A^{(1)}$ and $y > x$ in the $A^{(2)}$. For example, we change the guard $x > y$ in the $A^{(1)}$ to $x \geq y$ and the $y > x$ in the $A^{(2)}$ to $y \geq x$, which is one possible repair.

Discussions. The first example (Fig. 1) illustrates that the fault localization problem for a timed automaton is essentially solving a set of clock constraints that are collected from a counter-example trace. Since the constraints are either invariants at locations, or guards and resets on transition edges, they are expressed in linear real arithmetic theory [1]. The property φ_{AS} refers to a clock variable y, and thus φ_{EI} is chosen to include a set of delay values appearing in the counter-example trace. The example indicates that the proposed repair is considered by referring to a particular counter-example involving those delay values. Therefore, it is desirable to execute the BMC again to see whether the repair works as we intend. Remember that our problem is localizing faults automatically, but is not *debugging* automatically.

The second example (Fig. 2) involves two timed automata that are deadlocked at particular intermediate states. The generated counter-example shows that the automata are *stuck* at $\langle \ell_1, \ell_1 \rangle$. Although the reason for the deadlock is attributed to inconsistent guard conditions referring to clock variables, the property to check (φ_{AS}) is $\Diamond((at^{(1)} = l_2) \vee (at^{(2)} = l_2))$ and is independent of clocks. The formula φ_{EI} needs not include delay values, and thus can use only a counter-example transition sequence $(\bigwedge_{j=1..L} T(e^j)^{co})$.

Now, we study the formula φ_{EI} in detail. If we use the transitions $T(e^j)$ appearing directly in the counter-example such that $\varphi_{EI} = \bigwedge_j T(e^j)$, then $\varphi_{EI} \wedge \varphi_{AS}$ is inconsistent regardless of φ_{TF}. Since the counter-example trace ends with the stuck state $\langle \ell_1, \ell_1 \rangle$, the formula φ_{EI} contains a sub-formula, $(at_3^{(1)} = \ell_1) \wedge (at_3^{(2)} = \ell_1)$. On the other hand φ_{AS} refers to $(at_3^{(1)} = l_2) \wedge (at_3^{(2)} = l_2)$. Recall that both φ_{EI} and φ_{AS} are non-relaxable. The conjunction $\varphi_{EI} \wedge \varphi_{AS}$ is neither satisfiable nor relaxable at all. Alternatively, consider a situation where $\varphi_{EI} = \bigwedge_j T(e^j)^{co} = (\bigwedge_j \bigwedge_{e^j \in E(l_s^j)} \neg \tau(e^j))$. While a whole formula $\varphi_{EI} \wedge \varphi_{TF} \wedge \varphi_{AS}$ is unsatisfiable, some of $T(e^j)$ in φ_{TF} can be relaxed because each $T(e^j)$ is itself marked *soft* or relaxable in our failure model. Thus, the MCSes mentioned above were obtained.

Last, enumerating MCSes is time-consuming and a scalability problem remains. We may use an efficient method implemented in [8], which adopts a technique for blocking MCSes [15].

6   Related Work

Formula-based or consistency-based fault localization methods are applied to design debugging of VLSI circuits [19,21] or imperative programs [5,7–9]. The method combines the model-based diagnosis [18] and Boolean satisfiability [4]. The problem is finding a diagnosis, which is MCSes when the methods use maximum satisfiability. Partial maximum satisfiability is often preferred because it allows us a way of giving a *hint* for the relaxation by marking clauses as either soft or hard [7–9,21]. The precision and efficiency of finding potential root causes are dependent on the encoding of trace formulas [9]. In the application to imperative programs, the flow-insensitive trace formula [7] was proposed first. Since it is not adequate to deal with control flow bugs, in which branching conditions may be buggy, flow-sensitive trace formula is used [5]. Full flow-sensitive trace formula is equivalent to a program's control flow graph and is the most expressive. It is shown successful in finding multiple faults in a program [8].

In the applications to VLSI circuits and imperative programs, the trace formulas are deterministic in that an execution path is unique when we determine the input values completely. Timed automata have non-deterministic transitions [1]. Especially, discrete transitions and a delay transition is taken non-deterministically. This fact makes the fault localization problem complicated. Our approach in this paper is to use a sliced transition trace formula. It is similar to the flow-insensitive trace formula [7], but is different in that we use $T(e)^{co}$ but not $T(e)$ directly. $T(e)^{co}$ encodes a counter-example transition sequence by excluding all the transitions that are not taken. This encoding method is essential in localizing faults for deadlock cases as shown in the second example. Note that an accompanying paper [17] discusses cases for power consumption automata (PCAs) [16], in which PCAs are assumed to be *deterministic* weighted timed automata, and thus simplifies the fault localization problem.

7   Concluding Remarks

We reported a consitency-based fault localization method for timed automata using the partial maximum satisfiability. This work is still preliminary in that further study is needed for large example cases. It calls for an efficient algorithm to enumerate MCSes to counter the scalability problem (cf. [8,13,15]). There are also other important directions. First, the properties are extended from safety and bounded reachability to a wide class of LTL formulas. Second, introducing the proposed method to industrial strength tools such as UPPAAL [10] would be interesting in view of practice.

Acknowledgements. This work is partially supported by JSPS KAKENHI Grant Numbers 24300010 and 26330095.

References

1. Alur, R., Dill, D.L.: A theory of timed automata. TCS **126**, 183–235 (1994)
2. Alur, R.: Formal verification of hybrid systems. In: Proceedings of the EMSOFT 2011, pp. 273–278 (2011)
3. Biere, A., Cimatti, A., Clarke, E., Zhu, Y.: Symbolic model checking without BDDs. In: Cleaveland, W.R. (ed.) TACAS 1999. LNCS, vol. 1579, pp. 193–207. Springer, Heidelberg (1999)
4. Biere, A., Heule, M., Van Maaren, H., Walsh, T. (eds.): Handbook of Satisfiability. IOS Press, Amsterdam (2009)
5. Christ, J., Ermis, E., Schäf, M., Wies, T.: Flow-sensitive fault localization. In: Giacobazzi, R., Berdine, J., Mastroeni, I. (eds.) VMCAI 2013. LNCS, vol. 7737, pp. 189–208. Springer, Heidelberg (2013)
6. Dutertre, B., de Moura, L.: The Yices SMT Solver. http://yices.csl.sri.com
7. Jose, M., Majumdar, R.: Cause clue clauses : error localization using maximum satisfiability. In: Proceedings of the PLDI 2011, pp. 437–446 (2011)
8. Lamraoui, S.-M., Nakajima, S.: A formula-based approach for automatic fault localization of imperative programs. In: Merz, S., Pang, J. (eds.) ICFEM 2014. LNCS, vol. 8829, pp. 251–266. Springer, Heidelberg (2014)

9. Lamraoui, S.-M., Nakajima, S., Hosobe, H.: A hardened flow-sensitive trace formula for fault localization. In: Proceedings of the ICECCS 2015 (2015, to appear)

10. Larsen, K.G., Pettersson, P., Yi, W.: Uppaal in a nutshell. J. STTT 1(1–2), 134–152 (1997)

11. Liffiton, M.H., Sakallah, K.A.: On finding all minimally unsatisfiable subformulas. In: Bacchus, F., Walsh, T. (eds.) SAT 2005. LNCS, vol. 3569, pp. 173–186. Springer, Heidelberg (2005)

12. Liffiton, M.H., Sakallah, K.A.: Algorithms for computing minimal unsatisfiable subsets of constraints. Autom. Reasoning 40(1), 1–33 (2008)

13. Liffiton, M.H., Malik, A.: Enumerating infeasibility: finding multiple MUSes quickly. In: Gomes, C., Sellmann, M. (eds.) CPAIOR 2013. LNCS, vol. 7874, pp. 160–175. Springer, Heidelberg (2013)

14. Manna, Z., Pnueli, A.: The Temporal Logic of Reactive and Concurrent Systems. Springer, New York (1992)

15. Morgado, A., Liffiton, M., Marques-Silva, J.: MaxSAT-based MCS enumeration. In: Biere, A., Nahir, A., Vos, T. (eds.) HVC. LNCS, vol. 7857, pp. 86–101. Springer, Heidelberg (2013)

16. Nakajima, S.: Using real-time maude to model check energy consumption behavior. In: Bjørner, N., Boer, F. (eds.) FM 2015. LNCS, vol. 9109, pp. 378–394. Springer, Heidelberg (2015)

17. Nakajima, S., Lamraoui, S.-M.: Fault localization of energy consumption behavior using maximum satisfiability. In: Mousavi, M.R., Berger, C. (eds.) CyPhy 2015. LNCS, vol. 9361, pp. 99–115. Springer, Heidelberg (2015). doi:10.1007/978-3-319-25141-7_8

18. Reiter, R.: A theory of diagnosis from first principles. Artifi. Intell. 32(1), 57–95 (1987)

19. Safarpour, S., Mangassarian, H., Veneris, A., Liffiton, M.H., Sakallah, K.A.: Improved design debugging using maximum satisfiability. In: Proceedings of the FMCAD 2007, pp. 13–19 (2007)

20. Sorea, M.: Bounded model checking for timed automata. ENTCS 68(5), 116–134 (2002)

21. Zhu, C.S., Weissenbacher, G., Malik, S.: Post-silicon fault localization using maximum satisfiability and backbones. In: Proceedings of the FMCAD 2011, pp. 63–66 (2011)

Automated Program Debugging for Multiple Bugs Based on Semantic Analysis

Aishan Liu$^{(\boxtimes)}$, Li Li, and Jie Luo

Department of Computer Science, Beihang University, Beijing 100191, China
{liuaishan,lili,luojie}@nlsde.buaa.edu.cn

Abstract. Fault locating is a time-consuming process. In a previous paper, Liu proposed an algorithm named bounded debugging via multiple predicate switching (BMPS)[1], which try to find a successful execution trace by switching outcomes of multiple predicates. Substantively, BMPS focuses on the program faults which are caused by control flow. However, this kind of faults represent only a small fraction. In this paper, we present an algorithm combining BMPS with a semantic based debugging method, which is aimed at locating more than control flow related faults. The semantic based debugging algorithm generates a sequence of equations from the execution trace of a failed test case, and give a minimum faulty program segment according to solutions of the equations. Our algorithm can locate multiple faults in the program one by one through an iterative and interactive process. Moreover, an optimization based on use-define chain is applied to BMPS for improving efficiency of the algorithm, as well as some other methods. To evaluate out approach, we conduct experiment on Siemens suite. The result indicates that our method has significant improvement on both accuracy and efficiency.

Keywords: Automated debugging · Predicate switch · Semantic analysis

1 Introduction

Traditional program debugging is an arduous and manual process that requires a large number of time, effort, and a well comprehension of the code. Generally, traditional debugging consists of two steps: (1) program turns out an unexpected result or behavior; (2) developer re-executes the failed test case step by step and inspects the program state to find out the cause of the problem. Such process can be apparently time consuming, tedious and sometimes error-prone.

Researchers were more interested in utilizing computer power for program debugging since the processing power of machines has drastically increased. Therefore automated debugging techniques are being explored by researchers. Automated debugging basically consists of program slice based model, program state based model, statistical model and program spectrum based model [2,3].

In a previous paper [4], Zhang proposed an algorithm which switches the outcome of an instance of a single predicate and then inspect the so called

S. Liu and Z. Duan (Eds.): SOFL+MSVL 2015, LNCS 9559, pp. 86–100, 2016.
DOI: 10.1007/978-3-319-31220-0_7

switched predicate to find out the cause of the fault. After experiment evaluation, the author found their approach to be effective and practical. However, switching a single predicate could not be sufficient and useful in some situation. In 2010, Liu proposed the bounded debugging via multiple predicate witching algorithm (BMPS) which is to switch the outcome of instances of multiple predicates to locate bugs. However, both the algorithms are basically aimed at control flow related program bugs, and cost much time especially when the program contains amounts of predicates (e.g. conditional statements).

In this paper, we propose a method combining BMPS with Intra-function debugging algorithm (Sect. 2.2), which is aimed at locating multiple bugs including not only control flow related faults. We present an iterative and interactive approach for programmer to locate program bugs, which would provide developer with a minimum program segment containing faulty code. Some program would contain a lot of predicates, and many of them could be unrelated to the results or the variables with unexpected value. If we treat every predicate to be switchable, it would be really time consuming and redundant. So, we optimize the algorithm by applying use-define chain to reduce the number of predicates to be switched. Since our algorithm is interactive, programmer could mark some statements as errorless such that workload of predicate switching will be reduced.

2 Technical Background

2.1 BMPS

Bounded debugging via multiple predicate switching algorithm (BMPS) locates faults through switching the outcomes of instances of multiple predicates to get a successful execution where each loop is executed for a bounded number of times. The most important concept is critical predicate set. It is a set of predicates which could be switched to get the right execution or result of the program. Obviously, BMPS concentrated on the control flow related bugs in the program. By switching the outcomes of predicates, which could be the branch statements, the execution trace would go to another path leading to a right output under specified test case.

Figure 1 below depicts a small program example. In this program, inputs variables are a and b. However, the conditional statement in line 4 is faulty. Test

```
1.   int i=5,x;
2.   int a,b;
3.   read(a,b)
4.   if(i<a+b) //correct version: i<=a+b
5.     x=i+1;
6.   else
7.     x=i;
```

Fig. 1. Example of a Program.

case of $< a = 2, b = 3, x = 6 >$ is failed. As for this test case, the expected output is x=6, yet x is 5 after execution. If we switched the outcome of the predicate $i < a + b$ to $!(i < a + b)$, the execution trace could change from (1,2,3,7) to (1,2,3,5) which would lead to the right result. Thus, predicate $i < a + b$ is a critical predicate by which we could switch to get the right result.

For iterative programs, critical predicate set should be uncomputable. So the author considered depth k critical predicate set which is deduced from an execution path where each loop is executed at most k times.

For each predicate p in the program, we introduce a Boolean variable sw_p, and replace p with $\neg sw_p \wedge p \vee sw_p \wedge \neg p$. Given a program, we define the formula as below:

$$\Phi = IN \wedge S_1 \wedge ... \wedge (\neg sw_p \wedge p \vee sw_p \wedge \neg p) \wedge ... \wedge S_n \wedge OUT$$

IN is the input of the test case, S_i denotes the statements in the program and OUT means the assertion of the test case (usually the output or the result of the test case). After that, we convert Φ to conjunctive normal form (CNF) and feed it a SAT solver (e.g., z3, minisat, etc.) to solve the satisfiability problem. If the CNF is satisfiable, and the value of sw_p is true, which means the value of p is false, the execution trace goes to another path leading to the right result. Thus, the assertion holds and p could be a critical predicate to reveal the bugs.

Obviously, it is more convenient to switch the outcomes of some predicates if whole program is transferred to CNF [5]. Then, we resort to a SAT solver (e.g., z3, minisat, etc.) to solve the satisfiability problem.

2.2   Intra-function Debugging Algorithm

First of all, we give some brief definition to help depict our algorithm.

Definition 1 *(State). A state σ is defined as a k-tuple.*

$$\sigma : (x_1 \rightarrow n_1, ..., x_k \rightarrow n_k)$$

$x_i \rightarrow n_i$ *means the value of x_i is n_i, and denoted as $\sigma(x_i) = n_i$*

Definition 2 *(Environment). Assume S is the head of a conditional statement, and σ is the state when executing S. $\langle S, \sigma \rangle$ is called an Environment.*

Definition 3 *(Structure-S). Assume σ is a state, S is the statement executed under the state σ, and ϵ is the stack of Environment. Thus, the triple below is a Structure-S:*

$$\langle S, \sigma, \epsilon \rangle$$

Definition 4 *(Trace Stack). A stack is called a Trace Stack iff every element in the stack has the type of Structure-S.*

Definition 5 *(Structure-T). Assume $\langle S, \sigma, \epsilon \rangle$ is a Structure-S, π is the corresponding trace stack. A structure-T is denoted as below:*

$$\pi | \langle S, \sigma, \epsilon \rangle$$

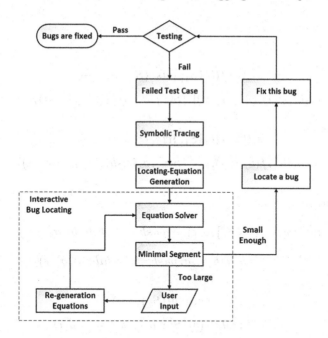

Fig. 2. Flow Diagram of Intra-function Debugging Algorithm.

Intra-function debugging algorithm uses semantic analysis to give developer a minimal faulty program segment. When a test case failed, the algorithm computes a minimal inconsistent program segment according to the input and output of the test case. Programmers are able to mark some statements to be errorless iteratively to reduce the scale of faulty program segment.

Figure 2 is the flow diagram of Intra-function debugging algorithm, which simply shows the flow and main steps of the method.

The algorithm includes four main steps:

(1) *Symbolic Execution.* Execute and trace the program by symbolic representation according to the input of the failed test case. Record the execution trace and program states.

The execution of program could be treated as many steps of compute. And every step is similar to a transition from a Structure-T to another.

-Assignment

$$\pi|\langle l : x = e, \sigma, \epsilon\rangle \to push(\langle l : x = e, \sigma, \epsilon\rangle)|\langle skip, \sigma[[e]_\sigma/x], \epsilon\rangle$$

$[e]_\sigma$ is the value of expression e under state σ.

-Sequence of Statemtents

$$\frac{\pi|\langle S_1, \sigma, \epsilon\rangle \to \pi'|\langle S_1', \sigma', \epsilon'\rangle}{\pi|\langle S_1; S_2, \sigma, \epsilon\rangle \to \pi'|\langle S_1'; S_2, \sigma', \epsilon'\rangle}$$

$$\pi|\langle skip; S, \sigma, \epsilon\rangle \to \pi|\langle S, \sigma, \epsilon\rangle$$

-Conditionals

If $[b]_\sigma = true$

$$\pi|\langle l : if(b)\{S_1; \}else\{S_2\}, \sigma, \epsilon\rangle \rightarrow$$

$$push(\langle l : if(b), \sigma, \epsilon\rangle, \pi)|\langle\{S_1; \}, \sigma, push(\langle l : if(b), \sigma\rangle, \epsilon)\rangle$$

If $[b]_\sigma = false$

$$\pi|\langle l : if(b)\{S_1; \}else\{S_2\}, \sigma, \epsilon\rangle \rightarrow$$

$$push(\langle l : if(b), \sigma, \epsilon\rangle, \pi)|\langle\{S_2; \}, \sigma, push(\langle l : if(b), \sigma\rangle, \epsilon)\rangle$$

-Loops

If $[b]_\sigma = true$

$$\pi|\langle l : while(b)\{S; \}, \sigma, \epsilon\rangle \rightarrow push(\langle l : while(b), \sigma, \epsilon\rangle, \pi)$$

$$|\langle\{S; \}l : while(b)S;, \sigma, push()\langle l : while(b), \sigma\rangle, \epsilon)\rangle$$

If $[b]_\sigma = false$

$$\pi|\langle l : while(b)\{S; \}, \sigma, \epsilon\rangle \rightarrow$$

$$push(\langle l : while(b)\{S; \}, \sigma, \epsilon\rangle, \pi)|\langle skip, \sigma, \epsilon\rangle$$

(2) *Locating-Equation Generation.* Generate a set of locating equations for every statement backwards from the beginning of breakpoint - a statement in which the value of specified variable is not expected.

In the second step of the algorithm, we generate locating-equation for every Structure-S in Trace Stack π. Thus we can specify the transition of Structure-S by solving equation set. Besides, the locating-equation sets are stored in a list, in which every element has a form of $(eq, \langle S, \sigma, \epsilon\rangle)$. Among them, eq denotes an equation set while $\langle S, \sigma, \epsilon\rangle$ is a Structure-S.

-Initial State

$$\pi|\rho$$

-Assignments

$$\frac{top(\pi) = \{l : x = e, \sigma, \epsilon\}last(\rho) = (eq, \{S, \sigma', \epsilon'\})x \in FV(eq)}{\pi|\rho \rightarrow pop(\pi)|append((eq[e/x], \{l : x = e, \sigma, \epsilon\}), \rho)}$$

$$\frac{top(\pi) = \{l : x = e, \sigma, \epsilon\}last(\rho) = (eq, \{S, \sigma', \epsilon'\})x \notin FV(eq)}{\pi|\rho \rightarrow pop(\pi)|\rho}$$

Given a Structure-S containing statement $l : x = e$ at the top of trace stack. If x appears in equation set eq, all the variable x in eq corresponding current Structure-S can be replaced with e. On the contrary, skip it.

-Conditionals

$$\frac{top(\pi) = \{l : if(b), \sigma, \epsilon\}last(\rho) = (eq, \{S, \sigma', \epsilon'\})}{\pi|\rho \rightarrow pop(\pi)|append((eq \cup \{b = [b]_\sigma\}, \{l : if(b), \sigma, \epsilon\}), \rho)}$$

Given a Structure-S containing head part $if(b)$ of the conditional statement, equation $b = [b]_\sigma$ is added to the equation set corresponding with the current Structure-S.

-Loops

$$\frac{top(\pi) = \{l : while(b), \sigma, \epsilon\} last(\rho) = (eq, \{S, \sigma', \epsilon'\})}{\pi|\rho \to pop(\pi)|append((eq \cup \{b = [b]_\sigma\}, \{l : while(b), \sigma, \epsilon\}), \rho)}$$

The rule is the same as the former.

(3) *Equation Solver.* Find the first equation set $\rho[m]$ in the equation set list that has no solution. The statement block corresponded to the equation set is crucial. Statements from the corresponding statement block in $\rho[m]$ to $\rho[1]$ could be a minimal faulty program segment.

The equation set with no solution implies that under no state σ could the statements in [m] be executed to get the expected result.

(4) *Iteratively Minimize Segment.* The first-time locating segment might be too large for programmer to find out the real place of the faults. An iterative process need to be performed to make it easier for the programmer to locate faults. Programmer needs to give an expected value of a variable in the segment, and repeat from step 1 to minimize the faulty segment until code fragment is considered small enough for programmer to locate the cause of fault.

3   Bug Localization Framework

Intra-function debugging algorithm generates the locating equation for every statement in the program and then solve the equation set to get a faulty program segment. The algorithm performs better on computational faults than other kinds of faults (especially the control flow related faults). When the execution trace goes to a wrong path caused by some faulty predicates (branches in program), the algorithm may give an irrelevant program segment which could lead to a bad localization. It is obvious that BMPS could solve the control flow related fault, while Intra-function debugging algorithm is opposite. We propose an algorithm combined with the two methods, therefore it can deal with both the control flow related and compute related faults.

Firstly, we use Intra-function algorithm to give a coarse-grained faulty program segment according to the expected variable value given by programmer. It definitely reduce the space and the number of predicates need to be switched. Then we call BMPS to switch the outcomes of the predicates contained in the program segment. Also, programmer needs to check the limited number of statements in the segment to eliminate the compute related fault. One pass may solve one single bug. An iterative process need to be done if the program consists of multiple bugs. Programmer needs to give another expected value of a variable in the segment, and repeat the steps above to minimize the faulty segment step by step.

If the locating result turns out unsatisfiable, we may use BMPS for the whole program. As we said before, if the problem is caused by control flow faults and the execution trace goes to the wrong path, the Intra-function debugging algorithm would give an irrelevant program segment leading to a bad localization result. This pass is aimed to deal with the program under such a situation. The disadvantage is that the full scale switch would consume much more time and space. More variables and paths would increase the number of variables and clauses in the SAT problem (satisfiability problem), which would make it more difficult and complex to solve the problem.

The overview of our algorithm is given in Fig. 3. The algorithm has 5 main steps.

Step 1: Find Faulty Value

When facing a failed run, inspect the input and output of test case to identify a proper variable with unexpected value.

Step 2: Reduce Faulty Program Segment

Run Intra-function debugging algorithm to get a minimal faulty program segment.

Step 3: Small Scale Predicate Switch

Run BMPS in the small segment of faulty program. Only the predicates in the segment is switchable, which means they are the candidates to be switched.

Step 4: Iterative Debugging and Locating

Repeatedly run step2 and step3 to get a more precise result in order to fix multiple bugs.

Step 5(Additional): Full Scale Predicate Switch

Run BMPS for the whole program if the results above seems to be unsatisfiable.

Fig. 3. Algorithm Overview.

4   Optimization

In the previous paper, the author proposed the prototype of bounded debugging via multiple predicate switching algorithm. It is an excellent algorithm, however, optimization could be made somewhere.

4.1   Use-Definition Chain

A Use-Definition Chain (UD Chain) is a sparse representation of data-flow information about variables [6]. A UD chain connects a use to all the definitions that may flow to it. Abstractly a UD chain is a function from a variable and a basic-block-position pair to sets of basic-block-position pairs, one for each use or definition, respectively. Concretely, they are generally represented by linked lists. They can be constructed by solving the reaching definitions data-flow problem for a procedure and then using the resulting information to build the linked list.

Making the UD chain is a step in liveness analysis, so that logical representations of all the variables can be identified and tracked through the code.

- *Use of Variable.* If variable, v, is on the RHS of statement $s(j)$, there is a statement $s(i)$ with $i < j$ and $min(j - i)$, that it is a definition of v and it has a use at $s(j)$ (or, in short, when a variable, v, is on the RHS of a statement $s(j)$, then v has a use at statement $s(j)$).

- *Definition of Variable.* When a variable, v, is on the LHS of an assignment statement, such as $s(j)$, then $s(j)$ is a definition of v. Every variable has at least one definition by its declaration (or initialization).

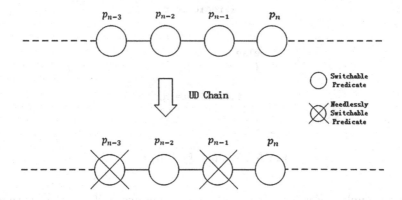

Fig. 4. Use-Definition Chain.

In out algorithm, we use UD chain to eliminate the redundant predicates need to be switched. When a test case failed, it means the result turned out wrong and the values of some variables were different from the expectation. When we get the UD chain of a variable, the statements which use the variable or related variable would be gathered. Of course, we can acquire the predicates in the statement sets. We treat these predicates as switchable and more suspicious ones than that are not in the sets.

As it is showed in Fig. 4, BMPS treats every predicate to be switchable. There are at least n predicates treated as candidates in the program. Then, BMPS may switch any of them to find out an execution path to get the right result. However, after the process of UD chain, we get a chain of predicates which is related to the variable with unexpected value. In another words, these predicates may influence the value of the variable with wrong value, and the faults may lie in these predicates. On the contrary, the other predicates may be unrelated to the variable and would not be needed to be switched so that we can save more time and space.

4.2   Predicate Switch Strategy

As we have already stated, in order to get the right results we have to switch conditional branch outcomes till we find some predicates which could be switched to make the program produce the correct output. It is our goal to develop a switching strategy to make the algorithm more practical and effective.

- *Manually set limits*. Although we have implemented UD chain to the algorithm, some predicates could also be eliminated from the switchable predicate set. Programmer could mark some predicates to be not switched to make it more effective.

```
if(Predicate-1)
{
    ...
    if(Predicate-m)
    ...
}
else
{
    ...
    if(Predicate-n)
    ...
}
```

Fig. 5. Example of a Program.

The example in Fig. 5 is a small program. It contains an if-else block with various conditional branch in each sub-block. They are all predicates in switchable predicate set and may be switched to get right result. However, if it is certain that the execution path go into if part of the very first predicates (Predicate-1), it can be eliminated from the switchable predicate set. As for this case, it would at least reduce a half of the total spend in space and time. This action would make the algorithm more smart.

- *Increasingly number of predicates to be switched at a time*. Although we are aiming at the program with multiple bugs, sometimes only one predicate switch could lead to the right result and this may always happen in fact. Thus, we limit the number of predicates to be switched from one to all. After experiment, we found that most test case with control flow related bugs could be solved by only switching a small amount of predicates. Firstly, we only switch one predicate at a time, if we cannot get to the right result or the programmer are not satisfied with it, we increase the number of predicates to be switched at a time. Every time, we add the number by one. But, this may spend more time than the normal algorithm.

- *Last executed first switched ordering*. In the previous paper, Zhang and Gupta have presented that execution of faulty code (i.e. root cause of a failed run) is often not far away from the point at which the program fails (e.g., program crashes or it produces a wrong output value). Therefore, we can switch the predicates in reverse order. That is to say, the predicate that is closer to the faulty results (i.e. the end of the program in some situation) is earlier to be switched.

4.3 Upper Bound for Loops

In the previous paper, Liu proposed to set an upper bound for the iterative programs manually. That is to say, when programmer face with a program with loops (e.g., while, for statements), he must give BMPS a number to describe the times the loop circulates. Like the usual model checker methodology, we unwind the loop by duplicate the loop body n times, where n is the unwinding limit. However, it is difficult for programmer to give an accurate number for the iteration times. So we use Loopus [7] , a tool that automatically compute loop bounds for C programs, to give the upper bound of loop time.

5   Experiment and Evaluation

We implement BMPS by using CBMC, a bounded model checker for ANSI C programs (Clarke, Kroening, and Lerda 2004) [8,9]. For the implementation of Intra-function debugging algorithm, we use LLVM to parse the input program and generate the symbolic execution trace. We solve the CNF and equation set by implementing the Z3 (a SAT solver). All of our experiments are performed on a 3.10 GHZ Intel Core 2 Duo CPU with 4 GB RAM.

- *CBMC*. The tool produces a Boolean formula for a C program. We add assume and assert statements to give program specification. Then we use z3 (a SAT solver) [10] to check the formula generated by CBMC. If the formula is satisfiable, it means we generate a counter-example that meet the expected result. Let p_i be a predicate in the program, we replace p_i with the expression $sw_i?nondet\_bool(): p_i$. In the expression, sw_i is a Boolean variable and the function $nondet\_bool()$ returns a non-deterministic Boolean value. The expression controls the execution to go p_i or $\neg p_i$. Finally, We add $assume()$ to give the expected results of the variable; and $assert(0)$ to make the program stoppable.

- *Static Program Slice*. We use static data and control flow analysis to acquire a set of program statements related to the specified variable [11,12]. After predicate switch, we get an execution path where some predicate have already been switched. It is not apparent for the programmers to find out the localization of faults if we just show these switched predicate statement to them. Thus, we use static program slice to give programmer a set of statements that influence the switched predicates which may help to reveal the bugs.

5.1 Experiment Result

We use Siemens suite for experiment and evaluation. It consists of 7 base programs. Each of them have a number of faulty versions and test case. All the programs (implemented in C language), test cases and defect data can be downloaded from the website http://www-static.cc.gatech.edu/aristotle/Tools/ subjects at Georgia Tech. We used TCAS program and REPLACE program in the Siemens suite. The TCAS program constitutes an aircraft collision avoidance system with 173 lines of code and 41 faulty versions.

Table 1. Results of running our algorithm on TCAS

Version	#ErrNum	DetectReduce	RunTime	ErrorType
v1	1	96	0.26	Control Flow
V2	1	95	0.24	Control Flow
V3	1	98	0.28	Control Flow
V4	1	96	0.29	Control Flow
V5	1	72	0.55	Compute
V6	1	97	0.31	Control Flow
V7	1	78	0.56	Compute
V8	1	79	0.49	Compute
V9	1	96	0.31	Control Flow
V10	2	98	0.29	Control Flow
V11	2	98	0.28	Control Flow
V12	1	97	0.25	Control Flow
V13	1	71	0.47	Compute
V14	1	75	0.44	Compute
V15	3	69	0.45	Compute
V16	1	72	0.49	Compute
V17	1	75	0.50	Compute
V18	1	77	0.41	Compute
V19	1	78	0.47	Compute
V20	1	95	0.26	Control Flow
V21	1	96	0.28	Control Flow
V22	1	98	0.25	Control Flow
V23	1	96	0.29	Control Flow
V24	1	97	0.26	Control Flow
V25	1	97	0.30	Control Flow
V26	1	79	0.50	Add Code
V27	1	74	0.52	Add Code
V28	1	95	0.30	Control Flow
V29	1	96	0.28	Control Flow
V30	1	95	0.29	Control Flow
V31	2	70	0.51	Add Code
V32	2	71	0.52	Add Code
V33	4	–	–	Crash
V34	1	97	0.31	Control Flow
V35	1	98	0.27	Control Flow
V36	1	78	0.47	Compute
V37	1	97	0.29	Control Flow
V38	1	–	–	Crash
V39	1	98	0.29	Control Flow
V40	2	97	0.31	Control Flow
V41	1	96	0.28	Control Flow

Table 1 below shows the result of running our algorithm on TCAS. **#ErrNum** is the total number of bugs in program, **DetectReduce** means the reduction of code needs to be checked after running our algorithm, **RunTime** is the running time of algorithm, **ErrorType** is the type of error in a program. Among the 41 versions, 4 versions add some codes to the original version, 2 versions crash, 11 versions are compute related bugs, the others are control flow related bugs. The experiment result shows that our approach deals well with the versions containing control flow related bugs. It reduces at least 95 % of the detection scope, because we use modified BMPS. For the general control flow related bugs, it can figure out a set of predicates which could be switched to get to the expected result. The number of predicates in the set is not more than 10 as usual. After examining the predicates, the exact localizations of bugs are detected. As for the compute related bugs, our approach gives a minimal suspicious program segment. It reduces 75 % of the detection scope averagely. Furthermore, these program segments are context-sensitive which could help the programmer to understand the cause of bugs.

As for the run time of the algorithm, it runs about 0.3 s for the program with control flow related bugs averagely and 0.51 s for those with compute related bugs. The run time of the former ones are more than the latter ones, because we run an additional full scale predicate switch if the small scale predicate switch cannot find a critical predicate set.

Obviously, our approach is better than BMPS. Firstly, it cannot deal with the compute related bugs. Secondly, BMPS may give the programmer an irrelevant predicate to reveal the bugs. For example, Fig. 6 below is a segment of TCAS. The output of TCAS is the variable *alt_sep*, and a conditional statement is placed at the end of the program, which means after executing this conditional statements the execution of TCAS is over. Suppose that *alt_sep* is expected to be *UNRESOLVED*, but the value is *UPWARD_RA* for some reason. Thus, there are some bugs in program. But, when using BMPS, we could always switch the predicates in this conditional statement to get the right result which would absolutely conceal the real bugs. In our approach, programmer can mark this conditional statement to be errorless manually, then the algorithm would find out the real locations of bugs.

```
if (need_upward_RA && need_downward_RA)
    alt_sep = UNRESOLVED;
else if (need_upward_RA)
    alt_sep = UPWARD_RA;
else if(need_downaward_RA)
    alt_sep = DOWNWARD_RA;

return alt_sep;
```

Fig. 6. Example of TCAS.

As for the REPLACE program, it has 564 lines of code, and 32 faulty versions. Among the 32 versions, 2 versions miss code, 2 versions add code, 19 versions are control flow related faults. It has many loops, our algorithm could effectively reduce the number of candidate switchable predicates, which could apparently reduce the total running time. But we cannot deal with the situation that code are missing.

Also, we intentionally combine the control flow bug related version with the other version to form some new versions with multiple bugs for TCAS program. Our approach could deal with these situation in about 4 iterative processes averagely. The run time could not be counted, for the process is an iterative subprocedures with programmer.

6   Related Work

In a previous paper, the author (Zhang, Gupta and Gupta) firstly proposed an algorithm to locate faults through automated predicate switch. They demonstrated that by forcibly switching the outcome of a predicate at runtime the program state can be modified. But they only switch one single predicate at a time. In 2010, Liu and Li presented a first step towards a theoretical exploration of program debugging algorithm (BMPS). They switch multiple predicates at a time in order to get a successful execution result.

Griesmayer et al. [13] gives a fault localization algorithm for C programs by constructing a modified program that allows a given number of expressions to be changed arbitrarily. They use the counterexample trace from a Model Checker (CBMC). Because every expression could be modified, the search space is extremely large. Like what we did in our approach, for an expression e, they introduce a Boolean variable sw and replace e with $sw?nondet() : e$. But, our search space is smaller than theirs for control flow related problem.

BugAssist [14] minimizes a given error trace obtained from bounded model checking using a Max-SAT algorithm. When a test case failed, BugAssist generates an execution trace and transfers it into an unsatisfiable formula combined with the input and the assertion. Thus, it has an apparent limitation that only executable statements can be part of the minimized error trace, which means only the bugs in the executable statements could be revealed. They treat bug locating problem as a partial maximum satisfiability problem which asks what is the maximum number of clauses that can be satisfied by any assignment. However, bug locating is a SAT problem in our paper. Also, we can locate bugs in the statement that is not executed under specified test case.

Many bug locating work uses the difference and comparison between the error trace and successful trace. Groces approach [15] calls CBMC to get a failing run firstly, then computes the difference between a failing run and a closest correct run. Ball et al. [16] call a model checker several times and compares the counterexamples to a successful trace. They believe that the faults are those transitions that do not appear in a correct trace. Our approach does not need to compare the successful trace and the error trace, thus we need less information.

For the control flow related bug, our approach gives an exact location of the bug instead of a code fragment.

7 Conclusion

In this paper, based on Liu et al.'s work on automated debugging via multiple predicate switching, we proposed an algorithm combined BMPS with Intrafunction debugging method. So it would not only deal with the control flow related bugs, but also the compute related bugs. We optimize the algorithm by Use-Define chain, strategy for predicate switching and automated upper bound for loops. The search space for our approach is much reduced compared with the former algorithm. The results turned out that it is promising and more efficient.

8 Future Work

In the furture, we would like to extend the algorithm to fit pointer better. Moreover, a full implementation should be developed, and sufficient experiments should be made.

References

1. Liu, Y., Li, B.: Automated program debugging via multiple predicate switching. In: AAAI (2010)
2. Wong, W.E., Debroy, V.: A survey of software fault localization. Department of Computer Science, University of Texas at Dallas, Technical report UTDCS-45 9 (2009)
3. Cleve, H., Zeller, A.: Locating causes of program failures. In: Proceedings of the 27th International Conference on Software Engineering, pp. 342–351. ACM (2005)
4. Zhang, X., Gupta, N., Gupta, R.: Locating faults through automated predicate switching. In: Proceedings of the 28th International Conference on Software Engineering, pp. 272–281. ACM (2006)
5. Challenge, D.: Satisfiability: Suggested format. DIMACS Challenge, DIMACS (1993)
6. Muchnick, S.S.: Advanced Compiler Design Implementation. Morgan Kaufmann, San Francisco (1997)
7. Sinn, M., Zuleger, F.: Loopus-a tool for computing loop bounds for c programs. In: WING@ ETAPS/IJCAR, Citeseer, pp. 185–186 (2010)
8. Clarke, E., Kroning, D., Lerda, F.: A tool for checking ANSI-C programs. In: Jensen, K., Podelski, A. (eds.) TACAS 2004. LNCS, vol. 2988, pp. 168–176. Springer, Heidelberg (2004)
9. Clarke, E., Kroening, D., Yorav, K.: Behavioral consistency of c and verilog programs using bounded model checking. In: Design Automation Conference, Proceedings, pp. 368–371. IEEE (2003)
10. de Moura, L., Bjørner, N.S.: Z3: an efficient SMT solver. In: Ramakrishnan, C.R., Rehof, J. (eds.) TACAS 2008. LNCS, vol. 4963, pp. 337–340. Springer, Heidelberg (2008)

11. Weiser, M.: Program slicing. In: Proceedings of the 5th International Conference on Software Engineering, pp. 439–449. IEEE Press (1981)
12. Agrawal, H., Horgan, J.R.: Dynamic program slicing. In: ACM SIGPLAN Notices, vol. 25, 246–256. ACM (1990)
13. Griesmayer, A., Staber, S., Bloem, R.: Automated fault localization for C programs. Electron. Notes Theoret. Comput. Sci. **174**, 95–111 (2007)
14. Jose, M., Majumdar, R.: Cause clue clauses: error localization using maximum satisfiability. ACM SIGPLAN Notices **46**, 437–446 (2011)
15. Groce, A., Chaki, S., Kroening, D., Strichman, O.: Error explanation with distance metrics. Int. J. Soft. Tools Technol. Transf. **8**, 229–247 (2006)
16. Ball, T., Naik, M., Rajamani, S.K.: From symptom to cause: localizing errors in counterexample traces. In: ACM SIGPLAN Notices. vol. 38, pp. 97–105. ACM (2003)

Model Checking and Verification

Model Checking Process Scheduling over Multi-core Computer System with MSVL

Xinfeng Shu[1(✉)] and Zhenhua Duan[2]

[1] School of Computer Science,
Xi'an University of Posts and Communications, Xi'an 710061, China
shuxf@xupt.edu.cn
[2] Institute of Computing Theory and Technology,
Xidian University, Xi'an 710071, China
zhhduan@mail.xidian.edu.cn

Abstract. To solve the problem that software testing cannot meet the verification needs of process scheduling over multi-core computer system, a model checking approach with MSVL is adapted to verify the correctness of process scheduling. Firstly, the grammar of MSVL is briefly introduced; further, a general model supporting the most commonly used scheduling algorithms for multi-core computer is formalized by MSVL program; finally, as a case study, the safeness of the processes scheduler with the earliest deadline first(EDF) scheduling algorithm over a 2-core CPU is verified with MSV toolkit, which indicates the proposed approach can effectively solve the verification problems of process scheduling over multi-core CPU.

Keywords: Process scheduling · System modeling · Verification · Model checking

1 Introduction

Process scheduler is a critical component of the modern operating system. Its correctness is one of the most important factors affecting the safety and reliability of the computer system. How to ensure the correctness of the process scheduling is of great importance to the system developer. Currently, testing is the most important means to check the correctness of process scheduling. However, the method can only show the existence of the errors, but can not prove their absence. What's more, the executions of the processes over multi-core CPU become really parallel, and each process proceeds in a unpredictable speed under the influence of other processes. Hence, the classical testing method can hardly meet the verification needs of process scheduling under such circumstance.

This research is supported by Natural Science Foundation of Education Bureau of Shaanxi Province, China (No.11JK1037, No.15JK1678), Natural Science Foundation of Shaanxi Province, China (No.2015JM6359), the NSFC Grant No.61133001, No.61202038, No.61272117, No.61272118 and No.61322202.

S. Liu and Z. Duan (Eds.): SOFL+MSVL 2015, LNCS 9559, pp. 103–117, 2016.
DOI: 10.1007/978-3-319-31220-0_8

In the past decade, quite some researches have been down in formal specification and verification of process scheduling with various approaches. In [1], the authors employ the μCRL process algebra to model the scheduling and apply the μCRL model checker toolset to find the near-optimal solutions. In [2], the author uses Promela to describe a job-shop scheduling problems and adds Branch-and-Bound techniques to the LTL property to find a solution effectively. In [3], the real-time system with a preemptive scheduling policy is modeled as a scheduling time Petri Net and the timed properties are verified using HyTech, an automatic tool for the analysis of embedded systems.

Projection Temporal Logic (PTL) [4–6] is an interval based first order temporal logic with a key temporal construct, $(P1, ..., Pm)prjQ$, and supports both finite and infinite time. Further, Propositional Projection Temporal Logic (PPTL), the propositional subset of PTL, has the expressiveness power of the full regular expressions [7], which can be used to specify the properties of the hardware or software systems to be verified.

The language Modeling, Simulation and Verification Language (MSVL) is an executable subset of PTL with framing technique [8,9]. It supports the commonly used data types (e.g., char, integer, pointer, ...), data structures (e.g., array, user-defined structure, list, ...), boolean and arithmetic expressions. Besides, MSVL provides many powerful programming statements, such as frame, if, while, parallel ($\|$), ..., and has ability to model, simulate and verify the concurrent and reactive systems within a same logical system [10].

In recent years, MSVL has been successfully applied to verify the typical hardware and software systems such as virtual memory and embedded operating system [11–15]. This paper extends the application of MSVL based model checking approach to verify the process scheduling in a multi-core CPU computer system. To this end, a general system model supporting the typical periodic and non-periodic processes as well as the most commonly used scheduling algorithms is formalized by MSVL program. Then, an example is given to illustrate how this method works.

The rest of paper is organized as follows. In the next section, the language MSVL is briefly introduced. In Sect. 3, the system model of process scheduling over multi-core CPU is formalized. In Sect. 4, a case study is given to show how the proposed method works. Finally, conclusions are drawn in Sect. 5.

2 Modeling, Simulation and Verification Language

The language MSVL is an executable subset of PTL [5]. The grammar of MSVL consists of expressions and statements, where expressions can be regarded as the PTL terms, and statements as the PTL formulas [9,11].

Expression. Let D denote the data domain, which includes integers, string, lists, sets, etc. The expression e and boolean expression b of MSVL are defined inductively as follows:

$$e :: = d \mid x \mid \bigcirc e \mid f(e_1, \ldots, e_m)$$
$$b :: = true \mid false \mid e_1 = e_2 \mid \rho(e_1, \ldots, e_m) \mid \neg b \mid b_1 \wedge b_2$$

where $d \in D$ is a constant; $x \in V$ is a variable; f is a function and ρ is a predicate both defined over D.

Statement. The elementary statements in MSVL are defined as follows:

(1) Immediate Assign $\quad x \Leftarrow e$

(2) Unit Assignment $\quad x := e$

(3) Conjunction $\quad S_1 \ and \ S_2 \stackrel{def}{=} S_1 \wedge S_2$

(4) Selection $\quad S_1 \ or \ S_2 \stackrel{def}{=} S_1 \wedge S_2$

(5) Next $\quad next \ S \stackrel{def}{=} \bigcirc P$

(6) Always $\quad always \ S \stackrel{def}{=} \square P$

(7) Termination $\quad empty \stackrel{def}{=} \neg \bigcirc true$

(8) Skip $\quad skip \stackrel{def}{=} \bigcirc \varepsilon$

(9) Sequential $\quad S_1 ; S_2 \stackrel{def}{=} (S_1, S_2) \ prj \ empty$

(10) Local $\quad exist \ x : S \stackrel{def}{=} \exists x : S$

(11) State Frame $\quad lbf(x)$

(12) Interval Frame $\quad frame(x)$

(13) Projection $\quad (S_1, \ldots, S_m) \ prj \ S$

(14) Condition $\quad if \ b \ then \ S_1 \ else \ S_2 \stackrel{def}{=} (b \rightarrow S_1) \wedge (\neg b \rightarrow S_2)$

(15) While $\quad while \ b \ do \ S \stackrel{def}{=} (b \wedge S)^* \wedge \square(\varepsilon \rightarrow \neg b)$

(16) Await $\quad await(b) \stackrel{def}{=} \bigwedge_{x \in V_b} frame(x) \wedge \square(\varepsilon \leftrightarrow b)$

(17) Parallel $\quad S_1 \| S_2 \stackrel{def}{=} ((S_1 ; true) \wedge S_2) \vee (S_1 \wedge (S_2 ; true))$
$$\vee \ (S_1 \wedge S_2)$$

where x is a variable, e is an arbitrary expression, b is a boolean expression, and $S_1, \ldots, S_m, S$ are all MSVL statements. The immediate assignment $x \Leftarrow e$, unit assignment $x := e$, $empty$, $lbf(x)$ and $frame(x)$ are basic statements, and the left composite ones.

The immediate assignment $x \Leftarrow e$ can be defined as $x = e \wedge p_x$, where sub-formula $x = e$ denotes the value of variable x is equal to that of the arithmetic expression e, and atomic proposition p_x is the assignment flag for variable x. The unit assignment $x := e$ can be defined as $\bigcirc x = e \wedge \bigcirc p_x$, which means the value of variable x in the next equals to that of e and the assignment flag p_x holds in the next state.

The state frame statement $lbf(x)$ means that the value of x in the current state is equal to that in the previous state if there is no assignment to x, i.e., its assignment flag p_x does not hold; and the interval statement $frame(x)$ means that variable x always keeps its old value in the previous state if variable x is not assigned with a new value. The means of the left statements can be found in [10, 11] and hence are omitted here.

To use MSVL to formal verification, a model checking tool named MSV toolkit has been developed. It has three modes, i.e., modeling, simulation and verification, where simulation finds a model for the MSVL program, while modeling finds all models, and verification is based on the model checking approach.

3   Modeling of Process Scheduling over Multi-core CPU

Figure 1 gives a sketch of process scheduling in a typical multi-core computer system. The hardware resource of the system contains a m-core CPU($m \geq 1$), and $n(n \geq 1)$ I/O devices of all kinds. The process queues manage all the processes waiting for the CPU or other I/O device. Whenever a resource is free, the Process Scheduler will select an appropriate process with a standing request for the resource and put it to execute. The computer system allows many processes to execute concurrently, however, a resource can only be occupied by one process at any time.

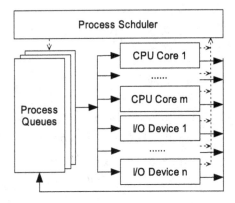

Fig. 1. Sketch of process scheduling over Multi-core CPU

3.1   Resource Description

Since one kind of hardware may have many physical devices, e.g., CPU may have more than 2 cores, we introduce the concept of logical device for the convenience of resource allocation. The name of the logical device is in fact the kind name of the corresponding physical device. Moreover, we assign each logical (physical) device a unique non-negative integer to identify each device. Thus, a process only needs to apply for logical devices during its execution, and the scheduler will allocate the specific physical ones to it and enable the process to run.

Let N_0 and N_1 be the set of non-negative and positive integers respectively. The logical and physical device can be depicted as follows.

Definition 1 (Physical Device). A physical device $pdev$ is a tuple defined as

$$pdev:: = (id, status, ldid, cproc),$$

where $id \in N_0$ is the device identifer; $status \in \{0, 1\}$ is the device status (0 denotes idle, 1 means busy); $ldid$ is the identifier of the corresponding logical device; $cproc$ is the process currently using the device.

Definition 2 (Logical Device). A logical device $ldev$ is a tuple defined as

$$ldev:: = (id, type, dlist, pque),$$

where $id \in N_0$ is the device identifer; $type \in \{0, 1\}$ is the device type (0 denotes exclusive, and 1 means shareable); $dlist$ is the list of the physical devices belonging to the logical device; $pque$ is the queue of the processes standing for the device.

3.2 Process Description

Intuitively, the execution of a process is in fact alternatively using different resource for a certain time in sequence according to the process code. Thus, from the view point of using the resources, the process code can be depicted by a sequence of resource requirement. To this end, we employe *Resource Requirement List* (RRL) to describe the code of a process.

Definition 3 (Resource Requirement List). Let id be the identifier of a logical device, and $t \in N_1$ be the time of the device to use. The resource requirement section (RRS) sec, composed resource requirement section (CRRS) cse and resource requirement list (RRL) rrl are defined inductively as follows:

$$sec:: = (id, t)$$
$$rss:: = sec \mid rss_1, rss_2$$
$$cse:: = (rss, t)$$
$$rrl:: = rss \mid cse^n \mid cse^\omega$$

where RRS (id, t) denotes needing device id for t units of time; CRRS (rss, t) $(t \geq \sum_{sec \in rss} sec.t)$ is used to describe the resource requirement of a periodic task, which means the period lasts t units of time and the resource requirement within a period is rss. $cse^n (n \in N_1)$ and cse^ω are used to describe the finite and infinite periodic tasks respectively. The former represents the CRRS cse will be repeat for n times, and the later stands for the CRRS cse will be repeat for infinitely many times.

Now we give two examples to show how RRL works to describe a process. Without loss of generality, we suppose the computer is equipped with the devices as shown in Table 1. If the RRLs of process P_1 and P_2 are as follows:

$$rrl_1 = (1, 10), (4, 5), (1, 2), (2, 10)$$
$$rrl_2 = ((1, 1), (3, 2), (1, 2), 10)^\omega$$

then, the rrl_1 of process P_1 denotes P_1 will use the devices CPU, HD, CPU, PRT with the lasting time 10, 5, 2, 10 in sequence. Further, rrl_2 means the process P_2 is a infinite periodic task with time period 10, and moreover, it needs CPU, NET and HD for 1, 2 and 2 units of time respectively in a task period.

Table 1. Check list between logical devices and physical ones

Logical Device			Physical Device	
ID	Name	Type	ID	Name
1	CPU	1	1	CPU Core 1
			2	CPU Core 2
2	PRT	0	3	Laser Printer
3	NET	0	4	Network Card
4	HD	0	5	Hard Disk

In consideration of modeling needs for the typical scheduling algorithms, we employ a 8-tuple to describe a process defined as follows.

Definition 4 (Process). The process *proc* is define as:

$$proc:: = (pid, rrl, ldid, pro, stime, ltime, tslice, dline)$$

where $pid, ldid, pro, stime, ltime, tslice, dline \in N_0$; pid is the identifier of the process; rrl is the resource requirement list; $ldid$ is the identifier of the logical device that the process is currently standing for; pro denotes the priority; $stime$ records the start time when the process begins to apply for the current resource; $ltime$ stores the left required time for current device; $tslice$ records the time slice used in a time sharing system; $dline$ keeps the deadline of the current period and it takes effect only if the process is a periodic task.

3.3 System Modeling

The modeling strategy of process scheduling over multi-core computer system is depicted in Fig. 2. The system model consists of three parts, i.e., Scheduler, Physical Devices and System Clock. Each of them will be formalized by a subprogram with MSVL in the following subsections. For simplicity, we ignore the execution time of the Scheduler.

Roughly speaking, the task of the Scheduler is to allocate resource for the waiting process. Firstly, the Scheduler keeps on waiting for the scheduling signal *sigSch*, which denotes there exist some processes applying for system resources. In case of *sigSch* received, it sets variable $cStatus = 0$ to pause the System Clock and allocates needed resources to the standing processes according to scheduling algorithm. Then, the Scheduler sends signal *sigRun* to the allocated resources and enable them to run. Moreover, it set variable $cStatus = 1$ to resume System

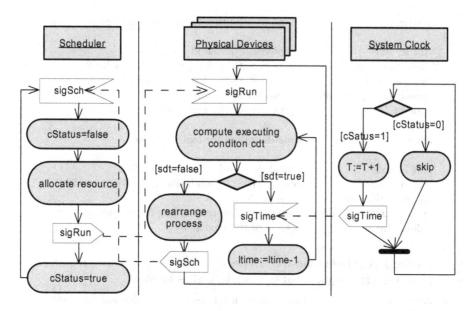

Fig. 2. Activity diagram of the system model

Clock again. After that, the Schedule continues to wait for the occurrence of another scheduling event.

For each physical device, we design a subprogram to describe its running. The execution of a process on a device is abstracted as the decreasing left required time of the resource under the driven of the signal *sigTime* from the System Clock. Initially, the physical device keeps idle and waits for the coming of signal *sigRun*. When the signal *sigRun* arrives, the device computes the executing condition *cdt* (the details can be found in Subsect. 3.3). If *cdt* holds, the device decreases the left required time *ltime* by 1 on the arriving of signal *sigTime* and continues to run the process; otherwise, it rearranges the process int.o the waiting process queue according to the left resource requirement and send a signal *sigSch* to the Scheduler. Finally, the device goes on waiting for another execution.

The task of System Clock is to keep the synchronization among physical devices like a real computer does. It just keeps on increasing the system time T and sending signal *sigTime* to each physical device in case of *cStatus* = 1.

In the following, we firstly employ MSVL structures to describe the data structures used in system modeling, and then use MSVL functions to simulate the running of Physical Device, Scheduler and System Clock.

Data Structures. We use linked list to manage the data of logical devices, physical devices and processes. According to the Definitions 1 and 2, the types of list nodes for physical device and logical device are defined respectively with MSVL as follows.

```
struct pdev_t                // node definition for physical device
{
    int id and               // physical device id
    int status and           // device status:0 for free and 1 for busy
    int ldid and             // corresponding logical device id
    process_t *cproc and     // pointer of the process using the device
    pdev_t *nexts            // pointer of the next node
};
struct ldev_t                // node definition for logical device
{
    int id and               // logical device id
    int type and             // device type:0 for exclusive and 1 for shareable
    pdev_t *dlist and        // physical device list
    process_t *pque and      // queue of processes standing for the device
    ldev_t *nexts            // pointer of the next node
};
```

According to the Definition 3, the types of list nodes for resource requirement section and resource requirement list are defined as follows.

```
struct sec_t                 // node definition for resource requirement section
{
    int id and               // logical device id
    int t and                // time required
    sec_t *nexts             // pointer of the next node
};
struct rrl_t                 //node definition for resource requirement list
{
    sec_t *secs and          // pointer of the resource requirement sections
    int ptime and            // 0 for non periodic task, otherwise the period time
    int reptimes and         // 0 denotes the task is an infinite periodic task,
                             //   otherwise, the number of periods to be repeated
    rrl_t *nexts             // pointer of the next node
};
```

The list node type for processes (Definition 4) is defined as follows.

```
struct process_t             //node definition for process
{
    int pid and              // identifier of the process
    rrl_t *rrl and           // resource requirement list
    int ldid and             // identifier of the logical device
    int pro and              // priority
    int stime and            // start time to wait for the device
    int ltime and            // left required time
    int tslice and           // time slice
    int dline and            // deadline of the current period
    process_t *nexts         // pointer of the next node
};
```

Table 2. Priority functions of typical scheduling algorithms

Algorithm name	Function definition
First Come First Service(FCFS)	$Hp(P_i, P_j) \stackrel{\text{def}}{=} P_i.stime < P_j.stime$
Shortest Process First(SPF)	$Hp(P_i, P_j) \stackrel{\text{def}}{=} P_i.ltime < P_j.ltime$
Highest Response Ratio Next (HRRN)	$Hp(P_i, P_j) \stackrel{\text{def}}{=} (T - P_i.stime)/P_i.ltime$ $< (T - P_j.stime)/P_j.ltime$
Highest Priority Next(HPN)	$Hp(P_i, P_j) \stackrel{\text{def}}{=} P_i.pro < P_j.pro$
Round Robin(RR)	$Hp(P_i, P_j) \stackrel{\text{def}}{=} P_i.st < P_j.st$
Multilevel Feedback Queue (MFQ)	$Hp(P_i, P_j) \stackrel{\text{def}}{=} (P_i.pro = P_j.pro$ $\text{and } P_i.pro < P_j.pro)$ $\text{or } (P_i.pro < P_j.pro)$
Rate Monotonic(RM)	$Hp(P_i, P_j) \stackrel{\text{def}}{=} P_i.ltime < P_j.ltime$
Earliest Deadline First(EDF)	$Hp(P_i, P_j) \stackrel{\text{def}}{=} P_i.dline < P_j.dline$

Scheduler Modeling. The priority of a process to acquire CPU or I/O devices is decided by the scheduling algorithm. Let $Hp(P_i, P_j)$ be the priority function between processes P_i and P_j which are both waiting for a same resource. Based on the data items of the process, it is not hard to write out the priority function for a commonly used scheduling algorithms. Table 2 gives the definitions of the priority functions for the typical scheduling algorithms, where variable T records the current system time. One can chooses the corresponding priority function in case of scheduling verification.

Let $ldSet, sigSch, cStatus$ be the variables saving the header pointer of the logical device list, scheduling signal and status of System Clock respectively. Further, we use the attribute $status$ of physical device to keep its running signal. Moreover, we employ boolean variable $alPrem$ to denotes whether the shared resource allows to be preempted according to the scheduling algorithm. Note that, before calling function Sch, the processes in the waiting queue of a logical device must be arranged on the descending ordered of priority according to the scheduling algorithm.

According to the strategy depicted in Fig. 3, the function Sch for the Scheduler in MSVL is as follows.

```
function Sch(ldev_t *ldSet, int *sigSch, int alPrem, int *cStatus)
{
    frame (pLogDev, pPhyDev, fPhyDev, rtn ) and (
    ......;                    /* Define and initialize local variables*/
        while (true) {
            await(*sigSch=1) ;         /*Wait for the scheduling signal*/
            *sigSch:=0 and *cStatus:=0;   /*Pause the system clock */
            pLogDev:=ldSet;
            while (pLogDev!=NULL) { /*Process each logical device*/
                pPhyDev:=pLogDev→dlist;
                /*Firstly, allocate the idle physical devices to processes*/
```

```
while( pPhyDev!=NULL and pLogDev→pque!=NULL ) {
    ......; /* allocate the idle device*/
};
/*Then, preempt device from the process with lower priority*/
if(alPrem=1 and pLogDev→type=1) then { /*shareable device*/
    fPhyDev:=pLogDev→dlist;
    while( fPhyDev !=NULL and pLogDev→pque!=NULL){
        pPhyDev:=pLogDev→dlist→nexts;
        while (pPhyDev!=NULL){    /* compare the priority*/
            rtn:=Hp(pPhyDev, fPhyDev, rtn);
            if (0=rtn) then {
                fPhyDev:=pPhyDev
            }; pPhyDev:=pPhyDev→nexts
        };
        ......;     /* preempt the device*/
    }
};
pLogDev:=pLogDev→nexts;
}
*cStatus:= 1; /* Resume the System Clock */
}
)
};
```

In function Sch, if the scheduling signal $sigSch$ arrives (i.e., $*sigSch := 1$), the Scheduler firstly turns off the scheduling signal (i.e., $*sigSch := 0$) and pauses the System Clock (i.e., $*cStatus := 0$). Then, the Scheduler traverses each logical device and allocates the corresponding physical devices to the waiting processes. For a given logical device, the Scheduler firstly allocates its idle physical devices to the standing processes. After that, if scheduling algorithm allows preemption (i.e., $alPrem = 1$) and the logical device is shareable (i.e., pLogDev→type=1) as well as there still exists some waiting processes, the Scheduler will preempt some physical devices from the process with lower priority and allocate them to the waiting higher priority processes. Function $Hp(pPhyDev, fPhyDev, rtn)$ compares the priorities between the two given processes. If the priority of the former one is above than or equal to that of the second one, it returns 1, otherwise 0.

Device Modeling. Let $dev, ldSet, sigSch, sigTime$ be the variables saving physical device, the header pointer of the logical device list, scheduling signal and system time signal respectively. The activities of dev given in Fig. 3 are formalized with a MSVL function $PhyDev$ as follows.

```
function PhyDev(pdev_t *dev, ldev_t *ldSet, int *sigSch, int *sigTime)
{
    frame( devID, rtn) and (
        ......;                    /* Define and initialize local variables*/
```

```
while (true) {
    await(dev→status=1) ;      /*Wait for the running signal*/
    while(dev→cproc→ltime> 0 and dev→cproc→tslice> 0) {
        await(*sigTime=1);              /*Wait for system clock*/
        ......; /*Decrease left required time and time slice by 1*/
    };
    if(dev→cproc→ltime> 0) then { /*Run out of time slice*/
        AddToLogDev(ldSet, dev→cproc, dev→cproc→ldid )
    }else {
        /* Compute the next resource requirement */
        rtn:=NextReqDev(dev→cproc, &devID, rtn);
        if(rtn> 0) then {
            AddToLogDev(ldSet, dev→cproc, devID)
        }
    }
    dev→status:=0 and *sigSch:=1;   /*Set scheduling signal*/
}
)
};
```

In function *PhyDev*, if the running signal arrives (i.e., dev→status=1), the device begins to repeatedly decrease the left required time and time slice of current process by 1 until either of which equals to 0. Subsequently, if the current time slice runs out (i.e., dev→cproc→ltime> 0), the process is added back to the corresponding waiting queue by calling function *AddToLogDev*. Otherwise, the device computes the next resource requirement by calling function *NextReqDev* and adds the process to the waiting process queue of logical device *devID*. Finally, the device sets its status to idle (i.e., dev→status:=0) and sends the scheduling signal to the Scheduler (i.e., *sigSch:=1).

System Clock Modeling. The task of System Clock is relative simple. It just keeps on increasing the system time T and generating signal *sigTime* to synchronize physical devices in case of *cStatus* = 1. Let $T, cStatus, sigTime$ be the variables saving the system time, the status of System Clock and system time signal respectively. Function *SysClock* formalizing the System Clock is as follows.

```
function SysClock(int *T , int *cStatus, int *sigTime)
{
    while (true) {
        if(*status=1) then { /*Run out of time slice*/
            *T:=*T+1 and *sigTime:=1
        }else {
            *sigTime:=0 and skip
        }
    }
};
```

3.4 Specification of the Whole System

Let $sigSch, sigTime, cStatus, T$ be the variables saving the scheduling signal, system time signal, system clock status and system time respectively. Further, let $ldArray, pdArray, prArray, secArray, rrlArray$ be the arrays keeping the data of logical devices, physical devices, processes, resource requirement sections as well as resource requirement lists respectively. Since all the physical devices, the Scheduler and the System Clock run concurrently in the computer system, the whole process scheduling over a multi-core computer system can be described by the following MSVL function.

```
function System()
{
    frame(sigSch, sigTime, T, cStatus, ldArray, pdArray, prArray,
        secArray, rrlArray) and (
        ......; //Definitions for local variables
        Init(ldArray, pdArray, prArray, secArray, rrlArray);
        Sch(ldArray, &sigSch, 1, &sigRun, &cStatus) ||
            ||_pdev∈pdArray PhyDev(pdev, ldArray, &sigSch, &sigRun, &sigTime)
        || SysClock(&T, &cStatus, &sigTime)
    }
    )
};
```

where function $Init$ initiates the sets of logical devices, physical devices as well as processes. The function will be specified according to the computer system to be verified.

4   Verification Example

In this section, we employ the system model formalized above to verify the process scheduling over a multi-core computer system.

4.1 System Description

Without loss of generality, let the hardware of the computer consist of a 2-core CPU, and 3 different I/O devices named by Laser Printer, Network Card and Hard Disk which only support exclusive access mode. The check list between logical devices and physical devices is given in Table 1. Moreover, the scheduler of the computer selects the algorithm of Earliest Deadline First (EDF), a preemptive real-time scheduling algorithm, to select a process.

Suppose 3 processes P_1, P_2 and P_3 are read to run and their original resource requirement lists are as follows:

$$P_1 : ((4,3), (1,5), (2,3), 12)^{10}$$
$$P_2 : ((1,4), (3,3), (4,2), 10)^{\omega}$$
$$P_3 : ((3,4), (1,8), (2,5), 18)^{\omega}$$

where P_1 is a finite periodic task, P_2, P_3 are both infinite periodic tasks. After being loaded into the memory, each process will be assigned to the standing process queue belonging to the logical device it initially applies for.

Thus, function *Init* of the system model are defined as follows.

function Init(ldev_t ldArray[ ], pdev_t pdArray[ ], process_t prArray[ ],
        sec_t secArray[ ], rrl_t rrlArray[ ])
{
    frame(i) and (
        int i and i<==0 and empty;
        while (i< 10) {
            ......; /*Initialize each array into a linked list respectively*/
        };
        ldArray[0].id<== 1 and ldArray[0].dlist<==&pdArray[0] and
            ldArray[0].type<== 1 and pdArray[1].nexts<==NULL and
            ldArray[0].pque<==NULL and empty;
        ......; /*Initialize the other logical devices*/
        pdArray[0].id<== 1 and pdArray[0].cproc<==NULL and
            pdArray[0].status<== 0 and pdArray[0].ldid<== 1 and empty;
        ......; /*Initialize the other physical devices*/
        prArray[0].pid<== 1 and prArray[0].ldid<== 4 and
            prArray[0].stime<== 0 and prArray[0].ltime<== 0 and
            prArray[0].rrl<==&rrlArray[0] and rrlArray[1].nexts<==NULL and
            prArray[0].tslice<== 0 and prArray[0].dline<== 0 and empty ;
        ......; /*Initialize other processes and their resource requirements*/
)
};

After completing the modeling program, we execute the modeling program in the MSV interpreter and analyze the result. The screenshot result of modeling is given in Fig. 3.

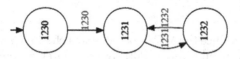

Fig. 3. The result of system modeling

4.2 System Verification

In the following, we use the MSV toolkit to verify the safety property of the process scheduling over the computer, i.e., the task within a period finish successfully before the coming of deadline for each process. It is equivalent to verify that for any process *prc*, the left required resource time *ltime* plus the system

PPTL Formula:

[](p1 and p2 and p3)

Propositions Define:

define p1: T+pdArray[0].ltime<= pdArray[0].dline
define p2: T+pdArray[1].ltime<= pdArray[1].dline
define p3: T+pdArray[2].ltime<= pdArray[2].dline

Fig. 4. The PPTL formula to be verified

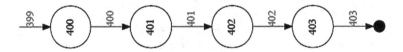

Fig. 5. The result of verification

time T must be less than or equal to the deadline *dline* of current period at any time. The property is depicted in MSVL as follows:

$$safeSch \overset{def}{=} \bigwedge_{prc \in prArray} always(T + prc.ltime \leq prc.dline).$$

The definition of the property in PPTL formula is depicted in Fig. 4. The result of the verification is given in Fig. 5, which shows property *safeSch* is not satisfied at state 403.

5   Conclusion

In this paper, we introduce the MSVL based model checking method to verify the safeness of process scheduling over multi-core computer system. A general model for process scheduling is formalized that it can be easily used to verifying all kinds of commonly used scheduling algorithms and typical periodic/nonperoid tasks, and the only work need to do is just adjust necessary parameters. However, the execution time of the process scheduler is ignored. In the future, we will improve the system model to be more close to a real computer. Besides, we will extend the application of the method to more area, such as embedded system, operating system, cloud computing, etc.

References

1. Wijs, A., van de Pol, J., Bortnik, E.M.: Solving scheduling problems by untimed model checking. STTT **11**(5), 375–392 (2009)
2. Ruys, T.C.: Optimal scheduling using branch and bound with SPIN 4.0. In: Ball, T., Rajamani, S.K. (eds.) SPIN 2003. LNCS, vol. 2648, pp. 1–17. Springer, Heidelberg (2003)
3. Lime, D., Roux, O.H.: Formal verification of real-time systems with preemptive scheduling. Real-Time Syst. **41**(2), 118–151 (2009)
4. Duan, Z.: An extended interval temporal logic and a framing technique for interval temporal logic programming. Ph.D. thesis, University of Newcastle Upon Tyne, May 1996
5. Duan, Z.: Temporal Logic and Temporal Logic Programming. Science Press, Beijing (2005)
6. Duan, Z., Tian, C., Zhang, L.: A decision procedure for propositional projection temporal logic with infinite models. Acta Inf. **45**(1), 43–78 (2008)
7. Tian, C., Duan, Z.: Expressiveness of propositional projection temporal logic with star. Theor. Comput. Sci. **412**(18), 1729–1744 (2011)
8. Duan, Z., Koutny, M.: A Framed Temporal Logic Programming Language. J. Comput. Sci. Technol. **19**, 333–344 (2004)
9. Duan, Z., Yang, X., Koutny, M.: Framed temporal logic programming. Sci. Comput. Program. **70**(1), 31–61 (2008)
10. Duan, Z., Tian, C.: A unified model checking approach with projection temporal logic. In: Liu, S., Araki, K. (eds.) ICFEM 2008. LNCS, vol. 5256, pp. 167–186. Springer, Heidelberg (2008)
11. Wang, M., Duan, Z., Tian, C.: Simulation and verification of the virtual memory management system with MSVL. In: Proceedings of the 2014 IEEE 18th International Conference on Computer Supported Cooperative Work in Design (CSCWD), pp. 360–365, May 2014
12. Cui, J., Duan, Z., Tian, C., Zhang, N., Zhou, C.: Model Checking μ C/OS-III Multi-task System with TMSVL. In: Butler, M., Conchon, S., Zaïdi, F. (eds.) Formal Methods and Software Engineering. Lecture Notes in Computer Science, vol. 9407, pp. 187–200. Springer, Switzerland (2015)
13. Yu, Y., Duan, Z., Tian, C., Yang, M.: Model checking C programs with MSVL. In: Liu, S. (ed.) SOFL 2012. LNCS, vol. 7787, pp. 87–103. Springer, Heidelberg (2013)
14. Bin, Y., Duan, Z., Tian, C.: Bounded model checking of traffic light control system. Electr. Notes Theor. Comput. Sci. **309**, 63–74 (2014)
15. Ma, Q., Duan, Z., Zhang, N., Wang, X.: Verification of distributed systems with the axiomatic system of MSVL. Formal Asp. Comput. **27**(1), 103–131 (2015)

A Method Based on MSVL for Verification of the Social Network Privacy Policy

Xiaobing Wang[✉] and Tao Sun

Institute of Computing Theory and Technology and ISN Laboratory,
Xidian University, Xian 710071, People's Republic of China
xbwang@mail.xidian.edu.cn, 307882479@qq.com

Abstract. A lot of privacy issues exist in the social network for its data information is excessively public and spreads quickly. This paper presents a method of modeling the social networking system and verifying its privacy policy based on the temporal logic programming language MSVL, which is an executable subset of Projection Temporal Logic. First of all, select an appropriate social networking system and simplify it. Then, model the system with an MSVL program and describe its privacy policy with a Propositional Projection Temporal Logic formula. Next, execute the program with the formula in the modeling, simulation and verification platform of MSVL. Finally, we can improve or modify the verified privacy policy according to the results.

Keywords: MSVL · Social networks · Privacy policy · Verification

1 Introduction

The development of Six Degrees of Separation theory introduces the early concept of the social network into the Internet and creates a Social Networking Site (SNS) [1]. Currently, SNS has penetrated into every aspects of our lives and works. Broadly speaking, SNS is an online community which is created by a group of people with the similar interests and activities. It provides them with a rapid exchange and approach to share all kinds of information, and brings great convenience of their lives and works. Typical SNSs include Facebook, Twitter, YouTube, LinkedIn, etc.

Many privacy problems are found in different SNSs at present [2]. The causes of these problems are mainly three points. (1) The users' own negligence leads to leak of privacy. Such as some users fill in personal privacy of sensitive data when they register the system, or download the Internet file indiscriminately, these are likely to bring potential risk of personal privacy data. (2) The SNSs' unsound privacy policy mechanisms lead to the leak of privacy. Such as the data storage of many SNSs are not enough safe, and the access to the privacy information

---

X. Wang—This research is supported by the NSFC Grant Nos. 61133001, 61272118, 61272117, 61322202, 61402347, 61420106004, 91418201, and the Fundamental Research Funds for the Central Universities Nos. JB140320, JB140308.

S. Liu and Z. Duan (Eds.): SOFL+MSVL 2015, LNCS 9559, pp. 118–131, 2016.
DOI: 10.1007/978-3-319-31220-0_9

of users is not strict, these are likely to be used by hackers. (3) The third-party applications lead to the leak of privacy. Such as, some SNSs allow the third-party applications to embed into the sites for their own benefits without checking their safety. As a result, the criminals will be able to embed malicious code into the third-party applications to steal users' personal privacy data.

As we known, a lot of methods are proposed to address privacy problems in SNS. XBook [3] has been deployed on Facebook as an independent third-party application and can indeed prevent the other applications deployed on Facebook from leaking user privacy. Security mechanisms based on third-party applications are also studied for social networking platform in [4]. An information dissemination model based on the online social network is proposed in [5], which takes into account the impact of the node degree and propagation mechanism. A social networking system model based on Petri nets [6] and an effective algorithm for friend suggestion are established. In addition, Privacy Policy Framework (PPF) [7] is invented for social network privacy policy, which includes a formal model, a knowledge-base logic and a formal privacy policy language. Moreover, the Poporo tool [8,9] selects an application developed with Java as the social networking system to study, and describes the privacy policy set of the system with B method called Matelas [10]. The main features of some famous online social networking platforms such as Facebook, Twitter, Google+ and Diaspora are summarized in [4], then a graph-based modeling method is proposed to describe and measure the privacy policy and security.

Modeling, Simulation and Verification Language (MSVL) is an executable subset of Projection Temporal Logic (PTL) and developed as a temporal logic programming language, by which concurrent systems can be modeled, simulated and verified [11]. This paper extends the MSVL applications to the social network privacy policy, and the main contributions are as follows. (1) A novel method for verification of the social network privacy policy is proposed based on MSVL. (2) An application is illustrated to show how this method works. With these contributions, the language MSVL can be used to model, simulate and verify the social network privacy policy in the real world.

The rest of the paper is organized as follows. Section 2 briefly introduces a unified model checking approach based on MSVL. In Sect. 3, a method based on MSVL for modeling SNS and verifying the privacy policy is proposed. Then, Sect. 4 provides a case study to show how to use this method. Finally, conclusions are drawn in Sect. 5.

2   A Unified Model Checking Approach

PTL is a first-order temporal logic which has a key temporal operator prj [12], and Propositional PTL (PPTL) [13] is a propositional subset of PTL which excludes variables, quantifiers and predicates. PPTL can be used to describe properties of concurrent systems, and it has already been proved that the expressiveness of

PPTL is the same as the full regular expressions [14]. The language MSVL [15] is a temporal logic programming language which is an executable subset of PTL. PPTL and MSVL can be used for the purpose of modeling, simulation and verification of software and hardware systems [11].

A unified model checking approach with PTL is based on Normal Form Graph (NFG) [16]. By modeling a system with an MSVL program p, and specifying the desirable property of the system with a PPTL formula φ, whether or not the system satisfies the property (whether or not $p \rightarrow \varphi$ is valid) can equivalently be checked by evaluating whether or not $\neg(p \rightarrow \varphi) \equiv p \wedge \neg \varphi$ is unsatisfiable. The satisfiability of a formula in the form of $p \wedge \neg \varphi$ is checked by constructing the NFG of $p \wedge \neg \varphi$, and then inspecting whether or not there exist paths in the NFG.

As it is shown in Fig. 1, the MSV platform is the tool of executing MSVL program, and it has three modes: simulation, modeling and verification. Simulation is finding a model for the MSVL program, while modeling is finding all models. Verification is based on the above unified model checking approach.

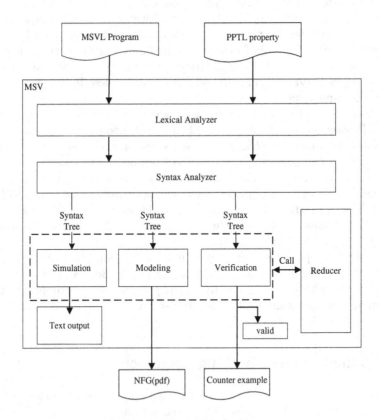

Fig. 1. The MSV platform

3 A Method Based on MSVL for Verification of the Social Network Privacy Policy

We adopt the unified model checking approach for the verification of the social network privacy policy. The method is briefly introduced as follows. Firstly, we select an appropriate social networking system, simplify it and model it with an MSVL program. Then, we describe some privacy policies with PPTL formulas. Next, we execute the program with formulas in the MSV platform with modeling, simulation and verification modes separately. Finally, we can improve or modify the related privacy policy according to the result. The sketch of this verification method is shown in Fig. 2.

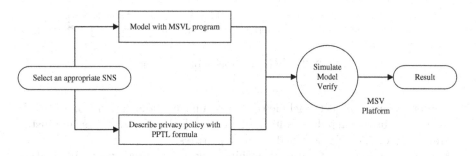

Fig. 2. The sketch of the verification method

3.1 The Specific Process of Modeling

In Fig. 3, at first, we select an appropriate system and simplify it to abstract the core elements and the main operations, then model with an MSVL program. Second, we select some privacy policies to be described with PPTL formulas. Finally, we can execute the modeling program and PPTL formulas in the MSV platform with simulation, modeling and verification modes. The specific process is as follows in details.

Step 1 Select an appropriate system and simplify it. Real SNSs include complex data structures and cumbersome user operations, so they are very difficult to model. In order to give an easy understanding of the verification method and highlight a system feature, firstly we select an appropriate SNS and simplify it. As is known to all, the core elements of SNSs such as Facebook, Twitter, Google+ and Diaspora are user, content, relationship between users and operations on content as follows.

1. User: the most main subject of the online social networking system, including the personal information of the user like ID number, name, sex, age, job, email, address and hobbies. And most SNSs encourage user fill in real name when the user creates the personal account, but it is not mandatory. As is known to all, filling in real name is conducive to realizing the function of SNS searching, that is Facebook.

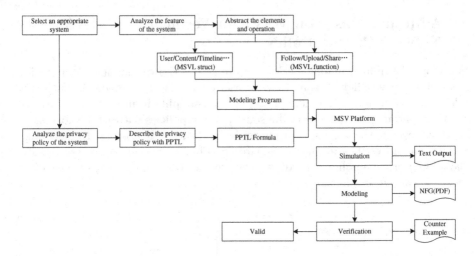

Fig. 3. The specific process of modeling

2. Content: content objects include text, link, image, audio and video, etc. Such as, Twitter users can publish 140 words or less which is called tweets, and Instagram is an online SNS designed to share pictures.
3. Friendship: it describes the relationship between two users. Generally speaking, there are two main kinds of user relationship, one is the real-name strong relation like Facebook, the other is non-real-name weak relationship like Twitter.
4. Operation: it includes uploading, commenting, tagging, reminding, sharing and sending messages to a user or a group, etc.

So, in the verification method we only need to take into account the core elements and discard the other non-core elements. Then, we use the struct data type in MSVL as the base data type in the modeling, and use MSVL functions to simulate the user operations.

Step 2 The modeling process. Firstly, we use MSVL struct type to describe the user, content, user profile in the SNS, and use a linked list to describe the friends list and personal timeline of the user.

Struct of User represents the user in the system which includes ID, name, sex, age, job, email, address, like and friend list.

```
struct User
{
    int     ID      and
    string  name    and
    string  sex     and
    int     age     and
    string  job     and
    string  email   and
```

```
        string   address  and
        string   like     and
        Fri*     friends
};
```

Struct of Content represents the content in the system which includes Id, time of creation, type of content, substance and belonger.

```
struct Content
{
    int    id       and
    string time     and
    string type     and
    string substance and
    string belonger
};
```

Struct of UserPage represents the user profile in the system which includes belonger, user, current time, current mood and timeline.

```
struct UserPage
{
    string   name     and
    User*    u        and
    string   date     and
    string   mood     and
    Timeline* tl
};
```

Struct of Fri represents the friend list struct in the system which includes name of the friend and nexts pointer.

```
struct Fri
{
    string name      and
    Fri*   nexts
};
```

Struct of Timeline represents the timeline of user profile which includes time, belonger, shared, substance and nexts pointer.

```
struct Timeline
{
    string   time     and
    string   belonger and
    int      quote    and
    string   substance and
    Timeline* nexts
};
```

Secondly, we use MSVL functions to simulate the user operations, and they can be divided into three kinds: the operation of user himself, the operation between users and the operation of user to content. As they are shown as follows.

1. The operation of user himself:

```
function Register
function Create_Content
function Page_field
function Show_timeline
```

2. The operation between users:

```
function Follow
function Notfollow
```

3. The operation of user to content:

```
function Upload
function Delete
function View
function Share
```

3.2 The Common Privacy Policy

As is known to all, almost all the online SNS has the feature that each object must be associated at least to one user (i.e., the belonger), and each user must own at least one object (i.e., the personal user profile). The process of building and destroying associations is subject to the security policies implemented by the SNS. Online SNSs provide their privacy policies: such as one option blocks cookies that don't include a privacy policy, another blocks cookies that can save your contact information without your approval and user can set stranger can not view the personal profile of the user. However, such enforcements are seldom sufficient to avoid misuses. The current privacy and security policies are non-standardized and user-dependent, so we introduce some common privacy policies in online SNS as follows. Then we select one or more common privacy policies to describe and verify in the next section.

1. The permission setting of viewing the user personal information, general including only me, friends and public;
2. The permission setting of viewing the content which the user uploaded, general including friends and public;
3. The permission setting of sharing and commenting the content which the user uploaded, general including friends, public and forbid;
4. Add friend setting, general including question, friend of friend and public;
5. Advertisement pushing setting, general including allow and forbid;
6. Blacklist someone (the user in the blacklist cant make any operation on the user).

3.3   Verification of Privacy Policy

After completing the modeling program with MSVL, we can execute the modeling program with simulation and modeling in the MSV platform and analyze the results. And then if the results are reasonable and correct, we select some common privacy policies in Sect. 3.2 to describe with PPTL formulas. Finally, we can verify whether these privacy policies are correct or not by executing the modeling program together with PPTL formulas in the verification mode of MSV platform. If the verification result is invalid, the MSV platform will return an NFG of a counter example. We should analyze the exist defect of our model and the verified privacy policy according to the NFG, and then find the potential privacy issues in the online SNS and modify them.

4   An Application

4.1   Modeling of SNS

Firstly, we select the most famous SNS Facebook as our model prototype. As is known to all, the core elements of Facebook are Friendship and Timeline. We discard the other non-core elements and some complex operations of Facebook to build up a small similar system with MSVL as shown in Fig. 4.

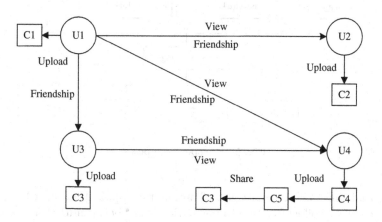

Fig. 4. A small system instance

In the system, there are four users (modeling program initiates three users u1, u2 and u3, then registers a new user u4 through the function Register in the modeling process), five contents (modeling program initiates four contents c1, c2, c3 and c4, then creates a new content c5 by the user through the function Create_Content in the modeling process). The four users have separate profiles, u1 and u2, u3, u4 are all friends, u3 and u4 are friends too. In the modeling program, the Upload function means the user uploads a content into the system, the View function means two users with friendship can view each other's contents, the Share function means the user shares the content belong to his friends and view in his own timeline once he shares the content successfully.

Then we use an MSVL program to model the system, and the specific process is following as shown in Fig. 5.

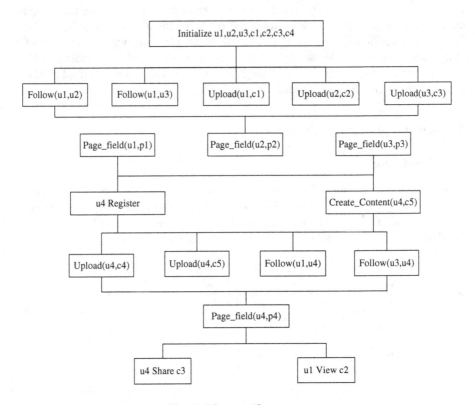

Fig. 5. The specific process

1. Initializing three Users u1, u2, u3 and four contents c1, c2, c3, c4;

2. Executing Follow function to make friendships between u1 and u2, u1 and u3; then executing Upload function to let u1, u2 and u3 upload contents c1, c2 and c3 separately;

3. Executing Page_field function to create user profiles for u1, u2 and u3;

4. Executing Register function to register a new user u4 and executing the Create_Content function to create a new content c5;

5. Executing Follow function to make friendships between u3 and u4, u1 and u4; then executing Upload function to let u4 upload contents c4 and c5;

6. Executing Page_field function to create user profile for u4;

7. Executing Share function to let u4 share c3 of u3, and executing the View function to let u1 view c2 of u2.

The Main Part of Modeling Program Code

```
Follow(u1,u2,fri1,fri2);
Follow(u1,u3,fri1,fri3);
Upload(u1,c1,p1,tl1);
Upload(u2,c2,p2,tl2);
Upload(u3,c3,p3,tl3);
Page_field(p2,u2,fri2,tl2);
output("Welcome, please register !\n") and skip;
register_flag := Register(u4,RValue);
if(register_flag = 1)
then
{ output("Congratulation, register successfully!
  Now you can create a new content. \n") and skip
}else{ skip    };
create_flag := Create_Content(c5,RValue);
if(create_flag = 1)
then
{   output("Congratulation, create content successfully!
    Now you can upload your content.\n") and skip
}else{ skip };
Upload(u4,c4,p4,tl4);
Upload(u4,c5,p4,tl5);
output("Congratulation, upload content successfully!
    Now you can add some friends.\n") and skip;
Follow(u3,u4,fri3,fri4);
Follow(u1,u4,fri1,fri4);
Page_field(p1,u1,fri1,tl1);
Page_field(p3,u3,fri3,tl3);
output("Congratulation, add friends successfully!
    Now you can create your user profile.\n") and skip;
Page_field(p4,u4,fri4,tl5);
share_flag := Share(u4,c3,p4,tl6,RValue);
if(share_flag = 1)
then
{   output("Shared successfully,
  now you can view it in your timeline.") and skip
}else{ skip    };
Show_timeline(p4,tl6);
view_flag := View(u1,u2,fri2,p2,tl2,c2,RValue);
if(view_flag = 1)
then
{ output("View successfully\n") and skip
}
else
{ output("View unsuccessfully\n") and skip
})};
```

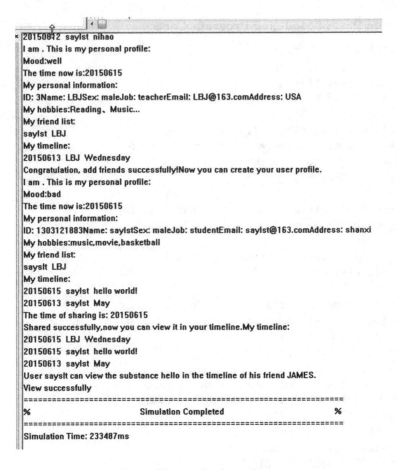

Fig. 6. The result of simulation

After completing the modeling program, we execute the modeling program in the MSV platform with simulation and modeling modes, then analyze the results. The screenshot results of simulation and modeling are in Figs. 6 and 7 separately.

4.2 Verification of Privacy Policy

After simulation and modeling, we select two common privacy policy (2) and (3) in Sect. 3.2 to verify.

(2) The user can view the content of his friend
a. u2 can view c1 of u1;
b. u2 can view c3 of u3;

In (2), the View function implements traversing the Friend list of u1, if it contains u2, there would be follow_flag = 1. At the same time, the View function implements traversing the timeline of u1, if it contains c1, there would be upload_flag = 1.

Fig. 7. The result of modeling

That is to say, if it is satisfied with follow_flag = 1 and upload_flag = 1 at the same time, there would be view_flag = 1, then u2 can view c1 of u1.

PPTL Formula Verification
define p : follow_flag = 1;
define q : upload_flag = 1;
define s : view_flag = 1;

We need verification of $p \wedge q \rightarrow s$, and it can be converted to $\neg\ (p \wedge q) \vee s$, as it is shown in Fig. 8. The result of the verification shows (2)a is satisfied as shown in Fig. 9 and (2)b is not satisfied as shown in Fig. 10. The result proves that the privacy policy (2) is correct.

PPTL Formula:

!(p and q)or s

Propositions Define:

define p: follow_flag=1;
define q: upload_flag=1;
define s: view_flag=1;

Fig. 8. The PPTL formula

(3) The user can share the content of his friend
a. u4 can share c3 of u3;
b. u2 can share c3 of u3;

In (3), the Share function implements traversing the Friend list of u3, if it contains u4, there would be follow_flag = 1. At the same time, the Share function implements traversing the timeline of u3, if it contains c3, there would be upload_flag = 1. That is to say, if it is satisfied with follow_flag = 1 and upload_flag = 1 at the same time, there would be share_flag = 1, u4 can share the c3 of u3.

PPTL Formula Verification
define p : follow_flag = 1;
define q : upload_flag = 1;
define s : share_flag = 1;

We need verification of $p \wedge q \rightarrow s$, and it can be converted to $\neg (p \wedge q) \vee s$. The result of the verification shows (3)a is satisfied as shown in Fig. 9 and (3)b is not satisfied as shown in Fig. 10. The above results prove that the privacy policy (3) is also correct.

Fig. 9. The result of verification–satisfied

Fig. 10. The result of verification–unsatisfied

5   Conclusions

In this paper we propose a method for modeling the SNS and verifying the privacy policy in the system based on MSVL. The method firstly selects an appropriate SNS and simplify it to abstract the core elements and the main operations. Then the method models the simplified system with MSVL program and describes the privacy policies with PPTL formulas. Next the MSVL program and PPTL formulas are together executed in the MSV platform with simulation, modeling and verification modes separately. Finally, we can improve and modify the related privacy policies according to the executing results. If the result of verification is invalid, the MSV platform would return an NFG of a counter example. We should analyze the exist defect of our model and the verified privacy policies, and then find the potential privacy issues in the online SNS and modify it. In the future work we will improve the MSVL language and MSV platform to make the method can be applied to more complex SNS. Besides, we will improve the method to make it verify not only the current common privacy policies, but also the privacy policies defined by users.

References

1. Boyd, D., Ellison, N.: Social network sites: definition, history and scholarship. J. Comput. Mediated Commun. **13**, 210–230 (2007)
2. Gross, R., Acquisti, A.: Information revelation and privacy in online social networks. In: ACM Workshop on Privacy in the Electronic Society, pp. 71–80. ACM, New York (2005)
3. Hu, Q., Chen, Z.: Analysis of the protection of personal privacy in social networking environment. Netinfo Secur. **8**, 43–44 (2010)
4. Caviglione, L., Coccoli, M., Merlo, A.: Social Network Engineering for Secure Web Data and Services. IGI Global, Hershey (2013)
5. Zhang, Y., Liu, Y., Zhang, H., Cheng, H., Xiong, F.: The research of information dissemination model on online social network. Acta Physica Sinica **60**, 1–7 (2011)
6. Ding, J., Cruz, I., Li, C.: A formal model for building a social network. In: IEEE International Conference on Service Operations, Logistics, and Informatics, pp. 237–242. IEEE Press, New York (2011)
7. Pardo, R., Schneider, G.: A formal privacy policy framework for social networks. In: Giannakopoulou, D., Salaün, G. (eds.) SEFM 2014. LNCS, vol. 8702, pp. 378–392. Springer, Heidelberg (2014)
8. Catano, N., Kostakos, V., Oakley, I.: Poporo: a formal framework for social networking. In: 3rd International Workshop on Formal Methods for Interactive Systems, ECEASST, pp. 79–82, Berlin (2009)
9. Cataño, N., Hanvey, S., Rueda, C.: Poporo: a formal methods tool for fast-checking of social network privacy policies. In: Furia, C.A., Nanz, S. (eds.) TOOLS 2012. LNCS, vol. 7304, pp. 9–16. Springer, Heidelberg (2012)
10. Catano, N., Rueda, C.: Matelas: a predicate calculus common formal definition for social networking. In: Frappier, M., Glässer, U., Khurshid, S., Laleau, R., Reeves, S. (eds.) ABZ 2010. LNCS, vol. 5977, pp. 259–272. Springer, Heidelberg (2010)
11. Wang, M., Duan, Z., Tian, C.: Simulation and verification of the virtual memory management system with MSVL. In: 18th IEEE International Conference on Computer Supported Cooperative Work in Design, pp. 360–365. IEEE Press, New York (2014)
12. Duan, Z., Maciej, K.: A framed temporal logic programming language. J. Comput. Sci. Technol. **19**, 341–351 (2004)
13. Tian, C., Duan, Z., Zhang, L.: A decision procedure for propositional projection temporal logic with infinite models. Acta Informatica **45**, 43–78 (2008)
14. Tian, C., Duan, Z.: Expressiveness of propositional projection temporal logic with star. Theor. Comput. Sci. **412**, 1729–1744 (2011)
15. Wang, X., Duan, Z., Zhao, L.: Formalizing and implementing types in MSVL. In: Liu, S., Duan, Z. (eds.) SOFL+MSVL 2013. LNCS, vol. 8332, pp. 60–73. Springer, Heidelberg (2014)
16. Duan, Z., Tian, C.: A unified model checking approach with projection temporal logic. In: Liu, S., Maibaum, T., Araki, K. (eds.) ICFEM 2008. LNCS, vol. 5256, pp. 167–186. Springer, Heidelberg (2008)

A Case Study: SOFL + Model Checking for OSEK/VDX Application

Zhuo Cheng[1], Haitao Zhang[2(✉)], Yasuo Tan[1], and Yuto Lim[1]

[1] School of Information Science, JAIST, Nomi, Ishikawa 923-1292, Japan
{chengzhuo,ytan,ylim}@jaist.ac.jp
[2] School of Information Science and Engineering, Lanzhou University,
Tianshui Road, Lanzhou, Gansu, China
htzhang@lzu.edu.cn

Abstract. OSEK/VDX, a standard of automobile OS, was proposed to support the development of high-quality automotive applications. With its widely adopted, more and more automotive applications have been developed based on OSEK/VDX OS. As the continuously increasing complexity in the development of the applications, how to efficiently develop an application is becoming a challenge. A primary problem is the requirement specification may not be accurately and easily understood by the developers carrying out different tasks. The major reason is the usage of informal languages or notations in the specification. To solve this problem, formal specification provides a feasible solution. However, some difficulties (e.g., high requirement of significant abstraction and mathematical skills) has hindered the widely usage of formal methods. To address these difficulties, SOFL, a formal engineering methodology, has been proposed. In this paper, in order to investigate and study how SOFL can be used to help develop an OSEK/VDX application, we conduct a case study of cruise control system. Through the case study, we can see that SOFL specification can effectively help developer to develop an OSEK/VDX application throughout the development process.

1 Introduction

With consumers' insatiable appetite to pursue a better driving experience, more and more automotive applications have been developed. In order to support the development of high-quality automotive applications and resolve the problem of increasing software content in automobiles, OSEK/VDX [1,2], a standard of automobile OS, was proposed in 1994. It has been widely adopted by many automobile manufacturers to design and develop an automobile OS, such as BMW, Opel, and Volkswagen. With its widely adopted, a growing number of automotive applications have been developed based on OSEK/VDX OS. However, as the continuously increasing complexity in the development of applications, how to efficiently develop an application is becoming a challenge.

A primary problem is the requirement specification may not be accurately and easily understood by the developers carrying out different tasks. The major reason causing that problem is the notations and languages used in the specification

© Springer International Publishing Switzerland 2016
S. Liu and Z. Duan (Eds.): SOFL+MSVL 2015, LNCS 9559, pp. 132–146, 2016.
DOI: 10.1007/978-3-319-31220-0_10

lack of precise syntax and semantics. These notations and languages inevitably associate ambiguity and may lead to misunderstanding. To solve this problem, formal specification gives a feasible solution. With precise constrain of semantics and syntax, formal specification can precisely define behaviors of the software and provide a firm basis for next developers to design and verify the program.

However, there exist some difficulties in using formal methods. For example, it requires significant abstraction and mathematical skills; it usually costs more in time and human effort for analysis and design [3]. These difficulties have hindered the widely usage of formal methods. To address these difficulties, SOFL, a formal engineering methodology, has been proposed in [3,4]. It proposes changes to software process, notation, methodology, and support environments for constructing systems, which makes formal methods more practical and acceptable.

In this paper, in order to investigate and study how SOFL can be used to help develop an OSEK/VDX application, we conduct a case study of cruise control system. Through the case study, we can see that SOFL specification can effectively help developer to develop an OSEK/VDX application throughout the development process.

The remainder of this paper is organized as follows. Section 2 gives an overview of our developing process. The formal requirement specification of the cruise control system is shown in Sect. 3. In Sect. 4, the design and implementation of the system is given. Simulation and verification of the developed application is illustrated in Sect. 5. Section 6 concludes the paper and gives future work.

2   Overview

Our developing process is divided into three stages. The first stage is for requirement specification. Through a survey of various cruise control systems equipped in different kinds of automobiles, the primary functions of a cruise control system is given. According to the given functions, a formal requirement specification based on SOFL notations is documented.

According to the specification, the next stage is to design and implement the cruise control system. As the cruise control system is developed as an application running on an OSEK/VDX OS, the design and implementation needs to adhere the OSEK/VDX standard, which means the system should be implemented as a multi-threaded software. From the SOFL specification, we find the design and implementation is fairly intuitive. It means SOFL is suitable to construct a requirement specification for an OSEK/VDX application.

After implementation, the last state is verification. In order to completely check OSEK/VDX applications, model checking [8,9] as an exhaustive technique can be applied to verify OSEK/VDX applications. There exist many model checking methods that have been applied to verify general multi-threaded software [10] and sequential software [11]. However, these existing model checking methods cannot be directly employed to precisely verify OSEK/VDX applications, since the execution characteristics of OSEK/VDX applications are different from sequential software and general multi-threaded software. In order to

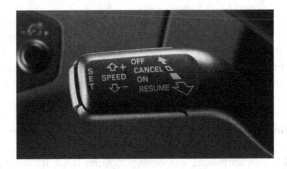

Fig. 1. Function buttons on the control lever of a cruise control system. (The figure is from the home page of Audi.)

apply existing model checking methods to verify the developed applications, we translate the cruise control system into a sequential software.

Moreover, based on SOFL specification, we can easily extract checking properties which are translated as assertions and inserted into the translated sequential software. After this, existing model checkers can be employed to verify the cruise control system.

3   Formal Requirement Specification

3.1   Cruise Control System

Cruise control system is a servomechanism that can maintain a constant vehicle speed as set by the driver. It accomplishes this function by measuring the vehicle speed, comparing it to the set speed, and automatically adjusting the throttle according to a control algorithm. It is usually used for long drives across highways. By using the cruise control system, drivers do not need to control the throttle pedal to maintain the speed of vehicles, which can alleviate the fatigue of drivers. Meanwhile, it can reduce the unnecessary change of speed, which usually results in better fuel efficiency. With these advantages, cruise control system has now been widely equipped in various brands of automobiles, such as BMW, Audi, and Volkswagen.

Cruise control systems developed by different automobile manufacturers usually have different auxiliary functions. Figure 1 shows the control lever of a cruise control system equipped in an Audi automobile. A driver can activate different functions by pressing the function buttons on the control lever. Button ON and OFF are to turn on and turn off the system, respectively. After system turns on, when the button SET is pressed, if the speed of the vehicle is within a specific speed interval which is supported by the cruise control system, the system will start to maintain current vehicle speed until the driver presses button OFF, or CANCEL, or steps on brake. SPEED+ and SPEED- is used to adjust the set speed when system keeps on maintain current vehicle speed. When SPEED+ is pressed, the set speed will be increased, and the system will increase current speed to the set speed and maintain the speed of vehicle at that level. The button CANCEL can temporarily turn off the system, meanwhile, the button RESUME can resume the system to the moment at which the system is temporarily turned off.

3.2 Requirement Specification

As our objective is to investigate whether SOFL can be used in developing an OSEK/VDX application, rather than develop a fully functional system, for simplicity, we only consider parts of the functions. Moreover, to the consideration of safety, a new CONFIRM button is provided.

After system turns on, the primarily functions required by a cruise control system are as follows (as function button SET in Fig. 1 is not considered in our design, in the following parts of the paper, system turns on means the system stars to maintain current vehicle speed).

1. Let the driver increase and decrease the value of the set speed. The set speed is required within a speed interval supported by the cruise control system. To the consideration of safety, a confirm operation is needed to confirm the setting.
2. Keep on maintaining the vehicle speed at the set value.

Although above specification is very simple, it still may cause misunderstanding. For example, the sentence "a confirm operation is needed to confirm the setting" does not clearly describe what will happen if the confirm operation is not performed. A designer may think that if an operation of increasing or decreasing is not followed by a confirm operation, the operation will be ignored. While another designer may think that the confirm operation is needed only when the driver has finished the setting (maybe after pressing button SPEED+ and SPEED- many times). In order to avoid any potential misunderstanding, as described above, formal notation can help greatly.

3.3 SOFL Specification

A SOFL specification is a hierarchical condition data flow diagram (CDFD) that is linked with a hierarchy of specification modules (s-modules) [4]. The CDFD comprises a set of condition processes and describes data flows between them, while the linked s-modules precisely defines the functionality of the components (condition process, data flow, data store) in the CDFD. Each condition process in the CDFD is linked with a c-process which is defined in the s-modules and describes functions in terms of pre and post conditions, within the specific specification context of the module [6]. More details about SOFL specification can refer [3,4].

The CDFD of the cruise control system is shown in Fig. 2, and the linked s-model is shown in Fig. 3. In Fig. 2, each box surrounded by narrow borders denotes a process, such as SET_adjust() and CRU_control(), which describes

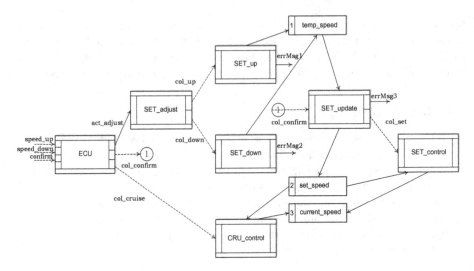

Fig. 2. Condition data flow diagram (CDFD) for the cruise control system.

an operation. It tasks inputs and produces outputs. Each directed line with a labeled variable name denotes a data flow. A solid line denotes an active data flow, while a dotted line denotes a control data flow. The box with a number and an identifier (e.g., temp_speed) is a data store which can be accessed by processes. A directed line from a data store to a process represents the process can read the data from the store, while a directed line from a process to a data store means the process can read, write, and update the data in the store. More details about the components used in the CDFD can refer [4,7].

The cruise control system comprises two primarily functions: set the desired vehicle speed (through increasing or decreasing the set speed) and maintain the vehicle speed at the set value. These two functions are triggered by ECU() (electronic control unit) process. Processes with names star with SET are for the first functions, and processes CRU_control() is for the second function. When the system is running, process ECU() keeps on monitoring the inputs of drivers. Different inputs will trigger different processes to achieve different functions. The selection of speed_up, speed_down, or confirm denotes the corresponding function button on the system control lever shown in Fig. 1 is pressed by the driver.

When button speed_up or speed_down is pressed, process ECU() will generate a data flow act_adjust to indicate which command has actually been selected, and passes this information to process SET_adjust(). Based on the value of act_adjust, process SET_adjust() will trigger either processes SET_up() (speed_up is selected) or SET_down() (speed_down is selected). Process SET_up() or SET_down() first reads the value of temp_speed from the data store, and try to update temp_speed by increasing or decreasing it with a constant value, respectively. As the cruise control system can only run within a designed speed interval, before updating the data, process SET_up() and SET_down() will first check if the updated value of temp_speed is within the interval. If not, an error message will be issued. Data temp_speed is a temporary data can be manipulated by process SET_up() and SET_down() and only after process SET_update() performs, the value of temp_speed can be assigned to set_speed. After process SET_up() or SET_down() completes the updates of temp_speed, it will sends the completion information to process SET_update(). Process SET_update() will assign data temp_speed to set_speed only after the confirm button is pressed. After process SET_update() assigns the value of temp_speed to set_speed, it will trigger process SET_control() to control current vehicle speed current_speed to the new set speed set_speed.

When no function button is pressed by the driver, it means the driver does not want to adjust the set speed and wants to maintain current vehicle speed, process CRU_control() will be triggered by process ECU(). Process CRU_control() maintains current vehicle speed current_speed to the value of set_speed based on a control algorithm.

s-module. Compared with the specification written in natural language given in Sect. 3.2, the functional abstraction expressed by the CDFD is obviously more comprehensible, especially, the dependency relations among processes can be clearly expressed. However, in order to completely define the CDFD, all the components (conditional process, data flows, data stores) in the CDFD must be precisely defined. To achieve this, the CDFD is linked with a s-model shown as in Fig. 3.

In the s-module, part **const** shows the constant variables used in the module. All the data flow variables, and data stores in the CDFD are defined in the **var** part. Each of them is defined in a specific data type. Keyword **inv** stands for invariant and indicates the properties that must be sustained throughout the entire specification. For example, min_sp <= set_speed <= max_sp in part **inv** means the setting value of the cruise control system must be larger than the maximum value that supported by the system and less than the minimum value. Function Controller() achieves the function of speed control based on a control algorithm. At this level of specification, the control algorithm has not been designed.

Process Init() is the initial process which performs only one time when the system stars up. We can see that, **pre** condition defines in the process Init() requires that current_speed should be less than max_sp and larger than min_sp. This ensures that the system can star up only when vehicle is running within the speed interval that supported by the cruise control system.

Each processes in the CDFD is linked with a **c-process**. It describes functions of the processes in terms of pre and post conditions in which predicate logic is adopted. For example, the post condition in c-process SET_adjust() means: if the value of data flow variable act_adjust is true, process SET_adjust() will trigger SET_up() by generating control signal col_up, otherwise act_adjust with a false value will make process SET_down() be triggered.

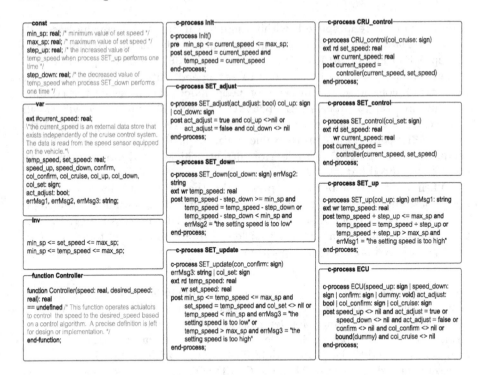

Fig. 3. s-module for the cruise control system.

4 Design and Implementation

4.1 Running Mechanism

Before starting to design and implement the cruise control system as an OSEK/VDX application, we should first obtain a preliminary understanding of the running mechanism of OSEK/VDX OS and its applications.

An OSEK/VDX application is developed as a multi-threaded software running on an OSEK/VDX OS. Tasks (i.e., threads) within the application are concurrently executed and can invoke service APIs to interact with OSEK/VDX OS modules. According to the service APIs invoked by a running task, the corresponding OS modules can dynamically change states of tasks.

Module: A general OSEK/VDX OS is composed of scheduler module, event process module, resource process module, interruption process module, and alarm process module. For simplicity, the cruise control system only interacts with the scheduler module of OSEK/VDX OS. Scheduler module in OSEK/VDX OS adopts static priority scheduling policy. A ready queue, shown in Fig. 4, is maintained to store identifiers of ready tasks. The ready queue is a composition of queues with different priorities. Tasks in the ready queue with the highest priority will be first scheduled to execute. For tasks with the same priorities, the scheduler module will schedule those tasks based on first in first out (FIFO).

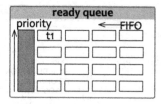

Fig. 4. Ready queue in an OSEK/VDX OS.

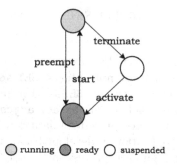

○ running ● ready ○ suspended

Fig. 5. States switch of the basic tasks.

Task states switching: There are two kinds of tasks, *basic task* and *extended tasks*, that can be proceeded in OSEK/VDX OS. The states of a basic task consist of **running** state, **suspended** state, and **ready** state. Compared with the basic tasks, an extended task has an unique state called **waiting** state which are used to interact with event process module. As the cruise control system does not interact with the event process module, tasks in the cruise control system are all defined as basic tasks. Figure 5 shows the states switch of basic tasks.

Service APIs: Scheduler module can respond to three kinds of API invocation.

- *TerminateTask():* a running task is moved to **suspended** state.
- *ActivateTask(tid):* task *tid* is moved from **suspended** state to **ready** state.
- *ChainTask(tid):* equivalent to the execution sequence *ActivateTask(tid) + TerminateTask().*

When one of these three service APIs is invoked by a running task, scheduler module will conduct corresponding operations to respond to the API invocation. This will change the states of the tasks according to the states switch rules shown in Fig. 5, and may lead to the context switch of tasks.

4.2 Design and Implementation as an OSEK/VDX Application

From the CDFD of the requirement specification, shown in Fig. 2, each conditional process in the CDFD achieves a specific function which is precisely defined in the corresponding c-process in the linked s-module shown in Fig. 3. Relations

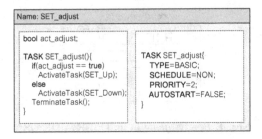

Fig. 6. Task $SET\_adjust()$.

between these processes are reflected via data flows (active data flow and control data flow) and data stores. For example, process SET_adjust() achieves a *selection* function, that is to activate process SET_up() or process SET_down() based on the value of input active data flow variable act_adjust. The relations between these three processes are reflected by control data flow col_up and col_down.

As an OSEK/VDX application is developed as a multi-threaded software, the intuitive idea is to design each process in the CDFD as a task within the application. Each active data flow variables can be implemented as a variable that can be accessed by the related tasks, and each control data flow variable can be treated as an invocation of service API *ActivateTask(tid)*, where *tid* is the identifier of the corresponding activated task. Based on this idea, the example of task $SET\_adjust()$ (i.e., the implementation of process SET_adjust()) is shown in Fig. 6. It consists of two files: *source code* file and *configuration* file. The source code file, shown in the left side, is used to present the concrete behaviors of the application. The configuration file, shown in the right side, is used to indicate the configuration data of tasks (e.g., priority).

Let's first focus on the source file of task $SET\_adjust()$. As shown in Fig. 6, the source file is written in C ++ programming language. The active data flow variable act_adjust is defined as a bool variable that can be accessed by task $SET\_adjust()$. The control data flow variables col_up and col_down are treated as invocation of service APIs *ActivateTask(SET_up)* and *ActivateTask(SET_down)* respectively, where task $SET\_up()$ and $SET\_down()$ are the implementation of process SET_up() and SET_down() respectively. According to the post condition of process SET_adjust() in the s-module, when the value of act_adjust is true, process SET_up() will be triggered. Reflected in the task $SET\_adjust()$, when the variable act_adjust is true, the service API *ActivateTask(SET_up)* will be invoked, which is to activate task $SET\_up()$. The *TerminateTask()* in the last line is to move task $SET\_adjust()$ itself to the suspended state. This service API is invoked when a task has completed its operation.

For the configuration file of a task, there are four items:

- TYPE: type of tasks (**BASIC** or **EXTENDED**).
- AUTOSTART: to indicate the initial states of tasks when system turns on (**TRUE**: ready or **FALSE**: suspended).

- SCHEDULE: to indicate if the task can be preempted by another ready task with higher priority (**FULL**: can or **NON**: cannot).
- PRIORITY: task priority (e.g., 1, 2 ...).

For the type of tasks, as mention in the last subsection, all the tasks in the cruise control system are defined as basic tasks.

As the setting of AUTOSTART, it depends on if a task needs to be activated by another task. Only the task that do not need to be activated by another task is set to has AUTOSTART as TRUE. Thus, according to the CDFD of the specification, only task $ECU()$ has AUTOSTART as TRUE.

For the setting of property SCHEDULE, it depends on tasks' specific running characteristics. For task $ECU()$, when system is running, it keeps on monitoring the input of the driver and activates another task. For example, when no function button is pressed, task $ECU()$ will activate task $CRU\_control()$. It expects $CRU\_control()$ can run immediately to achieve its function. When task $CRU\_control()$ completes its operation, task $ECU()$ continues to activate another task according to the input of the driver. If the setting of SCHEDULE is NON, the activated task $CRU\_control()$ can only run after task $ECU()$ is terminated. As task $ECU()$ keeps on running after system turns on, it means task $CRU\_control()$ will never run, which is an obviously wrong setting. Thus, the setting of SCHEDULE for task $ECU()$ should be FULL.

For other tasks, e.g., $SET\_adjust()$, it activates task $SET\_up()$ or $SET\_down()$, and then, it will be terminated by invoking service API $TerminateTask()$. To implement this running characteristic, both setting of property SCHEDULE can achieve. As a FULL setting of SCHEDULE may lead to more frequent context switch, we set SCHEDULE of all the tasks except task $ECU()$ as NON.

For the setting of PRIORITY, from the running characteristic of task $ECU()$ described above, we can see when a task is activated, it should preempt task $ECU()$. Thus, the priority of task $ECU()$ should be the lowest among all the tasks. For other tasks, as the setting of SCHEDULE is NON, any settings of PRIORITY that higher than the setting of $ECU()$ are reasonable.

Applying these ideas, based on the SOFL specification, we can implement the cruise control system as an OSEK/VDX application. The complete implementation is shown in Fig. 7.

5   Simulation and Verification

To completely check OSEK/VDX applications, we employ model checking to verify the developed application. As mentioned in Sect. 2, the existing model checking methods cannot be directly employed to precisely verify the OSEK/VDX applications, since the execution characteristics of OSEK/VDX applications are different from sequential software and general multi-threaded software.

As described in Sect. 4, an OSEK/VDX application is developed as a multi-threaded software. When it runs on OSEK/VDX OS, the executions of tasks within the application are dispatched by scheduler module, and the running task

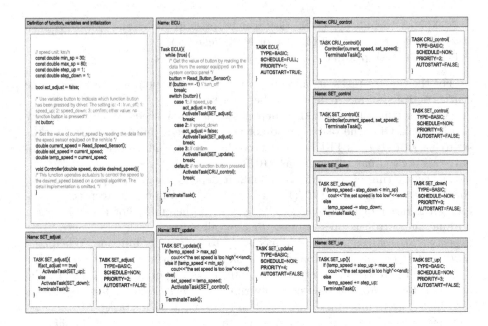

Fig. 7. Implementation of cruise control system as an OSEK/VDX application.

is explicitly determined by the scheduler according to task priorities and configuration data. Moreover, tasks can invoke service APIs supported by OSEK/VDX OS to dynamically change the states of tasks defined in the application, and the changed states will affect the scheduling of tasks.

On the one hand, if we directly apply the existing model checking methods for general multi-threaded software to verify OSEK/VDX applications, it is too imprecise because a lot of unnecessary interleavings of tasks will be checked by existing methods, and these unnecessary interleavings may result in spurious bugs in the verification. This is because, in the existing works for the general multi-threaded software (e.g., systemC programs), since the running thread cannot be explicitly determined, all of the possible interleavings of runnable threads are taken into account in the verification in order to completely check the target software. However, in OSEK/VDX applications, the running task is explicitly determined by OSEK/VDX scheduler. The difference of scheduling policy between the general multi-threaded software and OSEK/VDX applications makes it is unsuitable to employ existing model checking methods for the general multi-threaded software to check OSEK/VDX applications.

On the other hand, if we want to employ the model checking methods for sequential software to verify OSEK/VDX applications, the developed target application has to be translated into a sequential software in advance. To achieve this, a sequentialization approach proposed in [5] can be applied.

5.1   Sequentialization

The key idea of the sequentialization approach is to use a directed graph to represent the sequential program of an OSEK/VDX application. To construct the directed graph, a directed graph constructor as a simulator has been developed. A simplified OSEK/VDX OS model is included in the constructor to respond to the invoked service APIs. A tool named `autoC` has also been developed based on this approach. More details about the approach can be found in [5].

Through the sequentialization approach, based on the implementation shown in Fig. 7, the directed graph for the cruise control system is shown in Fig. 8. The definition of the directed graph is as follows.

DEFINITION: The directed graph is a tuple $\mathcal{G} = (V, v_0, v_e, E, L)$. V is the set of nodes, and a node $v \in V$ is a tuple $v = (pcs, osd)$, $pcs = [n^1, \ldots, n^m]$ is a array used to record current locations of the tasks $t_1, \ldots, t_m$ (m is the number of the tasks), osd is a set of values used to store the data within D of the OS model, where $D = \{runTask, readyQueue, suspendList\}$ is a set of data structures used to store the states of the tasks. In the data structure set D, $runTask$ which is a variable is used to store the tid of the running task (tid is task identifier). The $readyQueue$ is composed of queues with different priorities and used to store the $tids$ of tasks in the ready state. The data structures $suspendList$ are used to store the $tids$ of the tasks in the suspended state. $v_0 \in V$ is the start node, $v_e \in V$ is the end node. $E \subseteq V \times V$ is the set of directed edges. $L : E \to \bigcup \Sigma^{tid}$ is the labeling function from an edge $(v, v') \in E$ to a task statement $\alpha \in \bigcup \Sigma^{tid}$, where tid is task identifier, Σ^{tid} is the set of the statements of tasks tid, the expression of a statement $\alpha \in \Sigma$ is as follow:

$\alpha ::= condition \mid assignment \mid goto \mid assertion \mid \texttt{API}$

Note that, the invocation of service APIs are replaced as $goto$ statements in Fig. 8.

5.2   Verification

Before verifying the program, we should first extract checking properties from the requirement specification. We can easily extract checking properties from two parts of the SOFL specification. The first part is the post condition of a c-process in the s-module. A post condition in a c-process can be interpreted as assertions and inserted into the directed graph at the locations after the execution of the corresponding task.

For example, from the post condition of process `SET_adjust()`, we can know that task $SET\_adjust()$ will activate task $SET\_up()$ if the value of `act_adjust` is true, otherwise, it will activate task $SET\_down()$. Because each step of constructing the directed graph, the data within D which stores the states of tasks has been kept in the directed graph. This makes that we can know which task is running (in **running** state) and also can check whether a task is activated (in **ready** state) or not (in **suspended** state) at any node of the directed graph. Through searching the directed graph, we can know that task $SET\_adjust()$ runs

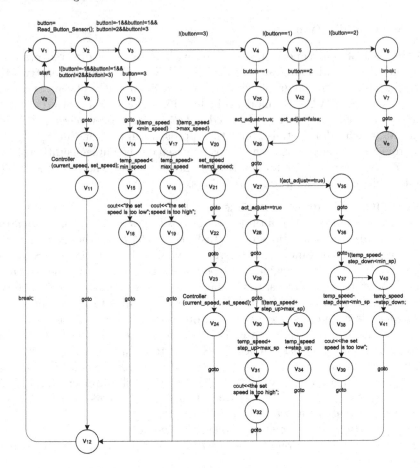

Fig. 8. Directed graph for cruise control system.

following nodes $\langle v_{27}, v_{28}, v_{29}, v_{30} \rangle$ (when act_adjust is true) or $\langle v_{27}, v_{35}, v_{36}, v_{37} \rangle$ (when act_adjust is false). Thus, we can insert $assert$(SET_up@$readyQueue$) after node v_{30} and $assert$(SET_down@$readyQueue$) after node v_{37}, where $tid@readyQueue$ means task tid is in the ready queue.

The second part is the part inv in the s-module. The part inv indicates properties that must be sustained throughout the entire specification. Thus assertions extracted from this part can be inserted into any locations from node v_0 to node v_e of the directed graph. Specific to the part inv of the s-module shown in Fig. 3, from relationship formula min_sp <= set_speed <= max_sp we can get two assertions: $assert$(set_speed <= max_sp) and $assert$(set_speed >= min_sp). Similarly, two assertions $assert$(temp_speed <= max_sp) and $assert$(temp_speed >= min_sp) can be extracted from relationship formula min_sp <= temp_speed <= max_sp. These assertions can be inserted into any locations from node v_0 to v_e. Note that, assign a value in interval [min_sp, max_sp] to current_speed is needed to check these assertions.

After inserting the assertions, the cruise control system has been translated into a sequential program. As the output target language of autoC is C programming language, in this study, we employ model checker CBMC to verify the program. The checking results indicate the developed application satisfies the checking properties discussed above.

6   Concluding Remarks

Through developing the cruise control system, we can see that SOFL specification can effectively help developer to develop an OSEK/VDX application throughout the development process. SOFL requirement specification can precisely define the behaviors of the software. From the specification, the design and implementation of the cruise control system is straightforward. A developer can easily develop and implement an OSEK/VDX application based on SOFL specification. Moreover, checking properties can be easily extracted from SOFL specification, which helps a lot for employing model checking technique to verify the developed applications.

For the future work, an important direction is to develop a tool to automatically generate assertions from SOFL specification and insert them into the translated directed graph.

References

1. OSEK/VDX Group. OSEK/VDX Operating System Specification 2.2.3. http://portal.osek-vdx.org/
2. Lemieux, J.: Programming in the OSEK/VDX Environment. CRC Press, Lawrence (2001)
3. Liu, S.: Formal engineering for industrial software development – an introduction to the sofl specification language and method. In: Davies, J., Schulte, W., Barnett, M. (eds.) ICFEM 2004. LNCS, vol. 3308, pp. 7–8. Springer, Heidelberg (2004)
4. Liu, S., Offutt, A.J., -Stuart, H., Sun, Y., Ohba, M.: SOFL: a formal engineering methodology for industrial applications. IEEE Trans. Softw. Eng. 24(1), 24–45 (1998)
5. Zhang, H., Aoki, T., Chiba, Y.: Yes! you can use your model checker to verify OSEK/VDX applications. In: Proceedings of the 8th IEEE International Conference on Software Testing, Verification and Validation, pp. 1–10, April 2015
6. Wang, X., Liu, S.: An approach to declaring data types for formal specifications. In: Liu, S., Duan, Z. (eds.) SOFL+MSVL 2013. LNCS, vol. 8332, pp. 128–147. Springer, Heidelberg (2014)
7. H.-Stuart, C., Liu, S.: An operational semantics for SOFL. In: Proceedings of the Asia-Pacific Software Engineering Conference, pp. 52–61, December 1997
8. Clarke, E.M., Grumberg, O., Long, D.E.: Model checking and abstraction. ACM Trans. Program. Lang. Syst. 16(5), 1512–1542 (1994)
9. Clarke, E.M., Emerson, E.A., Sifakis, J.: Model checking: algorithmic verification and debugging. Commun. ACM 152(11), 74–84 (2009)

10. Qadeer, S., Rehof, J.: Context-bounded model checking of concurrent software. In: Halbwachs, N., Zuck, L.D. (eds.) TACAS 2005. LNCS, vol. 3440, pp. 93–107. Springer, Heidelberg (2005)
11. Yang, Z., Wang, C., Gupta, A.: Model checking sequential software programs via mixed symbolic analysis. CM Trans. Des. Autom. Electron. Syst. 14(1), 1–26 (2009)

On Reachability Analysis of Updatable Timed Automata with One Updatable Clock

Yunqing Wen[1], Guoqiang Li[1(✉)], and Shoji Yuen[2]

[1] School of Software, Shanghai Jiao Tong University, Shanghai, China
{wyqwyq,li.g}@sjtu.edu.cn
[2] Graduate School of Information Science, Nagoya University, Nagoya, Japan
yuen@is.nagoya-u.ac.jp

Abstract. As an extension of *Timed Automata (TAs)*, *Updatable Timed Automata (UTAs)* proposed by Bouyer et al. have the ability to update clocks in a more elaborate way than simply reset them to zero. The reachability of general UTAs is undecidable, by regarding a pair of updatable clocks as counters updatable with incrementation and decrementation operations. This paper investigates the model of subclass of UTAs by restricting the number of updateable clocks. It is shown that the reachability of *UTAs with one updatable clock (UTA1s)* under diagonal-free constraints is decidable. The decidability is proved by treating a region of a UTA1 as an unbounded digiword, and encoding sets of digiwords that are accepted by a pushdown system where regions are generated on-the-fly on the stack.

1 Introduction

Timed Automata(TAs), introduced by Alur and Dill [1], are one of the most-studied and most-established models for real-time systems. Lots of work has been devoted to extensions of timed automata, with much interest for classes whose emptiness problem remains decidable.

Updatable Timed Automata(UTAs) [2,3] are extensions of timed automata, based on the possibility to update the clocks in an elaborate way such as increment and decrement operations and assignments to arbitrary values. Their decidability have been investigated in [4], and also a quite precise way the thin frontier between decidable and undecidable classes of updatable timed automata has been described. The undecidability is technically shown to simulate the Minsky machine in general, while the decidability is shown by the fact that the constructed regions are finitely many. Our motivation is to investigate an interesting subclass of UTAs existing between them.

This paper gives a positive answer for the reachability of *UTAs with one updatable clock (UTA1s)* with diagonal-free time constraints by constructing regions on-the-fly over the stack of *pushdown systems (PDSs)*. Our result expands the thin frontier between decidable and undecidable classes of updatable timed automata. The model can be effectively used into soft real-time system modelling and analysis, where the updatable clock is used to depict relative

© Springer International Publishing Switzerland 2016
S. Liu and Z. Duan (Eds.): SOFL+MSVL 2015, LNCS 9559, pp. 147–161, 2016.
DOI: 10.1007/978-3-319-31220-0_11

deadline, which can be flexibly modified according to different conditions and environments.

The rest of the paper is organized as follows. Section 2 gives an introduction of UTAs and PDSs. Section 3 introduces UTAs with one updatable clock. Section 4 introduces the notion of *digiwords*, which is equivalent to region [1], but provides us a more concise description. Section 5 shows the decidable reachability of UTA1s by encoding them to PDSs, based on the notion of digiwords. The related work is presented in Sects. 6 and 7 concludes the paper.

2   Preliminaries

For finite words $w = \gamma_1 \gamma_2 \ldots \gamma_n$, we denote $\gamma_i \in w$ for $0 \leq i \leq n$.

Let $\mathbb{R}^{\geq 0}$ and $\mathbb{N}$ denote the sets of non-negative real numbers and natural numbers respectively. Let $\mathbb{N}^\omega = \mathbb{N} \cup \{\omega\}$, where ω is the first limit ordinal. Let $\mathcal{I}$ denote the set of *intervals* over $\mathbb{N}^\omega$. An interval can be written as a pair of a lower limit and an upper limit in the form of either $(a, b), [a, b), [a, c], (a, c]$, where $a, c \in \mathbb{N}$, $b \in \mathbb{N}^\omega$, '(' and ')' denote open limits, and '[' and ']' denote closed limits. For a number $r \in \mathbb{R}^{\geq 0}$ and an interval $I \in \mathcal{I}$, we use $r \in I$ to denote that r belongs to I. Let $I \setminus I' = \{r \mid r \in I \wedge r \notin I'\}$.

Let $X = \{x_1, \ldots, x_n\}$ be a finite set of *clocks*. A *clock valuation* $\nu : X \to \mathbb{R}^{\geq 0}$, assigns a value to each clock $x \in X$. ν_0 represents all clocks in X assigned to zero. Given a clock valuation ν and a time $t \in \mathbb{R}^{\geq 0}$, $(\nu + t)(x) = \nu(x) + t$, for $x \in X$. A clock assignment function $\nu[y \leftarrow b]$ is defined by $\nu[y \leftarrow b](x) = b$ if $x = y$, and $\nu(x)$ otherwise. $Val(X)$ is used to denote the set of clock valuations of X.

Definition 1 (Clock Constraint). *Given a finite set of clocks X, we define diagonal-free constraints con_{df} and diagonal constraints con, respectively as follows:*

$$con_{df} ::= x \in I?$$
$$con ::= x \in I? \mid x - y \in I?$$

where $x, y \in X$ and $I \in \mathcal{I}$.

2.1   Updatable Timed Automata

Updatable Timed Automata (UTAs) [2–4], extended from TAs, provide a more flexible way to adjust the value of clock during location switches.

Definition 2 (Updatable Timed Automata). *A UTA is a tuple $\mathcal{A} = \langle Q, q_0, F, X, \Delta \rangle$, where*

- *Q is a finite set of control locations, with the initial location $q_0 \in Q$,*
- *$F \subseteq Q$ is the set of final locations,*
- *X is a finite set of clocks,*
- *$\Delta \subseteq Q \times \mathcal{O} \times Q$, where $\mathcal{O}$ is a set of operations. A transition $(q_1, \phi, q_2) \in \Delta$ is written as $q_1 \xrightarrow{\phi} q_2$, in which ϕ is either*

Local ϵ, *an* empty *operation*,
Test $x \in I?$ *or* $x - y \in I?$, *where* $x, y \in X$ *and* $I \in \mathcal{I}$,
Assignment $x \leftarrow I$, *where* $x \in X$ *and* $I \in \mathcal{I}$,
Increment $x := x + 1$, *where* $x \in X$ *or*
Decrement $x := x - 1$, *where* $x \in X$.

Given a UTA $\mathcal{A}$, we use $Q(\mathcal{A})$, $q_0(\mathcal{A})$, $F(\mathcal{A})$, $X(\mathcal{A})$ and $\Delta(\mathcal{A})$ to represent its set of control locations, initial location, set of final locations, set of clocks and set of transitions, respectively. We will use similar notations for other models.

Definition 3 (Semantics of UTAs). *Given a UTA* $\mathcal{A} = \langle Q, q_0, F, X, \Delta \rangle$, *a configuration is a pair* (q, ν) *of a control location* $q \in Q$, *and a clock valuation* ν *on* X. *The transition relation of the UTA is represented as follows,*

– Progress transition: $(q, \nu) \xrightarrow{t}_{\mathcal{A}} (q, \nu + t)$, *where* $t \in \mathbb{R}^{\geq 0}$.
– Discrete transition: $(q_1, \nu_1) \xrightarrow{\phi}_{\mathcal{A}} (q_2, \nu_2)$, *if* $q_1 \xrightarrow{\phi} q_2 \in \Delta$, *and one of the following holds,*
  - **Local** $\phi = \epsilon$, *then* $\nu_1 = \nu_2$.
  - **Test** $\phi = x \in I?$ *or* $\phi = x - x' \in I?$, $\nu_1 = \nu_2$ *and* $\nu_2(x) \in I$ *holds or respectively* $\nu_2(x) - \nu_2(x') \in I$ *holds.*
  - **Assignment** $\phi = x \leftarrow I$, $\nu_2 = \nu_1[x \leftarrow r]$ *where* $r \in I$.
  - **Increment** $\phi = x := x + 1$, $\nu_2 = \nu_1[x \leftarrow \nu_1(x) + 1]$.
  - **Decrement** $\phi = x := x - 1$, $\nu_2 = \nu_1[x \leftarrow \nu_1(x) - 1]$ *and* $\nu_1(x) \geq 1$ *holds.*

The initial configuration is (q_0, ν_0). *The transition relation is* $\rightarrow$ *and we define* $\rightarrow = \xrightarrow{t}_{\mathcal{A}} \cup \xrightarrow{\phi}_{\mathcal{A}}$, *and define* $\rightarrow^*$ *to be the reflexive and transitive closure of* $\rightarrow$. *Without confusion, we will later leave out the subscript* $\mathcal{A}$.

If only diagonal-free constraints appear in test transitions, the corresponding UTAs are called diagonal-free UTAs. Different from TAs, diagonal or diagonal-free constraints heavily affect decidability results of UTAs. We list a few undecidable subclasses of UTAs.

Proposition 1. *(Proposition 2 in [2]) UTAs without increment rules under diagonal-free constraints are undecidable.*

Proposition 2. *(Proposition 3 in [2]) UTAs without decrement rules under diagonal constraints are undecidable.*

2.2 Pushdown Systems

A *pushdown system* [5] is a transition system equipped with a finite set of control locations and a stack. The stack contains a word over some finite stack alphabet, whose length is unbounded. Hence, a pushdown system may have infinitely many reachable states.

Definition 4 (Pushdown Systems). *A pushdown system(PDS) is a quadruple* $\langle P, \Gamma, \Delta \rangle$ *where*

- *P is a finite set of states,*
- *Γ is finite stack alphabet,*
- *$\Delta \subseteq P \times \Gamma^{\leq 2} \times P \times \Gamma^{\leq 2}$ is a finite set of transitions, where $(p, v, q, w) \in \Delta$ is denoted by $\langle p, v \rangle \hookrightarrow \langle q, w \rangle$, and*

We use $\alpha, \beta, \gamma, \cdots$ to range over Γ, and $w, v, \cdots$ over words in Γ^*.

A configuration of $\mathcal{P}$ is a pair $\langle q, w \rangle$, where $q \in Q$ and $w \in \Gamma^*$. A transition relation $\Longrightarrow$ between configurations of $\mathcal{P}$ is defined by

$$\langle q, \gamma w' \rangle \Rightarrow \langle q', ww' \rangle \text{ if } \langle q, \gamma \rangle \hookrightarrow \langle q', w \rangle$$

The reflective and transitive closure of $\Rightarrow$ is denoted by $\Rightarrow^*$, and we write $c \stackrel{\sigma}{\Rightarrow}^n c'$ if $c \stackrel{r_1}{\Rightarrow} c_1 \stackrel{r_2}{\Rightarrow} \ldots c_n \stackrel{r_n}{\Rightarrow} c'$ for any $n \in \mathbb{N}$ and $c, c', c_i \in Q \times \Gamma^*$ with $1 \leq i \leq n$ and $\sigma = [r_1, r_2, \ldots, r_n]$.

3   Updatable Timed Automata with One Updatable Clock

We propose a subclass of UTAs in a different facet by restricting the number of updatable clocks to be one, rather than restricting the ability of updates.

Definition 5 (Updatable Timed Automata with One Updatable Clock). *A UTA with one updatable clock (UTA1) is a tuple $\mathcal{A} = \langle Q, q_0, F, X, c, \Delta \rangle$, where*

- *Q is a finite set of control locations, with the initial location $q_0 \in Q$,*
- *$F \subseteq Q$ is the set of final locations,*
- *$X = \{x_1, \ldots, x_k\}$ is a finite set of clocks, and c is the singleton updatable clock,*
- *$\Delta \subseteq Q \times \mathcal{O} \times Q$, where $\mathcal{O}$ is a set of operations. A transition $(q_1, \phi, q_2) \in \Delta$ is written as $q_1 \stackrel{\phi}{\to} q_2$, in which ϕ is either*
  Local *ϵ, an empty operation,*
  Test *$x \in I?$, where $x \in X \cup \{c\}$ is a clock and $I \in \mathcal{I}$ is an interval,*
  Assignment *$x \leftarrow I$, where $x \in X \cup \{c\}$ and $I \in \mathcal{I}$, or*
  Increment *$c := c + 1$, or*
  Decrement *$c := c - 1$.*

Remark 1. UTA1s defined in Definition 5 are diagonal-free. We do *not* discuss diagonal constraints between clocks, and our following proofs cannot be naturally extended to cover them.

Definition 6 (Semantics of UTA1s). *Given a UTA1 $\mathcal{A} = \langle Q, q_0, F, X, c, \Delta \rangle$, a configuration(state) is a pair (q, ν) of a control location $q \in Q$, and a clock valuation ν on $X \cup \{c\}$. The transition relation of the UTA1 is represented as follows,*

- Progress transition: $(q, \nu) \stackrel{t}{\to} (q, \nu + t)$, where $t \in \mathbb{R}^{\geq 0}$.

– Discrete transition: $(q_1, \nu_1) \xrightarrow{\phi} (q_2, \nu_2)$, if $q_1 \xrightarrow{\phi} q_2 \in \Delta$, and one of the following holds,
   • **Local** $\phi = \epsilon$, then $\nu_1 = \nu_2$.
   • **Test** $\phi = x \in I?$, $\nu_1 = \nu_2$ and $\nu_2(x) \in I$ holds.
   • **Assignment** $\phi = x \leftarrow I$, $\nu_2 = \nu_1[x \leftarrow r]$ where $r \in I$.
   • **Increment** $\phi = c := c + 1$, $\nu_2 = \nu_1[c \leftarrow \nu_1(c) + 1]$.
   • **Decrement** $\phi = c := c - 1$, $\nu_2 = \nu_1[c \leftarrow \nu_1(c) - 1]$ and $\nu_1(c) \geq 1$ holds.

The initial configuration is (q_0, ν_0).

Remark 2. Although only increment $(c := c + 1)$ and decrement $(c := c - 1)$ are considered in the Definition 5, arbitrary decrement operation can also be easily encoded by some adjustment to the UTA1s we defined. For example, $p \xrightarrow{c := c - d} q$, where d is some fixed positive integer, can be encoded in the following way, by introducing an extra clock x' and more locations $p_1, p_2, \ldots, p_d, p_{d+1}$: $p \xrightarrow{x' \leftarrow [0,0]}$ $p_1 \xrightarrow{c := c - 1} p_2 \xrightarrow{c := c - 1} p_3 \cdots p_d \xrightarrow{c := c - 1} p_{d+1} \xrightarrow{x' \in [0,0]?} q$.

Example 1. The UTA1 illustrated in Fig. 1 has three clocks, c, x_1 and x_2, among which c is the singleton updatable clock allowed to update in a different way.

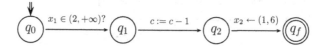

Fig. 1. An Example for UTA1s

One run of the UTA1 is as follows: $(q_0, \nu_0) \xrightarrow{2.5} (q_0, \nu_1) \xrightarrow{x_1 \in (2, +\infty)?}$ $(q_1, \nu_2) \xrightarrow{c := c - 1} (q_2, \nu_3) \xrightarrow{x_2 \leftarrow (1,6)} (q_f, \nu_4) \xrightarrow{5} (q_f, \nu_5)$, where

– $\nu_0 = \{\nu_0(c) = \nu_0(x_1) = \nu_0(x_2) = 0\}$,
– $\nu_1 = \nu_2 = \{\nu_1(c) = \nu_1(x_1) = \nu_1(x_2) = 2.5\}$,
– $\nu_3 = \{\nu_3(c) = 1.5, \nu_3(x_1) = \nu_3(x_2) = 2.5\}$,
– $\nu_4 = \{\nu_4(c) = 1.5, \nu_4(x_1) = 2.5, \nu_4(x_2) = 5.7\}$, and
– $\nu_5 = \{\nu_5(c) = 6.5, \nu_5(x_1) = 7.5, \nu_5(x_2) = 10.7\}$.

The first transition is a progress transition which elapses 2.5 time units, and each clock grows older for 2.5. The second transition tests whether the value of clock x_1 is greater than 2, and since it is so, a move from location q_0 to location q_1 happens. The sequent transition updates the particular clock c by decreasing one time unit and make a move from location q_1 to location q_2. The last but one transition randomly picks a value(in this run, 5.7 is picked) from the range $(1, 6)$ and assigns it to the clock x_2. The last transition is a progress transition which elapses 5 time units.

Definition 7 (Reachability Problem). *Given a UTA1 $A = \langle Q, q_0, F, X, c, \Delta \rangle$ and a state q, decide whether there exists a path from the initial configuration such as $(q_0, \nu_0) \rightarrow^* (q, \nu)$, for some ν.*

4   Digiword and Its Operations

We denote the powerset of D by $\mathcal{P}(D)$. Let $\mathcal{A} = (Q, q_0, F, X, c, \Delta)$ be a UTA1, and let n be the largest integer appearing in Δ. For $v \in \mathbb{R}^{\geq 0}$, $proj(v) = \mathbf{r}_i$ if $v \in \mathbf{r}_i \in Intv(n)$, where

$$Intv(n) = \{\mathbf{r}_{2i} = [i,i] \mid 0 \leq i \leq n\} \cup \{\mathbf{r}_{2i+1} = (i, i+1) \mid 0 \leq i < n\} \cup \{\mathbf{r}_{2n+1} = (n, \omega)\}$$

The idea of the following digitization is inspired by [6–10].

Definition 8. *Let $frac(x, t) = t - floor(t)$ for $(x, t) \in ((X \cup \{c\}) \times \mathbb{R}^{\geq 0})$, where t is clock x's value. A digitization $digi : Val(X \cup \{c\}) \to (\mathcal{P}((X \cup \{c\}) \times Intv(n)))^*$ is as follows. For $v \in Val(X \cup \{c\})$, let $Y_0, Y_1, \cdots, Y_m$ be sets that collect $(x, proj(t))$'s having the same $frac(x, t)$ for $(x, t) \in (X \cup \{c\}) \times \mathbb{R}^{\geq 0}$. Among them, Y_0 (which is possibly empty) is reserved for the collection of $(x, proj(t))$ with $frac(t) = 0$. We assume Y_i's except for Y_0 is non-empty, and Y_i's are sorted by the increasing order of $frac(x, t)$ (i.e., $frac(x, t) < frac(x', t')$ for $(x, proj(t)) \in Y_i$ and $(x', proj(t')) \in Y_j$, where $0 \leq i < j \leq m$).*

Example 2. In example 1, $n = 6$ and we have 13 intervals illustrated below.

```
0  r₁  1  r₃   2  r₅   3  r₇   4  r₉   5  r₁₁  6   r₁₃

  r₀      r₂      r₄      r₆      r₈     r₁₀     r₁₂
```

For the clock valuation ν_4 in Example 1, $digi(\nu_4)$ is $\{(c, \mathbf{r}_3), (x_1, \mathbf{r}_5)\}\{(x_2, \mathbf{r}_{11})\}$. Note that, for convenience we do not show the empty set Y_0 in $digi(\nu_4)$.

A word in $(\mathcal{P}((X \cup \{c\}) \times Intv(n)))^*$ is called *digiword*. If for a digiword $\bar{Y}$ there exists an clock valuation $\nu \in Val(X \cup \{c\})$ such that $digi(\nu) = \bar{Y}$, we call the word *well-formed digiword*.

Remark 3. For a finite set of clocks $X \cup \{c\}$, the set of *well-formed digiword* is finite. This is obvious, since there are a fixed number of clocks, which leads to a fixed number of combinations of digiword. This play an essential role in our encoding, ensuring the PDS has finite states.

Definition 9. *Let $\bar{Y} = Y_0 \cdots Y_m \in (\mathcal{P}((X \cup \{c\}) \times Intv(n)))^*$. We define digiword operations as follows.*

– **Insert$_I$** $insert(\bar{Y}, (x, \mathbf{r}_i))$ *for $x \in X \cup \{c\}$ inserts $(x, \mathbf{r}_i)$ to $\bar{Y}$ at*

$$\begin{cases} \text{either put into } Y_j \text{ for } j > 0, \text{ or} & \\ \qquad \text{put the singleton set } \{(x, \mathbf{r}_i)\} \text{ at any place after } Y_0 & \text{if } i \text{ is odd} \\ \text{put into } Y_0 & \text{if } i \text{ is even} \end{cases}$$

– **Delete** $delete(\bar{Y}, x)$ *for $x \in X \cup \{c\}$ is obtained from $\bar{Y}$ by deleting the element $(x, \mathbf{r})$ indexed by x.*
– **Increase** $increase(\bar{Y}, c)$ *is obtained from $\bar{Y}$ by replacing the element $(c, \mathbf{r}_i)$ indexed by c with element $(c, \mathbf{r}_{\min\{i+2, 2n+1\}})$.*

- **Decrease** $decrease(\bar{Y}, c, d)$ *and* $d \in \mathbb{N}$ *is obtained from* $\bar{Y}$ *by replacing the element* $(c, \mathbf{r}_i)$ *indexed by* c *with element* $(c, \mathbf{r}_{max\{i-d,0\}})$.
- **Shift.** *Let* $j \in [0..m]$ *and* $0 \leq i \leq 2n + 1$. *A shift* $\bar{Y} = Y_0 Y_1 \cdots Y_m \Rightarrow \bar{Y}' = Y_0' Y_1' \cdots Y_{m'}'$ *is defined as follows.*

$$
\begin{cases}
either \ \bar{Y}' = Y_0', Y_1', \cdots, Y_{m+1}' \ if \ Y_0 \neq \emptyset, Y_0' = \emptyset, Y_1' = \{(x, \mathbf{r}_{min\{i+1,2n+1\}}) \\
\qquad\qquad\qquad | \ (x, \mathbf{r}_i) \in Y_0\} \ and \ Y_j' = Y_{j-1} \ for \ j \in [2..m + 1]. \\
or \ \bar{Y}' = Y_0', Y_1', \cdots, Y_{m-1}' \ otherwise, \ Y_0' = \{(x, \mathbf{r}_{min\{i+1,2n+1\}}) \ | \ (x, \mathbf{r}_i) \in Y_m\}, \\
\qquad\qquad\qquad and \ Y_j' = Y_j \ for \ j \in [1..m - 1].
\end{cases}
$$

As convention, we define $\Rightarrow^*$ as reflexive transitive closure of $\Rightarrow$.

Example 3. Consider the digiword in Example 1, $digi(\nu_0) = \{(c, \mathbf{r}_0), (x_1, \mathbf{r}_0), (x_2, \mathbf{r}_0)\}$.

- after finite times shifts,
  $digi(\nu_1) = digi(\nu_2) = \{(c, \mathbf{r}_5), (x_1, \mathbf{r}_5), (x_2, \mathbf{r}_5)\}$
- after $decrease(digi(\nu_2), c, 2)$
  $digi(\nu_3) = \{(c, \mathbf{r}_3), (x_1, \mathbf{r}_5), (x_2, \mathbf{r}_5)\}$
- after $insert(delete(digi(\nu_3), x_2), (x_2, \mathbf{r}_{11}))$
  $digi(\nu_4) = \{(c, \mathbf{r}_3), (x_1, \mathbf{r}_5)\}\{(x_2, \mathbf{r}_{11})\}$
- after finite times shifts,
  $digi(\nu_5) = \{(c, \mathbf{r}_{13}), (x_1, \mathbf{r}_{13})\}\{(x_2, \mathbf{r}_{13})\}$

Equivalent to the *regions* [1] in nature, *well formed digiwords* are bisimilar to the clock valuations in the following sense:

$$\bar{Y}_1 \Rightarrow^* \bar{Y}_2 \ \text{if and only if} \ \forall \nu \in [\bar{Y}_1], \exists t \in \mathbb{R}^{\geq 0} \ \text{s.t.} \ \nu + t \in [\bar{Y}_2]$$

where, $[\bar{Y}] = \{\nu \mid \bar{Y} = digi(\nu)\}$.

5   Reachability for UTA1s

In this section, we show that the reachability problem of UTA1s is decidable. discretePDSs, which nicely enjoy decidable property of configuration reachability. The key idea is that when the updatable clock's value exceeds the maximum integer n, we push a special symbol into the stack to record the updates.

Definition 10. *For a UTA1* $\mathcal{A} = \langle Q, q_0, F, X, c, \Delta \rangle$, *there is a PDS* $\mathcal{P} = \langle P \times (\mathcal{P}((X \cup \{c\}) \times Intv(n)))^*, \{\bullet, \bot\}, \Delta_d \rangle$, *where the set of states* $P = Q \cup \{p' \mid p \in Q\}$ *and the initial configuration* $\kappa_0 = \langle (q_0, \{(x, \mathbf{r}_0) | x \in X \cup \{c\}\}), \bot \rangle$. Δ_d *consists of:*

- **Time Progress**
  1. $\langle (p, \bar{Y}), \bot \rangle \hookrightarrow \langle (p, \bar{Z}), \bot \rangle$, *where* $\bar{Y} \Rightarrow \bar{Z}$, *for* $(c, \mathbf{r}_i) \in Y_j \in \bar{Y}$ *and* $i \leq 2n - 1$.
  2. $\langle (p, \bar{Y}), \epsilon \rangle \hookrightarrow \langle (p, \bar{Z}), \bullet \rangle$, *where* $\bar{Y} \Rightarrow \bar{Z}$, *for* $(c, \mathbf{r}_i) \in Y_j \in \bar{Y}$ *and* $2n \leq i \leq 2n + 1$.

- **Local** $(p \xrightarrow{\epsilon} q \in \Delta)$
  $\langle(p,\bar{Y}),\epsilon\rangle \hookrightarrow \langle(q,\bar{Y}),\epsilon\rangle.$
- **Test** $(p \xrightarrow{x \in I?} q \in \Delta)$
  $\langle(p,\bar{Y}),\epsilon\rangle \hookrightarrow \langle(q,\bar{Y}),\epsilon\rangle$ *if* $r_i \subseteq I$ *for* $(x,\mathbf{r}_i) \in Y_j \in \bar{Y}.$
- **Assignment** $(p \xrightarrow{c \leftarrow I} q \in \Delta)$
  1. $\langle(p,\bar{Y}),\bullet\rangle \hookrightarrow \langle(p,\bar{Y}),\epsilon\rangle.$
  2. $\langle(p,\bar{Y}),\bot\rangle \hookrightarrow \langle(p',\bar{Y}),\bot\rangle.$
  3. $\forall \mathbf{r}_i \subseteq I \setminus \mathbf{r}_{2n+1}, \langle(p',\bar{Y}),\bot\rangle \hookrightarrow \langle(q, insert(delete(\bar{Y},c),(c,\mathbf{r}_i))),\bot\rangle.$
  4. $\langle(p',\bar{Y}),\epsilon\rangle \hookrightarrow \langle(p',\bar{Y}),\bullet\rangle,$ *if* $\mathbf{r}_{2n+1} \subseteq I.$
  5. $\langle(p',\bar{Y}),\bullet\rangle \hookrightarrow \langle(q, insert(delete(\bar{Y},c),(c,\mathbf{r}_{2n+1}))),\bullet\rangle,$ *if* $\mathbf{r}_{2n+1} \subseteq I.$
- **Assignment** $(p \xrightarrow{x \leftarrow I} q \in \Delta,$ *where* $x \in X)$
  $\forall \mathbf{r}_i \subseteq I, \langle(p,\bar{Y}),\epsilon\rangle \hookrightarrow \langle(q, insert(delete(\bar{Y},x),(x,\mathbf{r}_i))),\epsilon\rangle.$
- **Increment** $(p \xrightarrow{c := c+1} q \in \Delta)$
  1. $\langle(p,\bar{Y}),\epsilon\rangle \hookrightarrow \langle(q, increase(\bar{Y},c)),\epsilon\rangle,$ *for* $(c,\mathbf{r}_i) \in Y_j \in \bar{Y}$ *and* $i \le 2n-2.$
  2. $\langle(p,\bar{Y}),\epsilon\rangle \hookrightarrow \langle(q, increase(\bar{Y},c)),\bullet\rangle,$ *for* $(c,\mathbf{r}_{2n-1}) \in Y_j \in \bar{Y}.$
  3. $\langle(p,\bar{Y}),\epsilon\rangle \hookrightarrow \langle(q, increase(\bar{Y},c)),\bullet\bullet\rangle,$ *for* $(c,\mathbf{r}_i) \in Y_j \in \bar{Y}$ *and* $i \ge 2n.$
- **Decrement** $(p \xrightarrow{c := c-1} q \in \Delta)$
  1. $\langle(p,\bar{Y}),\bullet\bullet\bullet\rangle \hookrightarrow \langle(q,\bar{Y}),\bullet\rangle.$
  2. $\langle(p,\bar{Y}),\bullet\bullet \bot\rangle \hookrightarrow \langle(q, decrease(\bar{Y},c,1)),\bot\rangle.$
  3. $\langle(p,\bar{Y}),\bullet \bot\rangle \hookrightarrow \langle(q, decrease(\bar{Y},c,2)),\bot\rangle.$
  4. $\langle(p,\bar{Y}),\bot\rangle \hookrightarrow \langle(q, decrease(\bar{Y},c,2)),\bot\rangle$ *for* $(c,\mathbf{r}_i) \in Y_j \in \bar{Y}$ *and* $i \ge 2.$

In our encoding, we abuse the symbol ϵ in the left hand of the transition rule of PDS $\mathcal{P}$ to indicate that whatever the topmost symbol in the stack is, the transition can occur. This leads to a concise description for our encoding, which is equivalent to its counterpart with only standard transition rules. For example, $\langle(p,\bar{Y}),\epsilon\rangle \hookrightarrow \langle(q,\bar{Y}),\epsilon\rangle$ can be replaced with two transition rules since there are only 2 symbols in the alphabet: (1) $\langle(p,\bar{Y}),\bot\rangle \hookrightarrow \langle(q,\bar{Y}),\bot\rangle$ and (2) $\langle(p,\bar{Y}),\bullet\rangle \hookrightarrow \langle(q,\bar{Y}),\bullet\rangle.$

Given a UTA1 $\mathcal{A}$, for each kind of its transitions, we have its counterpart in the $\Delta_d(\mathcal{P})$. Some transitions of $\mathcal{P}$, at the first look, may seem hard to understand. The following give a simple explanation for simulating *assignment* and *decrement*.

For an assignment of the form $x \leftarrow I$, PDS $\mathcal{P}$ proceed with two different cases: (1) $x = c$; (2) $x \ne c$. For the first case, $\mathcal{P}$ first need to pop all symbol $\bullet$ out of stack, then push a certain number of symbols $\bullet$ if needed, and finally perform *delete* and *insert* operations. For the latter case, much simpler, just directly perform *delete* and *insert* operations.

For a decrement of the form $c := c - 1$, PDS $\mathcal{P}$ proceed with four different cases: (1) $\nu(c) > n+1$; (2) $\nu(c) = n+1$; (3) $n < \nu(c) < n+1$; (4) $1 \le \nu(c) \le n$. For the first case, $\mathcal{P}$ merely pops out two symbols of $\bullet$. For the second and third cases, $\mathcal{P}$ pops out one or two symbol(s) of $\bullet$ and performs *decrease* operation. The difference between them is how much it decreases. For the last case, $\mathcal{P}$ merely performs *decrease* operation.

The following example shows the discretization of assignment transitions, decrement transitions.

Example 4. Consider the run in the Example 1.

- $(q_1, \nu_2) \xrightarrow{c:=c-1} (q_2, \nu_3)$, where $\nu_2 = \{\nu_2(c) = \nu_2(x_1) = \nu_2(x_2) = 2.5\}$ and $\nu_3 = \{\nu_3(c) = 1.5, \nu_3(x_1) = \nu_3(x_2) = 2.5\}$. Corresponding simulation: $\langle(q_1, digi(\nu_2)), \bot\rangle \hookrightarrow \langle(q_2, decrease(digi(\nu_2), c, 2)), \bot\rangle$.
- $(q_2, \nu_3) \xrightarrow{x_2 \leftarrow (1,6)} (q_f, \nu_4)$, where ν_3 is defined above and $\nu_4 = \{\nu_4(c) = 1.5, \nu_4(x_1) = 2.5, \nu_4(x_2) = 5.7\}$. Corresponding simulation: $\langle(q_2, digi(\nu_3)), \bot\rangle \hookrightarrow \langle(q_f, insert(delete(digi(\nu_3), x_2), (x_2, \mathbf{r}_{11}))), \bot\rangle$.

Definition 11. *Let ϱ be any configuration of a UTA1 such that $\varrho_0 = (q_0, \nu_0) \hookrightarrow^*$ $\varrho = (q, \nu)$. Define $[\![\varrho]\!]$ to be $\langle(q, digi(\nu)), \bullet^k \bot\rangle$, where $k = 2 \times floor(\nu(c) - n) + ceiling(frac(\nu(c)))$ if $\nu(c) > n$ otherwise $k = 0$. A configuration κ of PDS $\mathcal{P}$ with some ϱ and $\kappa = [\![\varrho]\!]$ is called an* encoded configuration.

Example 5. Consider the configuration (q_f, ν_5) in Example 1, where $\nu_5 = \{c = 6.5, x_1 = 7.5, x_2 = 10.7\}$. By Definition 11, $[\![(q_f, \nu_5)]\!] = \langle(q_f, digi(\nu_5)), \bullet \bot\rangle$, where $digi(\nu_5) = \{(c, \mathbf{r}_{13}), (x_1, \mathbf{r}_{13})\}\{(x_2, \mathbf{r}_{13})\}$.

Remark 4. For a UTA1's time progress transition $(p, \nu) \xrightarrow{t} (q, \nu')$, where $t \in \mathbb{R}^{\geq 0}$, there has a transition sequence of $[\![(p, \nu)]\!] \hookrightarrow \langle(p, \bar{Z}_1), w_1\rangle \hookrightarrow \langle(p, \bar{Z}_2), w_2\rangle \cdots \hookrightarrow [\![(q, \nu')]\!]$ to simulate it, which consists of finite many time *time progress* transitions of PDS.

Lemma 1. *Given a UTA1 $\mathcal{A}$, its associated PDS $\mathcal{P}$, and any configuration ϱ, ϱ' of $\mathcal{A}$.*

(Preservation) *If $\varrho \to \varrho'$ then $[\![\varrho]\!] \hookrightarrow^* [\![\varrho']\!]$.*
(Reflection) *If $[\![\varrho]\!] \hookrightarrow^* \kappa$,*
1. *there exists ϱ' such that $\kappa = [\![\varrho']\!]$ and $\varrho \to^* \varrho'$, or*
2. *κ is not an encoded configuration, and there exists ϱ' such that $\kappa \hookrightarrow^* [\![\varrho']\!]$ by transitions (of $\mathcal{P}$) and $\varrho \to^* \varrho'$.*

With Lemma 1, we have the following theorem.

Theorem 1. *The reachability of a UTA1 is decidable.*

The proof is given in Appendix A.

6   Related Work

After *timed automata(TAs)* [1] had been proposed by Alur and Dill, a lot of work has been devoted to extensions of TAs.

The extension that allows to compare the sum of two clocks with a constant has also been investigated in [1]. It leads to an undecidable class of automata. Periodic clock constraints defined in [11], can express properties like "the value of a clock is even" or "the value of a clock is of the form $0.5 + 3n$ where n is some integer. The corresponding class of automata is strictly more powerful than TAs if silent transitions are not allowed but otherwise coincides with the original model.

Controlled real-time automata, a parameterized family of TAs with some additional features like clock stopping, variable clock velocities and periodic tests has been proposed in [12]. Due to carefully chosen restrictions, controlled real-time automata remains decidable.

Recursive timed automata(RTAs) [13] is an extension of TAs with recursive structure. It has clocks by the mechanism of "pass-by-value". When the condition of "glitch-freeness",i.e. all the clocks of components are uniformly either by "pass-by-value" or by "pass-by-reference", the reachability is shown to be decidable.

Nested timed automata (NeTAs) [9,10,14] extend TAs with recursive structure in another way, which allow clocks of some TAs in the stack elapse simultaneously with the current running clocks during time passage. Those clocks are named *local clocks*, while clocks in other TAs kept unaltered clocks during time passage are named *frozen clocks*. It is proved that the reachability of NeTAs with both types of clocks and a singleton *global clock* that can be observed by all TAs is decidable, while that with two or more global clocks is undecidable [10].

The *updatable timed automata (UTAs)* [4] is a natural syntactic extension of TA. It enjoyed the possibility of updating the clocks in a more elaborate way than just simple reset in TA. The value of a clock could be reassigned to a basic arithmetic computation result of values of other clocks. The paper gave undecidability and decidability results for several specific cases. The decidability results were obtained through a generalization of the region graph proposed by Alur and Dill, while the undecidability results were obtained by reducing an undecidable problem on Minsky Machine [15] to the emptiness problem for a subclass of UTAs. The expressiveness of the UTAs was also investigated in the paper. Our model UTA1s, is actually a specific subclass of general UTAs by restricting the number of updatable clock to one.

A forward analysis of UTAs has been proposed in [16] for specific subclass of UTAs that do not use comparisons between clocks. Recently, a refined algorithm for specific subclass of UTAs with diagonal constraints has been proposed in [17].

7   Conclusion

This paper has investigated the reachability of UTA1s, UTAs with one updatable clock. By restricting the number of updatable clocks to one, the reachability of UTA1s is decidable, under the diagonal-free constraints. The decidability is proved by encoding the clock behavior of UTA1s to PDSs based on the notion of *digiword*. The key idea is to use a stack to record the time interval exceeding the maximum constant integer. As a result, the transitions in pushdown systems are finer than that of UTA1s.

UTA1s defined in Definition 5 only allow diagonal-free clock constraints. Our proof can not be extended to cover the UTA1s with diagonal clock constraints. We will further investigate the reachability for the UTA1s with diagonal clock constraints as a future work.

Acknowledgements. This work is supported by the NSFC-JSPS bilateral joint research project (61511140100), the National Natural Science Foundation of China (No. 61472240, 91318301, 61261130589), and JSPS KAKENHI Grant-in-Aid for Scientific Research(B) (15H02684, 25280023) and Challenging Exploratory Research (26540026).

A A Proof of Lemma 1

Proof. Let $\varrho = (q, \nu)$. Then $[\![\varrho]\!] = \langle (q, digi(\nu)), w \rangle$, where $w = \bullet^k \perp$ for some k. For preservation part, By case analysis of $\varrho \to \varrho'$.

1. **Time Progress:** $\varrho \xrightarrow{t} \varrho'$. By the digiword's region-like property, we have $digi(\nu) \Rightarrow^* digi(\nu + t)$. Proceed with two subcases:
   (a) If no stack operations involved (i.e. $\nu(c) + t \leq n$), then we have $[\![\varrho]\!] = \langle (q, digi(\nu)), w \rangle \hookrightarrow^* [\![\varrho']\!] = \langle (q, digi(\nu + t)), w \rangle$ by applying the first transition rule of time progress rules finite times. Note that in this subcase, $w = \perp$.
   (b) If $\nu(c) + t > n$, then we have $[\![\varrho]\!] = \langle (q, digi(\nu)), w \rangle \hookrightarrow^* [\![\varrho']\!] = \langle (q, digi(\nu + t)), w' \rangle$ by applying the first time progress rule finite times (maybe zero times if $\nu(c) \geq n$) and then applying the second time progress rule finite times.

2. **Local:** $\varrho = (p, \nu) \xrightarrow{\epsilon} \varrho' = (q, \nu)$. Then with the *Local* transition of PDS, $[\![\varrho]\!] = \langle (p, digi(\nu)), w \rangle \hookrightarrow [\![\varrho']\!] = \langle (q, digi(\nu)), w \rangle$.

3. **Test:** $\varrho = (p, \nu) \xrightarrow{x \in I?} \varrho' = (q, \nu)$. Then with the *Test* transition of PDS, $[\![\varrho]\!] = \langle (p, digi(\nu)), w \rangle \hookrightarrow [\![\varrho']\!] = \langle (q, digi(\nu)), w \rangle$, since $\exists (x, \mathbf{r}_i) \in Y_j \in digi(\nu)$ such that $\mathbf{r}_i \subseteq I$, where $digi(\nu) = Y_1 Y_2 \cdots Y_j \cdots Y_m$.

4. **Assignment:** $\varrho = (p, \nu) \xrightarrow{x \leftarrow I} \varrho' = (q, \nu[x \leftarrow d])$, where $d \in I$. We proceed with 2 cases:
   (a) If $x \neq c$, then we have $[\![\varrho]\!] = \langle (p, digi(\nu)), w \rangle \hookrightarrow [\![\varrho']\!] = \langle (q, digi(\nu[x \leftarrow d])), w \rangle$ by applying the first assignment rule of PDS $\mathcal{P}$: $\langle (p, \bar{Y}), \epsilon \rangle \hookrightarrow \langle (q, insert(delete(\bar{Y}, x), (x, \mathbf{r}_i)), \epsilon \rangle$, where $\bar{Y} = digi(\nu)$ and $d \in \mathbf{r}_i$.
   (b) Otherwise, $x = c$, proceed with two subcases, $d <= n$ and $d > n$.
   – $d <= n$: If $w = \bullet^k \perp$ for $k > 0$, we first need to pop all symbols of $\bullet$ out of stack, by repeatedly applying the second assignment rule of PDS k times, having $[\![\varrho]\!] = \langle (p, digi(\nu)), \bullet^k \perp \rangle \hookrightarrow^* \kappa = \langle (p, digi(\nu)), \perp \rangle$, otherwise define $\kappa = [\![\varrho]\!]$ since the stack already has no symbols of $\bullet$. Then by applying the third and fourth assignment rule, we have $\kappa \hookrightarrow \kappa' = \langle (p', digi(\nu)), \perp \rangle \hookrightarrow [\![\varrho']\!] = \langle (q, digi(\nu[x \leftarrow d])), \perp \rangle$.
   – $d > n$: If $w = \bullet^k \perp$ for $k > 0$, we first need to pop all symbols of $\bullet$ out of stack, by repeatedly applying the second assignment rule of PDS k times, having $[\![\varrho]\!] = \langle (p, digi(\nu)), \bullet^k \perp \rangle \hookrightarrow^* \kappa = \langle (p, digi(\nu)), \perp \rangle$, otherwise define $\kappa = [\![\varrho]\!]$, since the stack already has no symbols of $\bullet$. Next, we have $\kappa \hookrightarrow \kappa' = \langle (p', digi(\nu)), \perp \rangle$ by the third assignment rule. Then, by repeatedly applying the fifth assignment rule of $\mathcal{P}$ until we have $k = 2 \times floor(d - n) + ceiling(frac(d))$ symbols of $\bullet$ in stack,

we have $\kappa' \hookrightarrow^* \kappa'' = \langle (p', digi(\nu)), \bullet^k \perp \rangle$. Finally, by applying the last assignment rule of $mathcalP$, we have $\kappa'' \hookrightarrow [\![\varrho']\!] = \langle (q, digi(\nu[c \leftarrow d])), \bullet^k \perp \rangle\rangle$.

5. **Increment:** $\varrho = (p, \nu) \xrightarrow{c:=c+1} \varrho' = (q, \nu[c \leftarrow \nu(c) + 1])$. We proceed with 3 subcases:

   (a) If $\nu(c) \leq n - 1$, then we have $[\![\varrho]\!] = \langle (p, digi(\nu)), w \rangle \hookrightarrow [\![\varrho']\!] = \langle (q, increase(digi(\nu), c)), w \rangle = \langle (q, digi(\nu[c \leftarrow \nu(c) + 1])), w \rangle$ by applying the first transition increment rule of PDS $\mathcal{P}$.

   (b) If $n - 1 < \nu(c) < n$, then we have $[\![\varrho]\!] = \langle (p, digi(\nu)), w \rangle \hookrightarrow [\![\varrho']\!] = \langle (q, increase(digi(\nu), c)), \bullet w \rangle = \langle (q, digi(\nu[c \leftarrow \nu(c) + 1])), \bullet w \rangle$ by applying the second transition increment rule of PDS $\mathcal{P}$.

   (c) If $\nu(c) \geq n$, then we have $[\![\varrho]\!] = \langle (p, digi(\nu)), w \rangle \hookrightarrow [\![\varrho']\!] = \langle (q, increase(digi(\nu), c)), \bullet \bullet w \rangle = \langle (q, digi(\nu[c \leftarrow \nu(c) + 1])), \bullet \bullet w \rangle$ by applying the third transition increment rule of PDS $\mathcal{P}$.

6. **Decrement:** $\varrho = (p, \nu) \xrightarrow{c:=c-1} \varrho' = (q, \nu[c \leftarrow \nu(c) - 1])$. Note that only when $\nu(c) \geq 1$, can this transition happen. We proceed with 4 subcases:

   (a) If $\nu(c) > n + 1$, then we have $[\![\varrho]\!] = \langle (p, digi(\nu)), \bullet \bullet \bullet w' \rangle \hookrightarrow [\![\varrho']\!] = \langle (q, digi(\nu)), \bullet w' \rangle = \langle (q, digi(\nu[c \leftarrow \nu(c) - 1])), \bullet w' \rangle$ by applying the first transition decrement rule of PDS $\mathcal{P}$.

   (b) If $\nu(c) = n + 1$, then we have $[\![\varrho]\!] = \langle (p, digi(\nu)), \bullet \bullet \perp \rangle \hookrightarrow [\![\varrho']\!] = \langle (q, decrease(digi(\nu), c, 1)), \perp \rangle = \langle (q, digi(\nu[c \leftarrow \nu(c) - 1])), \perp \rangle$ by applying the second transition decrement rule of PDS $\mathcal{P}$.

   (c) If $n < \nu(c) < n + 1$, then we have $[\![\varrho]\!] = \langle (p, digi(\nu)), \bullet \perp \rangle \hookrightarrow [\![\varrho']\!] = \langle (q, increase(digi(\nu), c, 2)), \perp \rangle = \langle (q, digi(\nu[c \leftarrow \nu(c) - 1])), \perp \rangle$ by applying the third transition decrement rule of PDS $\mathcal{P}$.

   (d) If $1 \leq \nu(c) \leq n$, then we have $[\![\varrho]\!] = \langle (p, digi(\nu)), \perp \rangle \hookrightarrow [\![\varrho']\!] = \langle (q, increase(digi(\nu), c, 2)), \perp \rangle = \langle (q, digi(\nu[c \leftarrow \nu(c) - 1])), \perp \rangle$ by applying the fourth transition decrement rule of PDS $\mathcal{P}$.

For *reflection* part, by induction on the steps of $\hookrightarrow^*$.

Base step: Consider the case of $[\![\varrho]\!] \hookrightarrow \kappa$:

1. **Time Progress.** Obviously, $[\![\varrho]\!] \hookrightarrow \kappa$ by one of two time progress rules of PDS $\mathcal{P}$. Since digiwords have the region-like property, $digi(\nu) \Rightarrow \bar{Y}$ implies that there exists a clock valuation $\nu' \in Val(X \cup \{c\})$ such that $\nu' = \nu + t$ and $\nu' \in [\bar{Y}]$ for a real number t(more precisely, $0 < t < 1$). Proceed with two cases:

   (a) If $\nu(c) < n$, then $[\![\varrho]\!] \hookrightarrow \kappa$ by using the first time progress rule of PDS $\mathcal{P}$. In such case, we have $\kappa = \langle (p, \bar{Y}, \perp) \rangle = [\![\varrho']\!]$, where $\varrho = (p, \nu) \xrightarrow{t} \varrho' = (p, \nu')$.

   (b) If $\nu(c) \geq n$, then $[\![\varrho]\!] \hookrightarrow \kappa$ by using the second time progress rule of PDS $\mathcal{P}$. In such case, we have $\kappa = \langle (p, \bar{Y}), \bullet w \rangle = [\![\varrho']\!]$, where $\varrho = (p, \nu) \xrightarrow{t} \varrho' = (p, \nu')$.

2. **Local.** If $[\![\varrho]\!] \hookrightarrow \kappa$ for $p \xrightarrow{\epsilon} q$ being a transition in $\mathcal{A}$, then $\kappa = \langle (q, digi(\nu)), w \rangle = [\![\varrho']\!]$, where $\varrho' = (q, \nu)$.

3. **Test.** Similar with the case for **Local.**

4. **Assignment.** We only need to proceed with the first three cases, the other cases can not happen since the configuration is a *encoded configuration*(i.e. $[\![\varrho]\!]$).

   (a) If $[\![\varrho]\!] \hookrightarrow \kappa$ by applying the first assignment transition rule of PDS $\mathcal{P}$, then κ is a *encoded configuration*, since we have $[\![\varrho]\!] = \langle (p, digi(\nu)), w \rangle \hookrightarrow \kappa = [\![\varrho']\!] = \langle (q, insert(delete(digi(\nu), x), (x, \mathbf{r}_i))), w \rangle$, where $\varrho = (p, \nu) \xrightarrow{x \leftarrow I} \varrho' = (q, \nu[x \leftarrow d])$ for $d \in \mathbf{r}_i \in I$.

   (b) If $[\![\varrho]\!] \hookrightarrow \kappa$ by applying the second assignment transition rule of PDS $\mathcal{P}$, then the clock involved is c and κ may not be a *encoded configuration*. However, by applying the same rules finite times and then third assignment rule, $\kappa \hookrightarrow^* \kappa_1 = \langle (p, digi(\nu)), \bot \rangle \hookrightarrow \kappa_2 = \langle (p', digi(\nu)), \bot \rangle$, and then if $\mathbf{r}_i \in I$ for $i \leq 2n$, we have $\kappa_2 \hookrightarrow [\![\varrho']\!] = \langle (q, insert(delete(digi(\nu), c), (c, \mathbf{r}_i)), \bot \rangle$, by applying the fourth assignment rule, otherwise, we have $\kappa_2 \hookrightarrow^* \kappa_3 = \langle (p', digi(\nu)), \bullet^k \bot \rangle \hookrightarrow [\![\varrho']\!] = \langle (q, insert(delete(digi(\nu), c), (c, \mathbf{r}_i)), \bullet^k \bot \rangle$ by applying finite times of fifth assignment rule first and then the last assignment rule.

   (c) If $[\![\varrho]\!] \hookrightarrow \kappa$ by applying the second assignment transition rule of PDS $\mathcal{P}$, the proof is similar to the above case.

5. **Increment.** We proceed with three cases:

   (a) If it takes the first increment transition rule, then we can infer that $\nu(c) <= n - 1$. Thus we have $[\![\varrho]\!] \hookrightarrow \kappa = \langle (q, increase(digi(\nu), c)), w \rangle = [\![\varrho']\!]$, where $\varrho \xrightarrow{c:=c+1} \varrho'$.

   (b) If it takes the second increment transition rule, then we can infer that $n - 1 < \nu(c) < n$. Then we have $[\![\varrho]\!] \hookrightarrow \kappa = \langle (q, increase(digi(\nu), c)), \bullet w \rangle = [\![\varrho']\!]$, where $\varrho \xrightarrow{c:=c+1} \varrho'$.

   (c) If it takes the third increment transition rule, then we can infer that $\nu(c) \geq n$. Then we have $[\![\varrho]\!] \hookrightarrow \kappa = \langle (q, increase(digi(\nu), c)), \bullet \bullet w \rangle = [\![\varrho']\!]$, where $\varrho \xrightarrow{c:=c+1} \varrho'$.

6. **Decrement.** We proceed with four cases:

   (a) If it takes the first decrement transition rule, then we can infer that $\nu(c) > n + 1$. Then we have $[\![\varrho]\!] = \langle (q, digi(\nu)), \bullet \bullet \bullet w' \rangle \hookrightarrow \kappa = \langle (q, digi(\nu)), \bullet w' \rangle = [\![\varrho']\!]$, where $\varrho \xrightarrow{c:=c-1} \varrho'$. Note that $digi(\nu) = digi(\nu[\nu(c) \leftarrow \nu(c) - 1])$, since $\nu(c) > n + 1$.

   (b) If it takes the second decrement transition rule, then we can infer that $\nu(c) = n + 1$. Then we have $[\![\varrho]\!] = \langle (q, digi(\nu)), \bullet \bullet \bot \rangle \hookrightarrow \kappa = \langle (q, decrease(digi(\nu), c, 1)), \bot \rangle = [\![\varrho']\!]$, where $\varrho \xrightarrow{c:=c-1} \varrho' = (q, \nu')$ and $\nu'(c) = n$.

   (c) If it takes the third decrement transition rule, then we can infer that $n < \nu(c) < n + 1$. Then we have $[\![\varrho]\!] = \langle (q, digi(\nu)), \bullet \bot \rangle \hookrightarrow \kappa = \langle (q, decrease(digi(\nu), c, 2)), \bot \rangle = [\![\varrho']\!]$, where $\varrho \xrightarrow{c:=c-1} \varrho' = (q, \nu')$ and $n - 1 < \nu'(c) < n$.

   (d) If it takes the fourth decrement transition rule, then we can infer that $1 <= \nu(c) <= n$. Then we have $[\![\varrho]\!] = \langle (q, digi(\nu)), \bot \rangle \hookrightarrow \kappa = \langle (q, decrease(digi(\nu), c, 2)), \bot \rangle = [\![\varrho']\!]$, where $\varrho \xrightarrow{c:=c-1} \varrho' = (q, \nu')$.

Induction step: Assume $[\![\varrho]\!] \hookrightarrow^* \kappa' \hookrightarrow \kappa$. We proceed with two cases:

1. κ' is an *encoded configuration*, and by induction hypothesis $[\![\varrho]\!] \hookrightarrow^* \kappa' = [\![\varrho']\!]$. Then the proof is similar to the base step.
2. κ' is not an *encoded configuration*. Note that for our encoding, we have encoded configurations except for the second, third and fifth assignment rule. Here, we give a proof for the fifth assignment rule. The other cases are similar. Assume $\kappa' = \langle (p', \bar{Y}), w \rangle$ is obtained by applying the fifth assignment rule, we have $\kappa' \hookrightarrow \kappa = \langle (q, digi(\nu')), w \rangle = [\![\varrho']\!] = [\![(q, \nu')]\!]$ by applying the last assignment rule, where $\exists \nu \in [\bar{Y}]$ such that $\nu' = \nu[c \leftarrow d]$ for $d \in r_{2n+1}$. Finally, put together $\varrho \rightarrow^* \varrho'$.

References

1. Alur, R., Dill, D.L.: A theory of timed automata. Theor. Comput. Sci. **126**, 183–235 (1994)
2. Bouyer, P., Dufourd, C., Fleury, E., Petit, A.: Are timed automata updatable? In: Emerson, E.A., Sistla, A.P. (eds.) CAV 2000. LNCS, vol. 1855. Springer, Heidelberg (2000)
3. Bouyer, P., Dufourd, C., Fleury, É., Petit, A.: Expressiveness of updatable timed automata. In: Nielsen, M., Rovan, B. (eds.) MFCS 2000. LNCS, vol. 1893, pp. 232–242. Springer, Heidelberg (2000)
4. Bouyer, P., Dufourd, C., Fleury, E., Petit, A.: Updatable timed automata. Theor. Comput. Sci. **321**, 291–345 (2004)
5. Schwoon, S.: Model-checking pushdown system. Ph.D. thesis, Technical University of Munich (2000)
6. Ouaknine, J., Worrell, J.: On the language inclusion problem for timed automata: closing a decidability gap. In: Proceedings of the 19th IEEE Symposium on Logic in Computer Science (LICS'04), IEEE Computer Society, pp. 54–63 (2004)
7. Abdulla, P.A., Jonsson, B.: Verifying Networks of Timed Processes (Extended Abstract). In: Steffen, B. (ed.) TACAS 1998. LNCS, vol. 1384, p. 298. Springer, Heidelberg (1998)
8. Abdulla, P., Jonsson, B.: Model checking of systems with many identical time processes. Theor. Comput. Sci. **290**, 241–264 (2003)
9. Li, G., Cai, X., Ogawa, M., Yuen, S.: Nested timed automata. In: Braberman, V., Fribourg, L. (eds.) FORMATS 2013. LNCS, vol. 8053, pp. 168–182. Springer, Heidelberg (2013)
10. Li, G., Ogawa, M., Yuen, S.: Nested timed automata with frozen clocks. In: Sankaranarayanan, S., Vicario, E. (eds.) FORMATS 2015. LNCS, vol. 9268, pp. 189–205. Springer, Heidelberg (2015)
11. Choffrut, C., Goldwurm, M.: Timed automata with periodic clock constraints. J. Automata, Lang. Comb. **5**, 371–404 (2000)
12. Demichelis, F., Zielonka, W.: Controlled timed automata. In: Sangiorgi, D., de Simone, R. (eds.) CONCUR 1998. LNCS, vol. 1466, pp. 455–469. Springer, Heidelberg (1998)
13. Trivedi, A., Wojtczak, D.: Recursive timed automata. In: Bouajjani, A., Chin, W.-N. (eds.) ATVA 2010. LNCS, vol. 6252, pp. 306–324. Springer, Heidelberg (2010)

14. Wen, Y., Li, G., Yuen, S.: An over-approximation forward analysis for nested timed automata. In: Liu, S., Duan, Z. (eds.) SOFL+MSVL 2014. LNCS, vol. 8979, pp. 62–80. Springer, Heidelberg (2015)
15. Minsky, M.: Computation: Finite and Infinite Machines. Prentice-Hall, Upper Saddle River (1967)
16. Bouyer, P.: Forward analysis of updatable timed automata. Formal Methods in System Design **24**, 281–320 (2004)
17. Fang, B., Li, G., Fang, L., Xiang, J.: A refined algorithm for reachability analysis of updatable timed automata. In: Proceedings of the 1st IEEE International Workshop on Software Engineering and Knowledge Management (SEKM 2015 @ QRS 2015), IEEE Computer Society, pp. 230–236 (2015)

Algorithm and Transformation

Research on Formal Development
of Non-recursive Algorithms of Graph Search

Qimin Hu[1,2(✉)], Jinyun Xue[1,2], and Zhen You[1,2]

[1] National Networked Supporting Software International
S and T Cooperation Base of China,
Jiangxi Normal University, Nanchang, Jiangxi, People's Republic of China
[2] Key Laboratory of High Performance Computing Technology,
Jiangxi Normal University, Nanchang, Jiangxi, People's Republic of China
{qiminhu,yucy0405}@163.com, jinyun@vip.sina.com

Abstract. Formal method is key approach in developing safety critical systems. Graph search algorithms are very important software components. The paper tries to formally develop two non-recursive graph search algorithms, depth-first search and breadth-first search. This is a very challenge task because non-recursive graph search algorithms have low computing complexity with high logic complexity comparing with recursive graph search algorithms. The formal development of non-recursive algorithms involves formalization of specification, loop invariant and proof of the algorithmic programs. In this paper, we introduce PAR platform that support MDD of software with high reliability and safety. Specification language Radl of PAR platform was used to describe the program specification; Software modelling language Apla was used to describe algorithmic programs; the function of recursive definition was used to develop and denote the loop invariant, then the algorithmic programs was formally proofed. Finally, the correct algorithmic programs denoted by Apla were transformed to the programs of executable language; such as C++, Java, VB and C#, etc., based on the program generating systems in PAR platform. The most important innovation is defining recursive function to denote the loop invariant that makes the loop invariant precise and simple.

Keywords: Formal development · Loop invariant · Non-recursive graph search algorithms · PAR platform · Depth-first search · Breadth-first search

1 Introduction

A graph-searching algorithm can discover much information about the structure of a graph. Many algorithms begin by searching their input graph to obtain this structural information. Other graph algorithms are organized as simple elaborations of basic graph-searching algorithms. Techniques for searching a graph are at the heart of the field of graph algorithms [2]. The depth-first and breadth-first based graph searching algorithms have been widely applied in many field

© Springer International Publishing Switzerland 2016
S. Liu and Z. Duan (Eds.): SOFL+MSVL 2015, LNCS 9559, pp. 165–178, 2016.
DOI: 10.1007/978-3-319-31220-0_12

such as minimum spanning trees, double connected branch and strongly connected components of graphs, graph matching, flows in networks, Hamilton map, Dijkstra's shortest paths, graph planarity testing etc. Graph search algorithms are widely used in industrial areas, such as electronic circuits design, power flow management in electric networks.

Graph searching algorithms can be implemented with recursive or non-recursive method. Although recursive graph search algorithms have clear readability and low logic complexity, they have high computing complexity. Recursive algorithms may exhaust all memory space in case of searching large graph. Some executable languages do not support recursive mechanism. In the contrary, non-recursive graph search algorithms have high logic complexity and low computing complexity. Obviously, non-recursive graph search algorithms have much more practical value than recursive algorithms in industrial applications.

Non-recursive graph search algorithms are very important. But up to now, few researchers can give their formal specification, accurate loop invariants and formal proof. The related books and theses just describe their development in natural language and implement in executable language.

Existing techniques of developing loop invariant are only suitable for some simple problems. Complicated algorithmic programs such as graph search algorithms which have non-linear data structure, cannot get satisfiable loop invariant using these techniques.

The formalization is an challenge for those algorithms. We urgently need a new style to give formal specification and an innovation to give precise loop invariants for those algorithms.

In this paper, using specification language Radl to describe the program specification of depth-first and breadth-first graph searching algorithms. Using the innovation of defining recursive function to denote the loop invariants. With the support of executable program generating systems in PAR platform, the C++, C#, Java executable programs have been generated.

The paper was organized as follows. The Sect. 2 gives the related preliminary knowledge of PAR platform; The Sect. 3 elaborates formal development of non-recursive algorithm of depth-first search and breadth-first search of graph; The Sect. 4 shows the correct graph search executable algorithmic programs be generated automatically based on the PAR platform; The Sect. 5 described the related works; Finally a short conclusion was presented.

2   Preliminary

PAR means PAR (Partition-and-Recur) method [18, 21, 23, 25] and its supporting platform, called PAR platform. PAR is a long-term research projects supported by a series of research foundations of China. PAR method and PAR platform consists of specification and algorithm describing language Radl, software modeling language Apla, a set of rules for specification transformation and a set of automatic generating tools such as Radl to Apla generating system, Apla to

Java, C++, Cexecutable program generating systems. According to the methodology of MDD, PAR has been used in developing software with high reliability and safety, such as non-trivial algorithm programs [20,24], traffic scheduling system [17], bank account management system and electric control system.

There are two developing ways in using PAR method and PAR platform to develop algorithm. One way is writing specification and recurrence relation for problem solution in Radl language at first, then generating Apla program by Radl to Apla generating system, then generating executable program by Apla to executable program generating system. This way can be used to develop algorithms whose post-condition can be expressed by quantifier. The other way is writing loop invariant and Apla program at first, then proof the correctness of Apla program by loop invariant, then generating executable program.

2.1 Specification Language Radl

Radl (Recur-based Algorithm Design Language) used the idiomatic mathematical symbols and style to describe the algorithm specification, specification transformation rules and the recurrence relation. Radl is the front language of the Apla language, with mathematical referential transparency. Using the unified format $(Q_i : r(i) : f(i))$ given by Dijkstra to denote quantifiers, where Q can be $\forall$ (all quantifier), $\exists$ (exists quantifier), MIN (minimum quantifier), MAX (maximum quantifier), Σ (summation quantifier), etc., and i is a bounded variable, $r(i)$ is the variant range of i and $f(i)$ is a function.

2.2 Software Modelling Language Apla

Apla (Abstract Programming Language) is the software modelling language and the target language of Radl to Apla program generating system, and the source language of Apla to Java, C++, C, Dephi executable program generating system.

2.3 Predefined Generic Abstract Data Type of Apla

Apla language provides abundant predefine generic abstract data type, such as set, list, tree, graph, etc. Those ADT realized sufficient data abstraction and function abstraction. With those Predefined generic ADT supporting, the abstract program written in Apla language is very short and easy to understand and prove.

List. Apla language provides predefined generic abstract data type List. The description of ADT List's data and operations is given below:

Specify ADT list (sometype data, [size])
//data is called the data type of list elements
//size is called the upper bounds of the number of list elements
type list(sometype data, [size])
var

h, t: integer;   //h and t represent the head and tail
                                      of List;
S, T: list:=[], [];   //S and T is List
e: data; i, j: integer;   //e is element of List
Operator:
[e]   //List which contain just one element
[]   //empty List
#S   //the number of elements in List S
S[i]   //the element in List S, S.h $\leq$ i $\leq$ S.t
S[i..j]   //one sublist of List S, S.h $\leq$ i, j $\leq$ S.t
S↑T   //construct a new List by concatenating List S and T. "↑"
                 operation can conveniently express insert and delete
                 operations on the head, tail or central of List
endspec;

Weighted Directed Graph. Apla language provides a weighted directed graph predefined generic abstract data types. Undirected graph can be view as a directed graph, where each undirected edge can be seen as two opposite directed edges. Let digraph be a weighted directed graph, which is defined as:

Type digraph((datatype, [size1]), (datatype, [size2]) = record
V: set(vertex, [size1]);   //is called the node set of G
E: set(edge, [size2]);   //is called the edge set of G
End;

The definition of vetex and edge:
type vertex = record
d: datatype;   //d is the data of node
n: int;   //n is the number of node
f:0..1;   //f is the sign of whether the node be visited
end;
type edge = record
w: datatype;   //w is the weight of edge
h, t: vertex;   //h and t is the head node and tail node of the edge
f:0..1;   //f is the sign of whether the edge be visited
end;

The description of ADT Graph's data and operations is given below:

Specify ADT digraph((sometype data, int size1), (sometype data, int size2))
var
v: vertex;   //node of graph
e: edge;   //edge of graph
Operator:
G+v   //add node v into graph G
G+e   //add edge e into graph G

#(G.V)	//the amount of nodes in graph G
#(G.E)	//the amount of edges in graph G
G.out(u)	//the head nodes of edgets whose tail node is u
G.in(u)	//the tail nodes of edgets whose head node is u
G.arcvalue(v_1, v_2)	//the weight of the edge which connect node v_1, v_2

endspec;

3 Formal Development of Non-recursive Algorithm of Graph Search

There are three popular graph traversal methods: depth-first search (DFS), breadth-first search (BFS), and topological search. The topological search applies only to directed acyclic graphs.

Formally develop non-recursive algorithm of depth-first search and bread-first search of graph. Specification language Radl of PAR method describes the formal specification. The innovation of defining recursive function denotes the loop invariant. Then formally prove the correctness of the algorithm programs denoted by Apla language. Finally, get executable program such as C#, C++, Java etc. through the PAR platform generating systems.

With $G = (V, E)$ standing for connected graph, V is called all the nodes in G, E is called all the edges in G, V_1 is source node in G.

3.1 Formal Development of Non-recursive Algorithm of Depth-First Graph Search

Depth-first search traverses a graph following the deepest (forward) direction possible. The algorithm starts by selecting the lowest numbered node v and marking it as visited. DFS selects an edge (v, u), where u is still unvisited, marks u as visited, and starts a new search from node u. After completing the search along all paths starting at u, DFS returns to v. The process is continued until all nodes reachable from v have been marked as visited [16].

Depth-first search can be used to compute topological sort of directed acyclic graphs, strongly connected components of graph and construct the directed-graph representation in graph planarity testing algorithm.

Developing Non-recursive Algorithm of Depth-First Graph Search.

Construct the problem formal specification:

Using DFS (G.V_1) to represent the sequence of nodes of graph G by depth-first search from source node V_1, and Using X to store the sequence of nodes. The problem specification can be as follows.

Q: given a graph G = (V, E) and the node V_1
R: X = DFS (G.V_1) $\land$ perm (X, G.V), where perm (X, G.V) representing the nodes in G.V composed X in a certain order.

G.out (V_1) represents the node set adjacent to node V_1,
let G.out $(V_1) = V_{11}, V_{12}, \ldots V_{1n}$,
DFS $(G.V_1) = [V_1] \uparrow DFS (V_{11}) \uparrow DFS (V_{12}) \uparrow \ldots \uparrow DFS (V_{1n})$

Further spread DFS (V_{11}) as follows:
Let G.out $(V_{11}) = V_{111}, V_{112}, \ldots V_{11n}$,
DFS $(G.V_1) = [V_1] \uparrow [V_{11}] \uparrow DFS (V_{111}) DFS(V_{112}) \uparrow \ldots \uparrow DFS(V_{11n}) \uparrow$
DFS $(V_{12}) \uparrow \ldots \uparrow DFS (V_{1n})$

Construct the loop invariant with defining recursive function:
Based on the above deduction, we can use the following strategy to get the loop invariant of non-recursive abstract algorithm of depth-first graph search:

Introduce three variables X, S, q, variable X storage the nodes set which have been visited; S storage the nodes set which are waiting for visit; q is the node which is visiting now.

Because graph has non-linear data structure, we need to define recursive function to determine when the waiting node should be stored into or got out from S. According to the definition of depth-first graph search, S should be the First In Last Out stack.

Describe varying law of all the variables in the above strategy, we can constitute the loop invariant as following:

$$DFS (G.V1) = X \uparrow [q] \uparrow F[G.out(q) \uparrow S]$$

F[S] should be the list which be constituted by concatenating depth-first search list of each node in the stack F[S] with recursive definition as formula 1. G.out(q) in the recursive definition stands for the nodes adjacent to q and are not visited:

$$\begin{cases} F[S] = []; & \text{when S is empty;} \\ F[q \uparrow S] = [q] \uparrow F[G.out (q) \uparrow S] & \text{when q is the node which is not visited;} \\ F[q \uparrow S] = F[S] & \text{when q is the node which is visiting now;} \end{cases} \tag{1}$$

According to the above loop invariant with defining recursive function, we can get the following Apla program:

Apla program (omit the input and output statements)

```
procedure DFS (g: digraph; proc process(q: vertex(integer)));
type st = vertex(integer);
var X, S: list(st); q, v1:st; numv, nume, i:integer;
e1:edge(integer, integer); g: digraph((integer), (integer));
begin
X, q, S:=[], v1, [];
do    (q.f = 0) →   X:=X↑[q];
                    process(q.d);
                    foreach (i:0 ≤ i ≤ #(g.out(q))-1:
                    if g.out(q)(i).f=0 → S:=[g.out(q)(i)]↑S;);
```

```
      fi;
      q.f:=1;
 [](q.f = 1) ∧ (¬(S = [])) → q, S:=S[S.h], S[S.h+1..S.t];
od;
foreach(i:0 ≤ i ≤ #(X) -1:write(X[i].n, '','');));
end.
```

Procedure process(q.d) in above Apla program is abstract generic procedure which can be substituted by different concrete procedures to get different graph algorithms, for example connected components computing algorithm.

Proof of Non-recursive Algorithm of Depth-First Graph Search. In order to prove this algorithm, We use Dijkstra-Gries standard proof strategy [3,6]. The proof strategy contains five conditions: (1) Prove that ρ is true before execution of the loop begins. (2) Prove that $\{\rho \land Bi\}Si\{\rho\}$, for $1 \leq i \leq n$. That is, execution of each guarded command terminates with ρ true, so that ρ is indeed an invariant of the loop. (3) Prove that $\rho \land \neg BB \Rightarrow R$, i.e. upon termination the desired result is true. (4) Prove that $\rho \land BB \Rightarrow (t > 0)$, so that t is bounded from below as long as the loop has not terminated. (5) Prove that $\{\rho \land Bi\}$ t1:=t; $Si\{t < t1\}$, for $1 \leq i \leq n$, so that each loop iteration is guaranteed to decrease the bound function.

Because each node of graph will be pushed in stack and visited just one time, the termination of this algorithm is obvious. We just need to prove conditions (1), (2), (3). In Sect. 3.1, we get the loop invariant ρ is: DFS(V1) = $X \uparrow [q] \uparrow$ $F[G.out(q) \uparrow S]$. The proof steps are as following:

(1) Proof ρ is true when the loop begins

wp("X, q, S:=[], V_1, [];", ρ)
≡ DFS $(G.V_1)$ = $[] \uparrow V_1 \uparrow F[G.out(V_1)]$
≡ true

(2) Proof ρ is true after each execution of loop

wp("X, S:=X$\uparrow$[q], G.out(q)$\uparrow$S", ρ)
≡ DFS $(G.V_1)$ = $X \uparrow [q] \uparrow [q] \uparrow F[G.out(q) \uparrow G.out(q) \uparrow S]$
(from formula 1)
≡ DFS $(G.V_1)$ = $X \uparrow [q] \uparrow F[q \uparrow G.out(q) \uparrow S]$
(from formula 1)
≡ DFS $(G.V_1)$ = $X \uparrow [q] \uparrow F[G.out(q) \uparrow S]$
$\rho \land (q.f = 0) \Rightarrow DFS(G.V_1) = X \uparrow [q] \uparrow F[G.out(q) \uparrow S]$

at the same time:

wp("q, S:=S[S.h], S[S.h + 1..S.t];", ρ)
≡ DFS $(G.V1)$ = $X \uparrow [S[S.h]] \uparrow F[G.out(S[S.h]) \uparrow S[S.h + 1..S.t]]$
(from formula 1)
≡ DFS $(G.V_1)$ = $X \uparrow F[S[S.h] \uparrow S[S.h + 1..S.t]]$
≡ DFS (V_1) = $X \uparrow F[S]$
$\rho \land (q.f = 1) \land (\neg(S = [])) \Rightarrow DFS (V1) = X \uparrow F[S]$

(3) Proof ρ is true when the loop termination

$$\rho \wedge \neg(((q.f = 0) \vee (\neg(S = [])))) \Rightarrow R$$
$$\equiv \rho \wedge (q.f = 1) \wedge (S = []) \Rightarrow R$$
$$\equiv DFS\ (G.V_1) = X \Rightarrow R$$
$$\equiv true$$

3.2   Formal Development of Non-recursive Algorithm of Breadth-First Graph Search

Breadth-first search visits all nodes at distance k from the lowest numbered node v before visiting any nodes at distance $k + 1$. Breadth-first search constructs a breadth-first search tree, initially containing only the lowest numbered node. Whenever an unvisited node w is visited in the course of scanning the adjacency list of an already visited node u, node w and edge (u, w) are added to the tree. The traversal terminates when all nodes have been visited [16].

Many graph algorithms such as Prim minimum spanning trees, Dijkstra single source shortest paths algorithm, adopt the spirit of breadth-first search.

Developing of Non-recursive Algorithm of Breadth-First Graph Search.

Construct Problem Formal Specification: Using BFS $(G.V_1)$ to represent the sequence of nodes of graph G by breadth-first search from node V_1, and Using X to store the sequence of nodes, the problem specification can be as follows:

$$Q: \text{given a graph } G = (V, E) \text{ and the node } V_1$$

Definition 1 (Breadth-first Order). *Using $D(X_i)$ represents the least number of edges which be used to connect node V1 and node X_i. For any two node X_i, X_j in sequence X, if $i < j$, then $D\ (X_i) \leq D\ (X_j)$.*

The post-condition assertion described in natural language is as follows:

$$R1: X = BFS\ (V_1) \wedge perm\ (X, G.V), \text{ and any two nodes in X}$$
$$\text{corresponding to the "Breadth-first Order".}$$

It is far more difficult to spread $X = BFS(V_1)$ than $X = DFS(V_1)$. So, the definition of recursive function F[S] need to define in advance as formula 2:

$$\begin{cases} F[S] = []; & \text{when } S = [], \\ F[S] = [S.h] \uparrow F[S[h + 1..t] \uparrow G.out\ (S.h)] & \text{when } S \text{ is not empty} \end{cases} \quad (2)$$

So we can get formal post-condition assertion as follow:

$$R2: X = BFS\ (V_1) = [V_1] \uparrow F(G.out(V_1)) \wedge ((S \neq [] \wedge F[S] = [S.h]$$
$$\uparrow F[S[h + 1..t] \uparrow G.out(S.h)]) \vee (S = [] \wedge F[S] = []))$$

Constructing loop invariant with defining recursive function:

Introduce three variables X, S, Q, variable X storage the nodes set which have been visited; S storage the nodes set which are waiting for visit; q is the node which is visiting now.

Describe varying law of all the variables in the above strategy, we can constitute the loop invariant of graph breadth-first search algorithm as following:

$$\text{BFS }(G.V1) = X \uparrow [q] \uparrow F[S \uparrow G.out(q)]$$

F[S] should be the First In First Out sequence, with the recursive definition as formula 3. G.out(q) in the recursive function stand for the nodes adjacent to q and are not visited:

$$
\begin{cases}
F[S] = [] ; & \text{when S is empty;} \\
F[q \uparrow S] = [q] \uparrow F[S \uparrow G.out\ (q)]; & \text{when q is the node which is not visited,} \\
F[q \uparrow S] = F[S]; & \text{when q is the node which is visiting now;}
\end{cases}
\tag{3}
$$

According to the above loop invariant with defining recursive function, we can get the following Apla program:

Apla program (omit the input and output statements)

Procedure BFS (g: digraph; proc process(q: vertex(integer)));

type st = vertex(integer);

var X, S: list(st); q, v1:st; numv, nume, i: integer;

g: digraph((integer), (integer));

Begin

X, q, S:=[], v1, [];

do (q.f = 0) → X:=X ↑ [q];

            process(q.d);

            foreach (i:0 ≤ i ≤ #(g.out(q)) -1:

            if g.out(q)(i). f = 0 → S:=[S ↑ g.out(q)(i)];); fi;

            q.f:=1;

[](q.f = 1) ∧ (¬(S = [])) → q, S:=S[S.h], S[S.h + 1..S.t];

od;

end.

Proof of Non-recursive Algorithm of Breadth-First Graph Search.

In order to prove this algorithm, We use Dijkstra-Gries standard proof strategy as Sect. 3.1. Because each node of graph will be pushed in sequence and visited just one time, the termination of this algorithm is obvious. We just need to prove conditions (1), (2), (3) in proof strategy.

In Sect. 3.2, we get the loop invariant ρ is: BFS(G.V1) = X ↑ [q] ↑ F[S ↑ G.out(q)]. The proof steps are as following:

(1) Proof ρ is true when the loop begin

$wp($ "X, q, S:=[], V_1, [];", $\rho)$

$\equiv \text{BFS}(G.V_1) = [] \uparrow [V_1] \uparrow F[G.out(V_1)] \uparrow []$

$\equiv \text{true}$

(2) Proof ρ is true after each execution of loop

wp("X, S:=X↑[q], S↑G.out(q)", ρ)
$\equiv$ BFS(G.V_1) = X↑[q]↑[q]↑F[S↑G.out(q)↑G.out(q)]
(from formula 3)
$\equiv$ BFS(G.V_1) = X↑[q]↑F[q↑S↑G.out(q)]
(from formula 3)
$\equiv$ BFS(G.V_1) = X↑[q]↑F[S↑G.out(q)]
$\rho \wedge$ (q.f = 0) $\Rightarrow$ BFS(G.V_1) = X↑[q]↑F[S↑G.out(q)]

At the same time:

wp("q, S:=S[S.h], S[S.h + 1..S.t];", ρ)
$\equiv$ BFS(G.V_1) = X↑[S[S.h]]↑F[S[S.h + 1..S.t]↑G.out(S[S.h])]
(from formula 3)
$\equiv$ BFS(G.V_1) = X↑F[S]
$\rho \wedge$ (q.f = 1) $\wedge$ ($\neg$(S = [])) $\Rightarrow$ BFS(G.V_1) = X↑F[S]

(3) Proof ρ is true when the loop terminate

$\rho \wedge \neg$((q.f = 0) $\vee$ ($\neg$(S = []))) $\Rightarrow$ R
$\equiv \rho \wedge$ (q.f = 1) $\wedge$ (S = []) $\Rightarrow$ R
$\equiv$ BFS(G.V_1) = X $\Rightarrow$ R
$\equiv$ true

4   Generate Executable Program by Program Generating System in PAR Platform

The executable program can be generated automatically from the Apla to C++, JAVA, C#, Vb.net generating system in PAR platform.

The executable program generating system and the predefined abstract data type, such as "list", "weighted directed graph" and other library parts have been strictly tested and analysed. They can ensure semantic consistency between Apla program and executable program.

4.1   The Generation Steps of Program Generating System

As shown in Fig. 1, we choose the "C# program generating system" to generate executable C# program.

- Firstly, we click "New Apla" button and input the abstract algorithm described in Apla language. The algorithm is very short, only 4 lines core codes, in the left side of Fig. 1.
- Secondly, we click "Generate" button, the corresponding C# program which has dozens of codes in the right side of Fig. 1 will be generated.
- Thirdly, we click "Run" button, the C# program can run immediately.
- Finally, we can input the edges, nodes and source node of graph and test.

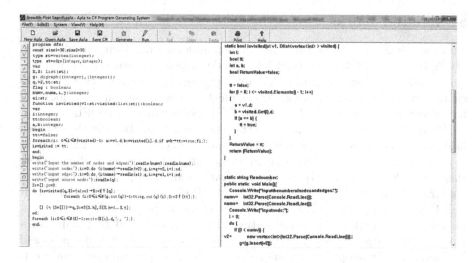

Fig. 1. Executable program generating system in PAR platform.

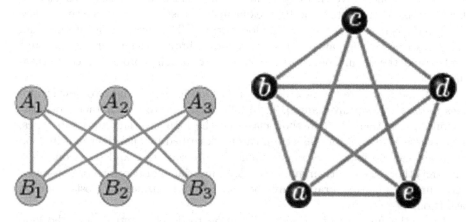

Fig. 2. Kuratowski K3, 3 graph.   **Fig. 3.** Kuratowski K5 graph.

4.2   The Results of Executable Programs Generated by Generating Systems

We input Kuratowski K3, 3 graph as Fig. 2 to test the depth-first graph search C# program, the result is A_1, B_1, A_2, B_2, A_3, B_3.

We input Kuratowski K5 graph as Fig. 3 to test the breadth-first graph search C# program, the result is c, b, d, a, e.

With no doubt, the program results are correct. We test the C# programs with many other test cases, the results are correct also.

5   Related Works

Up to now, existed related works about the developing non-recursive algorithm of graph search just describe their informal development process in natural language and implement them in executable language by program designer artificially. Few research about formal development of those algorithms was found in formal methods such as VDM [8], B [9], Z [1], Designware [15], SOFL [12].

Developing loop invariant is one of the most challenging tasks in the research field of formal methods. It contains a large amount of creative work. The amount of research work about the loop invariants is substantial and spread over more than three decades [7,10,11]. Gries gave four standard loop invariant developing strategies in [6]. Nguyen et al. in [13] and Rodriguez-Carbonell and Kapur in [14] generated polynomial loop invariants in simple program. B. Meyer summarized the international research status of loop invariants and gave loop invariants of twenty algorithms [5]. The loop invariant developing strategies proposed by Meyer mainly adopt the technique of transforming pre-condition and postcondition assertion [4].

In [2], Cormen gave the loop invariant of breadth-first search with natural language as 'At the test in line 10, the queue Q consists of the set of gray vertices (gray vertices means vertices waiting for visiting)'. This invariant is informal and can't describe varying law of all the variables. Through this invariant, we can't understand the nature of algorithm and can't formally prove the correctness also.

PAR method gave the new definition of loop invariant and two new strategies to develop loop invariants [19]. In [22], according to the character of postcondition assertion, PAR method classified the loop invariant into two types. One type is post-condition assertion can be described by quantifier and its loop invariant can be found by transforming the pre-condition and post-condition, and the other type can't. In most case, loop invariants of traversal of non-linear structure such as tree, graph, can't be found from transforming post-condition assertion.

Using the function of recursive definition to develop and denote the loop invariant, PAR method successfully developed the loop invariants of Pre-order, In-order, Post-order [26] non-recursive binary tree traversal algorithms and proof the correctness of them.

6   Conclusion

We formally develop non-recursive algorithms of graph depth-first search and breadth-first search with PAR method and PAR platform. Formal development gives us the formal specification, accurate loop invariant and proof of correctness of those algorithms. The executable programs generated by PAR platform can run correctly. The merits of this research can be summarized as following:

– The problem specification denoted by Radl language and abstract program described by software modelling language Apla are simple and accurate. It gave a simplified way to prove correctness.

- The formal development by PAR method can greatly improve program reliability. The formal specifications and abstract programs have been proof by loop invariants, the concrete executable programs are generated with a series of program generating systems which have been rigorously tested and static analysed.
- The simple and accurate loop invariants with function of recursive definition make formal development and proof of non-recursive graph search algorithms possible. The invariants would be very helpful for understanding the roles of every loop variable and nature of algorithms. The innovation of loop invariants developing technique can be used to other complex graph algorithms.

Summarily, the success in this research shows us the promise that PAR method can formally develop complex non-recursive graph search algorithms. We will do the research continuously and apply PAR method and PAR platform to develop more safety critical systems in industrial application.

Acknowledgments. The authors thank Professor David Gries for discussion about loop invariants in his tutorial lessons in FACS2013 hold in Jiangxi Normal University, Jiangxi Province, china.

This work was supported by the National Nature Science Foundation of China (Grant No. 61272075, No. 61462041), the major international cooperative research project (Grant No. 61020106009) from National Natural Science Foundation of China, the Natural Science Foundation of Jiangxi Province.

References

1. Abrial, J.R., Hayes, I.J., Hoare, T.: The Z Notation: A Reference Manual, 2nd edn. Oriel College, Oxford (1998)
2. Corman, T.H., Lieserson, C.E., Rivest, R.L., Stein, C.: Introduction to Algorithms, 2nd edn. MIT Press, Cambridge (2001)
3. Dijkstra, E.W.: A Discipline of Programming. Prentice Hall, New Jersey (1976)
4. Furia, C.A., Meyer, B.: Inferring loop invariants using postconditions. In: Blass, A., Dershowitz, N., Reisig, W. (eds.) Fields of Logic and Computation. LNCS, vol. 6300, pp. 277–300. Springer, Heidelberg (2010)
5. Furia, C.A., Meyer, B.: Inferring loop invariants: analysis, classification, and examples. To appear in ACM Comp. Sur. (2012). http://arxiv.org/abs/1211.4470
6. Gries, D.: The Science of Programming. Springer, New York (1981)
7. Henzinger, T.A., Hottelier, T., Kovács, L., Voronkov, A.: Invariant and type inference for matrices. In: Barthe, G., Hermenegildo, M. (eds.) VMCAI 2010. LNCS, vol. 5944, pp. 163–179. Springer, Heidelberg (2010)
8. Jones, C.B.: Systematic Software Development using VDM, 2nd edn. Prentice Hall, New York (1990)
9. Schneider, S.: B-Method. Palgrave, Basingstoke (2001)
10. Janota, M.: Assertion-based loop invariant generation. In: Proceedings of the 1st International Workshop on Invariant Generation (WING 2007) (2007)
11. Kovács, L., Voronkov, A.: Finding loop invariants for programs over arrays using a theorem prover. In: Chechik, M., Wirsing, M. (eds.) FASE 2009. LNCS, vol. 5503, pp. 470–485. Springer, Heidelberg (2009)

12. Liu, S.: Formal Engineering for Industrial Software Development. Springer, Heidelberg (2004)
13. Nguyen, T., Kapur, D., Weimer, W., Forrest, S.: Using dynamic analysis to discover polynomial and array invariants. In: 34th International Conference on Software Engineering (ICSE 2012), pp. 683–693. IEEE (2012)
14. Rodriguez-Carbonell, E., Kapur, D.: Generating all polynomial invariants in simple loops. J. Symb. Comput. **42**(4), 443–476 (2007)
15. Smith, D.R.: Designware: software development by refinement. In: Proceedings of the Eight International Conference on Category Theory and Computer Science, Edinburgh, September 1999
16. Wah, B.W., et al.: Wiley Encyclopaedias of Computer Science and Engineering. Wiley-Interscience, Hoboken (2008)
17. Wu, G., Xue, J.: PAR method and PAR platform used in development process of software outsourcing. Comput. Mod. 11.042 (2013)
18. Xue, J.: A unified approach for developing efficient algorithmic programs. J. Comput. Sci. Technol. **12**(4), 314–329 (1997)
19. Xue, J.: Two new strategies for developing loop invariants and their applications. J. Comput. Sci. Technol. **8**(2), 147–154 (1993)
20. Xue, J.: Formal derivation of graph algorithmic programs using partition-and-recur. J. Comput. Sci. Technol. **13**(6), 553–561 (1998)
21. Xue, J.: Methods of Programming. Higher Education Press, Beijing (2002)
22. Xue, J.: New concept of loop invariant and its application. In: The 3rd Colloquium on Logic in Engineering Dependable Software. Nanchang, China (2013)
23. Xue, J.: PAR method and its supporting platform. In: Proceedings of AWCVS 2006, Macao, 29–31 October 2006
24. Xue, J., Davis, R.: A simple program whose derivation and proof is also. In: Proceedings of the First IEEE International Conference on Formal Engineering Method (ICFEM 1997), p. 11. IEEE CS Press (1997)
25. Xue, J.: Implementation of model-driven development using PAR. In: Keynote Speech on the 6th International Workshop on Harnessing Theories for Tool Support in Software, Nanchang, China (2013)
26. Zuo, Z., You, Z., Xue, J.: Derivation and formal proof of non-recursive post-order binary tree traversal algorithm. Comput. Eng. Sci. **32**(3) (2013)

LtlNfBa: Making LTL Translation More Practical

Cong Tian, Jun Song, Zhenhua Duan$^{(\boxtimes)}$, and Zhao Duan

ICTT and ISN Lab, Xidian University, Xi'an 710071, People's Republic of China
zhhduan@mail.xidian.edu.cn

Abstract. We improve LTL2BA with a new algorithm for constructing Büchi automata from LTL formulas. The core of the new algorithm is a so called CF-normal form which presents an LTL formula in the current and future form. With the aid of well developed reduction rules in LTL2BA and new rules concerning combination of always and eventually operations, the improved translator named LTLNFBA is competitive with the current leading tools LTL3BA and SPOT.

Keywords: Linear temporal logic · Büchi automata · Generalized Büchi automata · Model checking · SPOT

1 Introduction

In model checking, a Linear Temporal Logic (LTL) [1] formula is often used to describe a desired property of the system to be verified. A model checker transforms the negation of this formula into a Büchi automata, builds the product of that automata with the system model, and then checks emptiness of the product automaton. Thus, constructing Büchi automata from LTL formulas is a significant process in LTL model checking and a scalable supporting tool is important in making LTL model checking practical.

The seminal theory of the transformation from LTL formulas to Büchi automata was worked out in the 80 s and the basic algorithms were developed during the 90 s in the last century. Originally, the transformation [2,3] was on mathematical simplicity, it was not appropriate for explicit model checking, since the automata constructed were always exponential in the size of the formula. On a demand-driven basis, an optimized translation [4] that avoided the exponential blow-up in many cases of practical interest was developed and used in the explicit model checker SPIN. Based on the optimization on the original transformation [5], symbolic model checkers such as NuSMV were developed. Also, a transformation via alternating automata was described in [6] motivated by mathematical simplicity [7]. As model-checking pervading into the industrial applications, efficient and applicable model checking algorithms are appealed.

This research is supported by the NSFC Grant Nos. 61133001, 61322202, 61420106004, 91418201, and 61272117.

S. Liu and Z. Duan (Eds.): SOFL+MSVL 2015, LNCS 9559, pp. 179–194, 2016.
DOI: 10.1007/978-3-319-31220-0_13

Thus, several improvements have been given to get a better translation tool from an LTL formula to an automaton during the last few years [8–13].

Considering the speed of the translators from LTL formulas to Büchi automata, LTL3BA [19] (improved version of LTL2BA [18]) and SPOT [21] are the leading tools. The underlying algorithms adopted by the two tools are different. In LTL3BA and LTL2BA, the translation proceeds in three steps: first, the given LTL formula is translated to a very weak alternating automaton (VWAA); second, the obtained VWAA is translated to a transition-based generalized Büchi automaton (TGBA); and third, the TGBA is transformed into a Büchi automaton (BA). Each of the three automata is simplified during the translation. SPOT translates a given LTL formula to a TGBA first by a tableau method presented in [22], and then a BA. In [20], experimental results on nine parametric formulas show that LTL3BA and SPOT are going nearly head-to-head.

In this paper, we improve LTL2BA with a new algorithm for constructing Büchi automata from LTL formulas. The new algorithm is based on a so called CF-normal form which presents an LTL formula in the current and future form. With the aid of well developed reduction rules and the new rules concerning combination of always and eventually operations, the improved translator named LTLNFBA is competitive with both LTL3BA and SPOT.

The reminder of the paper is organized as follows. The next section briefly presents the preliminaries including LTL and Büchi Automata. In Sect. 3, CF-normal forms are introduced for LTL formulas. Based on it, a transformation from LTL formulas to BA is presented in Sect. 4. Implementation and experimental results are given in Sect. 5.

2   Preliminaries

This section briefly presents LTL and Büchi automata.

2.1   Linear Temporal Logic

We use the terminology from [15]. Given a nonempty finite set AP of atomic propositions, the set of all LTL formulas over AP is the set of formulas built from elements in AP using negation ($\neg$), disjunction ($\vee$), next ($\bigcirc$), and until (U) operators. The syntax is presented as follows:

$$\phi ::= p \mid \neg\phi \mid \phi \vee \phi \mid \bigcirc \phi \mid \phi \, U \, \phi$$

where $p \in$ AP and ϕ is a well-formed LTL formula.

LTL formulas are interpreted in linear-time structures. A linear-time structure over AP is an infinite sequence $x = x(0), x(1), \cdots$ where each $x(i)$ is a valuation AP $\rightarrow \{true, false\}$. Whether or not a formula ϕ holds in a linear-time structure x at a position i, denoted by $x, i \models \phi$ is defined by the following semantics:

- $x, i \models p$ if $x(i)(p) = true$, for $p \in \mathsf{AP}$,
- $x, i \models \neg \phi$ if $x, i \not\models \phi$,
- $x, i \models \varphi \vee \psi$ if $x, i \models \varphi$ or $x, i \models \psi$,
- $x, i \models \bigcirc \varphi$ if $x, i+1 \models \varphi$, and
- $x, i \models \varphi \mathsf{U} \psi$ if there exists $j \geq i$ such that $x, i' \models \varphi$ for $i' \in \{i, i+1, ..., j-1\}$ and $x, j \models \psi$

The abbreviations $true$, $false$, $\wedge$, $\rightarrow$ and $\leftrightarrow$ are defined as usual. In particular, $true \overset{\text{def}}{=} \phi \vee \neg \phi$ and $false \overset{\text{def}}{=} \phi \wedge \neg \phi$ for any formula ϕ. In addition, eventually $(\Diamond \phi)$ and always $(\Box \phi)$ temporal constructs can be derived by $\Diamond \phi \overset{\text{def}}{=} true \mathsf{U} \phi$ and $\Box \phi \overset{\text{def}}{=} \neg \Diamond \neg \phi$, respectively.

It has been proved that any LTL formula can be transformed into a negation normal form where all negations are adjacent to atomic propositions by employing an auxiliary temporal operator $\bar{\mathsf{U}}$ [17]. Negation normal form of LTL is presented in Definition 1.

Definition 1 (Negation Normal Form). *For any $p \in \mathsf{AP}$, the set of LTL formula in negation normal form is defined by:*

$$\phi ::= p \mid \neg p \mid \phi \vee \phi \mid \phi \wedge \phi \mid \bigcirc \phi \mid \phi \mathsf{U} \phi \mid \phi \bar{\mathsf{U}} \phi$$

where $\neg(\phi \mathsf{U} \phi) \equiv (\neg \phi \bar{\mathsf{U}} \neg \phi)$ and $\neg(\phi \bar{\mathsf{U}} \phi) \equiv (\neg \phi \mathsf{U} \neg \phi)$.

The worst-case time complexity of transforming an LTL formula into negation normal form is linear in the length of ϕ, i.e. the number of symbols of ϕ, denoted by $|\phi|$. In what follows, useful logic laws for LTL are presented:

$$
\begin{aligned}
&\mathsf{L}_1 \ \neg \bigcirc \phi \equiv \bigcirc \neg \phi \\
&\mathsf{L}_2 \ \neg \ \phi \ \equiv \ \neg \phi \\
&\mathsf{L}_3 \ \neg \ \phi \ \equiv \ \neg \phi \\
&\mathsf{L}_4 \ \varphi \mathsf{U} \psi \equiv \psi \vee \varphi \wedge \bigcirc(\varphi \mathsf{U} \psi) \\
&\mathsf{L}_5 \ \varphi \bar{\mathsf{U}} \psi \equiv \psi \wedge (\varphi \vee \bigcirc(\varphi \bar{\mathsf{U}} \psi))
\end{aligned}
$$

2.2 Büchi Automata

We briefly present Büchi Automata (BA) and Transition-based Generalized Büchi Automata (TGBA) that will be used later in this paper.

Definition 2. *A Büchi automaton is a tuple $A = (\Sigma, Q, Q_0, \delta, F)$, where Σ is a finite alphabet, Q is a finite set of states, $Q_0 \subseteq Q$ is the set of initial states, $F \in 2^Q$ is a set of finial states, and $\delta : Q \times \Sigma \rightarrow Q$ is a transition function that maps a state and an input letter to a state in Q.*

A run of a BA on an infinite word $w = w_0, w_1, w_2, \cdots$ ($w_i \in \Sigma$ for each $i \geq 0$) is an infinite sequence of states $\rho = q_0, q_1, q_2, \cdots$ such that $q_0 \in Q_0$, and for each q_i, $i \geq 0$, $\delta(q_i, w_i) = q_{i+i}$. A run $\rho = q_0, q_1, q_2, \cdots$ is accepting if there exists some state $q \in F$ such that $q_i = q$ holds for infinitely many $i \in N_0$.

Generalized Büchi automata as well as transition-based generalized Büchi automata are immediate results of the transformations from temporal logic formulas to Büchi automata [17]. Recently, they are also used directly for model checking LTL formulas. We present here a minor modified version of the later and still named transition-based generalized Büchi automata.

Definition 3. *A transition-based generalized Büchi automaton is a tuple* $GA = (\Sigma, Q, q_0, F_v, \delta, G)$, *where* Σ *is a finite alphabet,* Q *is a finite set of states,* $Q_0 \subseteq Q$ *is the set of initial state,* F_v *is a set of final values,* $\delta : Q \times \Sigma \times 2^{F_v} \to Q$ *is a transition relation where each transition is labeled by a letter in* Σ *and a set of final values, and* $G = \{F_{fv} \mid fv \in F_v \text{ and } F_{fv} \text{ is the set of transtions where } fv \text{ occurs}\}$ *is a set of accepting sets.*

A run of a TGBA on an infinite word $w = w_0, w_1, w_2, \cdots$ $(w_i \in \Sigma$ for each $i \geq 0$) is an infinite alternating sequence of states and sets of final values $\rho = q_0, f_0, q_1, f_1, q_2, f_2 \cdots$ such that $q_0 \in Q_0$, for each $q_i \in Q$ and $f_i \in 2^{F_v}$, $i \geq 0$, $\delta(q_i, w_i, f_i) = q_{i+i}$. A run $\rho = q_0, f_0, q_1, f_1, q_2, f_2 \cdots$ is accepting if for each acceptance set $F_{fv} \in G$, $fv \in f_i$ for infinitely many $i \in N_0$.

3   CF-Normal Form for LTL

In what follows, CF-normal form (short for current and future normal form) is defined for LTL formulas. Originally, this normal form was used in [14,16] for dealing with Propositional Projection Temporal Logic (PPTL) formulas and in [23] for achieving stutter invariant LTL formulas. Because of different purpose, the definition in this paper is slightly different from the ones in [14,16,23]. Note that in the rest of the paper, when an LTL formula is mentioned, it indicates one in negation normal form.

Definition 4. *CF-normal form of an LTL formula* ϕ *is defined as follows,*

$$\phi \equiv \bigvee_i \beta_i \wedge \bigcirc \phi_i$$

where β_i *is a typical propositional logic formula (called state formula) in disjunction normal form, and* ϕ_i *an LTL formula without disjunction being the main operator.*

In CF-normal form, each $\beta_i \wedge \bigcirc \phi_i$, is called a literal where β_i indicates the proposition holding at the current state, and ϕ_i denotes that at the next state ϕ_i will hold. Thus, CF-normal form splits an LTL formula into the current and future parts. The following theorem shows that any LTL formula can be transformed into its CF-normal form.

Theorem 1. *Any LTL formula* ϕ *can be transformed to CF-normal form.*

Proof: The proof proceeds by induction on the structures of LTL formulas.
Base: If $\phi \in$ AP, we have $\phi \equiv \phi \wedge \bigcirc true$; if $\phi \equiv \neg\varphi$, $\varphi \in$ AP, we have $\phi \equiv (\neg\varphi) \wedge \bigcirc true$.
Induction: Suppose φ and ψ have been transformed into their CF-normal forms,

$$\varphi \equiv \bigvee_i \alpha_i \wedge \bigcirc \varphi_i$$
$$\psi \equiv \bigvee_j \beta_j \wedge \bigcirc \psi_j$$

we have,

- if $\phi \equiv \bigcirc\varphi$, $\phi \equiv true \wedge \bigcirc\varphi$.
- if $\phi \equiv \varphi \wedge \psi$,

$$\varphi \wedge \psi \equiv (\bigvee_i \alpha_i \wedge \bigcirc \varphi_i) \wedge (\bigvee_j \beta_j \wedge \bigcirc \psi_j)$$
$$\equiv \bigvee_i \bigvee_j (\alpha_i \wedge \beta_j) \wedge \bigcirc (\varphi_i \wedge \psi_j)$$

- if $\phi \equiv \varphi \vee \psi$,

$$\varphi \vee \psi \equiv \bigvee_i \alpha_i \wedge \bigcirc \varphi_i \vee \bigvee_j \beta_j \wedge \bigcirc \psi_j$$

- if $\phi \equiv \varphi \; \mathsf{U} \; \psi$,

$$\varphi \; \mathsf{U} \; \psi \equiv \psi \vee \varphi \wedge \bigcirc(\varphi \; \mathsf{U} \; \psi)$$
$$\equiv \bigvee_j \beta_j \wedge \bigcirc \psi_j \vee \bigvee_i \alpha_i \wedge \bigcirc \varphi_i \wedge \bigcirc(\varphi \; \mathsf{U} \; \psi)$$
$$\equiv \bigvee_j \beta_j \wedge \bigcirc \psi_j \vee \bigvee_i \alpha_i \wedge \bigcirc(\varphi_i \wedge (\varphi \; \mathsf{U} \; \psi))$$

- $\phi \equiv \varphi \; \bar{\mathsf{U}} \; \psi$,

$$\varphi \; \bar{\mathsf{U}} \; \psi \equiv \psi \wedge \big(\varphi \vee \bigcirc(\varphi \; \bar{\mathsf{U}} \; \psi)\big)$$
$$\equiv \psi \wedge \varphi \vee \psi \wedge \bigcirc(\varphi \; \bar{\mathsf{U}} \; \psi)$$
$$\equiv \bigvee_i \bigvee_j (\alpha_i \wedge \beta_j) \wedge \bigcirc(\varphi_i \wedge \psi_j) \vee \bigvee_j \beta_j \wedge \bigcirc \psi_j \wedge \bigcirc(\varphi \; \bar{\mathsf{U}} \; \psi)$$

Therefore, any LTL formula can be equivalently transformed to its CF-normal form.   □

Actually, the above proof provides an approach for transforming LTL formulas to CF-normal forms as illustrated in Algorithm 1. Note that in case

$$NF(P_1) \equiv \bigvee_i \alpha_i \wedge \bigcirc \varphi_i$$
$$NF(P_2) \equiv \bigvee_j \beta_j \wedge \bigcirc \psi_j$$

we have

$$NF\big(NF(P_1) \wedge NF(P_2)\big) \equiv \bigvee_i \bigvee_j (\alpha_i \wedge \beta_j) \wedge \bigcirc(\varphi_i \wedge \psi_j)$$

Note also that $DNF(P)$ denotes the disjunction normal form of a state formula (typical propositional logic formula) P.

Algorithm 1. $NF(P)$

Input: An LTL formula P in negation normal form
Output: CF-normal form of P

1: **case**
2: P is a propositional logic formula: **return** $DNF(P) \wedge \bigcirc true$;
3: P is $P_1 \vee P_2$: **return** $NF(P_1) \vee NF(P_2)$;
4: P is $P_1 \wedge P_2$: **return** $NF\big(NF(P_1) \wedge NF(P_2)\big)$;
5: P is $\bigcirc P_1$: **return** $true \wedge \bigcirc P_1$;
6: P is $P_1 U P_2$: **return** $NF(P_2) \vee NF\big(NF(P_1) \wedge NF(\bigcirc P_2)\big)$;
7: P is $P_1 \bar{U} P_2$: **return** $NF\big(NF(P_1) \wedge NF(P_2)\big) \vee NF\big(NF(P_2) \wedge NF(\bigcirc P_1)\big)$;
8: **end case**

4   From LTL Formulas to Büchi Automata

Now we show how LTL formulas can be equivalently transformed to Büchi automata by utilizing CF-normal form. We first transform an LTL formula to a TGBA.

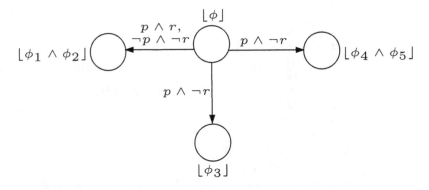

Fig. 1. Constructing graph structure of TGBA

The general idea for constructing TGBA is simple. To construct TGBA of ϕ, initially, a root node $\lfloor \phi \rfloor$ is created. Then we transform ϕ to its CF-normal form. As an example, suppose

$$\phi \equiv (p \wedge r \vee \neg p \wedge \neg r) \wedge \bigcirc(\phi_1 \wedge \phi_2) \vee p \wedge \neg r \wedge \bigcirc \phi_3 \vee p \wedge \neg r \wedge \bigcirc(\phi_4 \wedge \phi_5)$$

As illustrated in Fig. 1, three child nodes: $\lfloor \phi_1 \wedge \phi_2 \rfloor$, $\lfloor \phi_3 \rfloor$, and $\lfloor \phi_4 \wedge \phi_5 \rfloor$ of $\lfloor \phi \rfloor$ are created; and the following relations between the new created nodes and the old ones are produced:

$$\tau(\lfloor \phi \rfloor, p \wedge r) = \lfloor \phi_1 \wedge \phi_2 \rfloor$$
$$\tau(\lfloor \phi \rfloor, p \wedge \neg r) = \lfloor \phi_4 \wedge \phi_5 \rfloor$$
$$\tau(\lfloor \phi \rfloor, \neg p \wedge \neg r) = \lfloor \phi_1 \wedge \phi_2 \rfloor$$
$$\tau(\lfloor \phi \rfloor, p \wedge \neg r) = \lfloor \phi_3 \rfloor$$

To construct the whole graph structure of ϕ's TGBA, the procedure should be applied similarly on the new created nodes repeatedly until no new nodes can be produced.

There is little subtlety that has to be taken into account when translating $\varphi U\phi$: the formula ϕ must occur eventually, i.e. it cannot be postponed infinitely. For convenient, we say ϕ must be fulfilled as usual. However, whether ϕ in $\varphi U\phi$ is fulfilled is not explicitly presented in the graph structure obtained by repeatedly decomposing a formula by CF-normal form. For instance, Fig. 2 with out the set of final values (in red) on the edges shows the graph structure of formula

$$p \wedge \Box \bigcirc p \wedge ((\Box \bigcirc p)Uq)$$

constructed by CF-normal form. For the path $\langle \lfloor p \wedge \Box \bigcirc p \wedge ((\Box \bigcirc p)Uq) \rfloor \rangle^\omega$ that formed by the self-loop on node $\lfloor p \wedge \Box \bigcirc p \wedge ((\Box \bigcirc p)Uq) \rfloor$, q in $(\Box \bigcirc p)Uq$ is not fulfilled. Thus, such a path does not depict a model of formula $p \wedge \Box \bigcirc p \wedge ((\Box \bigcirc p)Uq)$. To precisely present models of a formula, accepting condition of TGBA are further defined on the graph structures obtained by CF-normal form. Roughly speaking, we decorate each edge in the graph with a set of final values indicating the set of until constructs which are involved in the original formula but not contained in the next state (the node this edge is connecting to). Intuitively, if $\varphi U\phi$ is not contained in the next state, $\varphi U\phi$ can be fulfilled at the next state. For the example, in Fig. 2, only one until construct $\Box \bigcirc pUq$ denoted by '1' is involved in the formula. Thus, the set of final values on each edge is:

$$(\lfloor p \wedge \Box \bigcirc p \wedge ((\Box \bigcirc p)Uq) \rfloor, p, \lfloor p \wedge \Box \bigcirc p \wedge ((\Box \bigcirc p)Uq) \rfloor) : \emptyset$$
$$(\lfloor p \wedge \Box \bigcirc p \wedge ((\Box \bigcirc p)Uq) \rfloor, p \wedge q, \lfloor p \wedge \Box \bigcirc p \rfloor) : \{1\}$$
$$(\lfloor p \wedge \Box \bigcirc p \rfloor, p, \lfloor p \wedge \Box \bigcirc p \rfloor) : \{1\}$$

In Fig. 2, the set of final values on each edge is pointed out in red.

The above transformation is formally presented in Algorithm 2. Alphabet Σ is composed of the set of conjunctions of atomic propositions or the negation of atomic propositions (line 1). F_v is the set of until constructs $\varphi U\phi$ appearing in

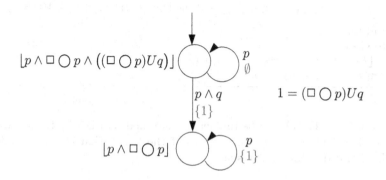

Fig. 2. Example TGBA (Color figure online)

P (line 2). St, a stack for storing the nodes that have not been decomposed, is initialized as empty (line 3). According to the given formula $P \equiv \bigvee_i \phi_i$, Q_0 is initialized by $\{\lfloor \phi_i \rfloor \mid P \equiv \bigvee_i \phi_i\}$ (line 4) and Q is initialized by Q_0 (line 5). For each node in Q, push it in St (lines 6–8). In case stack St is not empty, the top node $\lfloor \varphi \rfloor$ is popped and φ is transformed to CF-normal form $\varphi \equiv \bigvee_i \beta_i \wedge \bigcirc \varphi_i$ by Algorithm NF (lines 9–11). Subsequently, for each φ_i, if $\lfloor \varphi_i \rfloor \notin Q$, add $\lfloor \varphi_i \rfloor$ in Q and St (lines 12–15); produce a new transition $\delta(\lfloor \varphi \rfloor, \beta_i, F_v \setminus \{\psi_j \mid \varphi_i \equiv \bigwedge_j \psi_j$ and the main operator of ψ_j is $\mathsf{U}\}) = \lfloor \varphi_i \rfloor$ (line 16). Finally, in case stack St is empty, return TGBA $GA = (\Sigma, Q, q_0, F_v, \delta, G)$ where $G = \{F_f = \{\delta(q, \sigma, fv) = q' \mid f \in fv\} \mid f \in F_v\}$ (lines 19–20).

Algorithm 2. $TGBA(P)$

Input: An LTL formula P in negation normal form.
Output: TGBA $GA = (\Sigma, Q, q_0, F_v, \delta, G)$ of P.

1: $\Sigma = \{\bigwedge_i \dot{p}_i \mid p_i$ is an atomic proposition appearing in P and $\dot{p}_i$ denotes p_i or $\neg p_i\}$

2: $F_v = \{\varphi \mathsf{U} \phi \mid \varphi \mathsf{U} \phi$ occurs in $P\}$;

3: $St = \emptyset$;   /* Stack St is used to store the nodes that have not been decomposed*/

4: $Q_0 = \{\lfloor \phi_i \rfloor \mid P \equiv \bigvee_i \phi_i\}$;

5: $Q = Q_0$;   /* Initialization */

6: **for each** $\lfloor \varphi \equiv \bigwedge_j \varphi_j \rfloor \in Q$ **do**

7:    $push(St, \lfloor \varphi \rfloor)$;

8: **end for**

9: **while** St is not empty **do**

10:    $\lfloor \varphi \rfloor = top(St)$; $pop(St)$;

11:    transform φ to CF-normal form $\varphi \equiv \bigvee_i \beta_i \wedge \bigcirc \varphi_i$ by Algorithm NF;

12:    **for each** i **do**

13:      **if** $\lfloor \varphi_i \rfloor \notin Q$ **then**

14:        $Q = Q \cup \{\lfloor \varphi_i \rfloor\}$; $push(St, \lfloor \varphi_i \rfloor)$;

15:      **end if**

16:      $\delta(\lfloor \varphi \rfloor, \beta_i, F_v \setminus \{\psi_j \mid \varphi_i \equiv \bigwedge_j \psi_j$ and the main operator of ψ_j is $\mathsf{U}\}) = \lfloor \varphi_i \rfloor$;

17:    **end for**

18: **end while**

19: $G = \{F_f = \{\delta(q, \sigma, fv) = q' \mid f \in fv\} \mid f \in F_v\}$;

20: **return** $GA = (\Sigma, Q, q_0, F_v, \delta, G)$;

The obtained TGBA can be further transformed to a BA by the same algorithm used in LTL3BA [19]. Correctness of the translation is obvious and we omit the detailed proof to save space.

5 Implementation and Experimental Results

We have implemented a translator named LTLNFBA to transform LTL formulas to TGBA (and BA) based on the syntax and simplification rules in LTL2BA [18]. Besides the changed TGBA creating algorithm, we also add new rules to improve the transformation.

5.1 Improvements in Implementation

In addition to implement the new translating algorithm in LTL2BA, we integrate new rules to further improve the translation when dealing with formulas containing combination of always and eventually operators.

Let '1' denote the until construct $\Diamond p \equiv true U p$. To construct TGBA of $\Box \Diamond p$, we first transform $\Box \Diamond p$ to CF-normal form:

$$\Box \Diamond p \equiv \Diamond p \wedge \bigcirc(\Box \Diamond p)$$
$$\equiv \big(p \vee \bigcirc(\Diamond p)\big) \wedge \bigcirc(\Box \Diamond p)$$
$$\equiv p \wedge \bigcirc(\Box \Diamond p) \vee \bigcirc\big(\Diamond p \wedge (\Box \Diamond p)\big)$$

Thus, as illustrated in Fig. 3(1), there are two edges (drawn in blue) departing from the initial state $\lfloor \Box \Diamond p \rfloor$ that connecting to states $\lfloor \Box \Diamond p \rfloor$ and $\lfloor \Diamond p \wedge \Box \Diamond p \rfloor$, respectively. The final value of the one connecting to $\lfloor \Box \Diamond p \rfloor$ is $\{1\}$ and the other empty. Next, $\Diamond p \wedge \Box \Diamond p$ is transformed to CF-normal form:

$$\Diamond p \wedge \Box \Diamond p \equiv p \wedge \bigcirc \Box \Diamond p \vee \bigcirc(\Diamond p \wedge \Box \Diamond p)$$

Accordingly, two edges (drawn in red) departing from state $\lfloor \Diamond p \wedge \Box \Diamond p \rfloor$ that connecting to states $\lfloor \Box \Diamond p \rfloor$ and $\lfloor \Diamond p \wedge \Box \Diamond p \rfloor$ are created, respectively. The final value of the one connecting to $\lfloor \Box \Diamond p \rfloor$ is $\{1\}$ and the other empty. Consequently, by the simplification rule in LTL2BA:

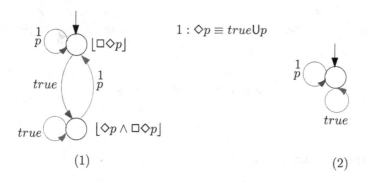

$$1 : \Diamond p \equiv true U p$$

(1)   (2)

Fig. 3. TGBA of $\Box \Diamond p$ (Color figure online)

Two different states s_1 and s_2 in a TGBA can be merged if for each transition (s_1, δ, fv, s) starting from s_1, there exist a transition (s_2, δ, fv, s) departing from s_2, and vice versa.

The TGBA in Fig. 3(1) is further simplified as shown in Fig. 3(2).

Consider CF-normal form of formula $\square\lozenge p$ again:

$$\square\lozenge p \equiv p \wedge \bigcirc(\square\lozenge p) \vee \bigcirc(\lozenge p \wedge (\square\lozenge p))$$

By the semantics of LTL formulas, $\square\lozenge p$ is equivalent to $\lozenge p \wedge (\square\lozenge p)$ in fact. Thus, we can directly produce TGBA of $\square\lozenge p$ in Fig. 3(2) without producing the TGBA in Fig. 3(1) first.

Further, for a formula in forms of $\square\lozenge p \wedge Q$ (p is a state formula and Q an arbitrary LTL formula) e.g. $\square\lozenge p \wedge \lozenge q$, by CF-normal form, we can obtain the TGBA as shown in Fig. 4(1) which can be simplified as the TGBA in Fig. 4(2). This simplification procedure can also be avoided by considering: $\square\lozenge p \equiv true \wedge \bigcirc\square\lozenge p$. Accordingly, when a formula in form of $\square\lozenge p \wedge Q$ occurs, we first equivalently represent $\square\lozenge p \wedge Q$ as $true \wedge (\square\lozenge p) \wedge Q$, and then construct TGBA via CF-normal forms. For instance, we represent $\square\lozenge p \wedge \lozenge q$ as $true \wedge \bigcirc(\square\lozenge p) \wedge \lozenge q$ first. Since

$$\square\lozenge p \wedge \lozenge q \equiv true \wedge \bigcirc(\square\lozenge p) \wedge \lozenge q$$
$$\equiv true \wedge \bigcirc(\square\lozenge p) \wedge (q \vee \bigcirc\lozenge q)$$
$$\equiv q \wedge \bigcirc(\square\lozenge p) \vee true \wedge \bigcirc((\square\lozenge p) \wedge \lozenge q)$$

TGBA shown in Fig. 4(2) can be constructed directly.

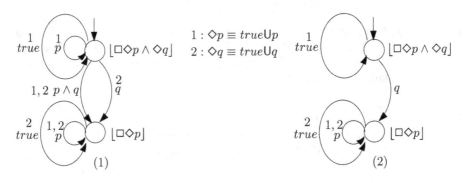

Fig. 4. TGBA of $\square\lozenge p \wedge \lozenge q$

5.2 Experimental Results

Preliminary version of LTLNFBA without the additional improvement discussed above outperforms LTL2BA but pales beside LTL3BA. By further implementing the additional rules for dealing with formulas in the forms of $\square\lozenge P$ and $\square\lozenge P \wedge Q$, where P is a state formula and Q an arbitrary LTL formula, LTLNFBA is competitive with both LTL3BA and SPOT. The source code of LTLNFBA as well as formulas involved in experiments presented in this paper can be found following http://web.xidian.edu.cn/ctian/en/ltlnfba.html. All experiments were done on a PC with one processor Intel(R) Core(TM) i7 CPU 550 @ 3.20 GHz, 3.24 GB RAM, and Microsoft Windows Xp Professional Version 2002 Service Pack 3 with VMWare workstation 9 (one core and 2 GB RAM)/32bit version of Ubuntu 12.04 LTS (gcc 4.6.3).

In the following, we compare the execution time (second) of LTLNFBA, LTL3BA (v1.0.2)[1], and SPOT (v1.2.1)[2] on nine parametric formulas from [18,19]. Note that only the time consumed by the transformation from LTL formulas to TGBA is considered since LTLNFBA and LTL3BA (v1.0.2) utilized the same technique for the transformation from TGBA to BA. We gradually increase the parameter of the formulas until a translator fails to finish the translation in 24 h limit or runs out of memory. The following are the nine parametric formulas.

$$\theta(n) = \neg\big((\Box\Diamond p_1 \wedge \cdots \wedge \Box\Diamond p_n) \to \Box(q \to \Diamond r)\big)$$
$$C_2(n) = \bigwedge_{i=1}^{n} \Box\Diamond p_i$$
$$U_2(n) = p_1 \mathsf{U}\big(p_2\mathsf{U}(\cdots p_{n-1}\mathsf{U}p_n)\cdots\big)$$
$$U_1(n) = \big(\cdots(p_1\mathsf{U}p_2)\mathsf{U}\cdots\big)\mathsf{U}p_n$$
$$Q(n) = \bigwedge_{i=1}^{n} (\Diamond p_i \vee \Box p_{i+1})$$
$$C_1(n) = \bigvee_{i=1}^{n} (\Box\Diamond p_i)$$
$$S(n) = \bigwedge_{i=1}^{n} \Box p_i$$

$$R(n) = \bigwedge_{i=1}^{n} (\Box\Diamond p_i \vee \Diamond\Box p_{i+1})$$
$$E(n) = \bigwedge_{i=1}^{n} \Diamond p_i$$

Experimental results on the above nine formulas are illustrated in Figs. 5 and 6 where the horizontal axis presents the concrete value of n and the vertical axis shows the time (second) consumed for constructing the TGBA. It shows that for formulas $\theta(n)$, $U_2(n)$, $S(n)$, and $C_2(n)$, LTLNFBA outperforms both LTL3BA and SPOT obviously. For the formula $C_1(n)$, LTLNFBA works better than both LTL3BA and SPOT in case $n > 2000$. For the two formulas $E(n)$ and $R(n)$ LTLNFBA outperforms SPOT and nearly goes hand in hand with LTL3BA. Finally, for the last two formulas $U_1(n)$ and $Q(n)$, LTLNFBA lists in the middle.

We also compare the size of the TGBA produced by the three tools on the nine parametric formulas. For the 7 formulas $\theta(n)$, $U_1(N)$, $U_2(N)$, $S(n)$, $E(n)$, $C_1(n)$, and $C_2(n)$, the numbers of the states and transitions of the TGBAs produced by the three tools are completely the same.

---

[1] sourceforge.net/projects/ltl3ba/files/ltl3ba/.
[2] spot.lip6.fr/wiki.

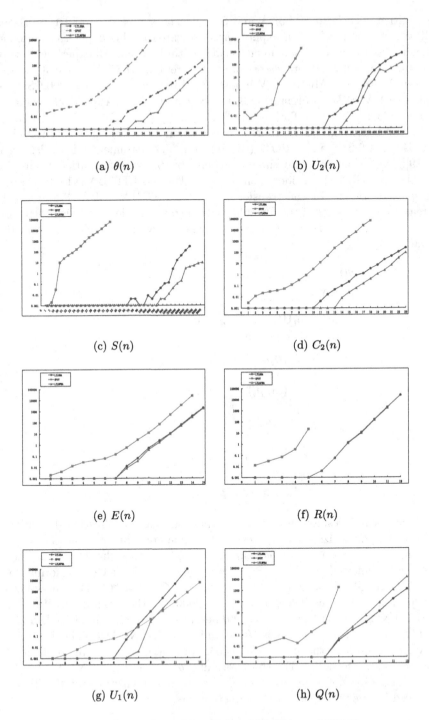

(a) $\theta(n)$

(b) $U_2(n)$

(c) $S(n)$

(d) $C_2(n)$

(e) $E(n)$

(f) $R(n)$

(g) $U_1(n)$

(h) $Q(n)$

Fig. 5. Comparison of LtlNfBA, LTL3BA, and SPOT

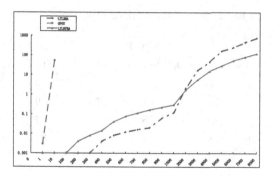

Fig. 6. Comparison of LTLNFBA, LTL3BA, and SPOT on $C_1(n)$

Table 1 presents the size of the TGBAs of formula $R(n)$ produced by the three tools. It shows that SPOT produces smaller TGBAs than both LTL3BA and LTLNFBA, and the TGBAs created by LTL3BA and LTLNFBA are completely the same in size. Recall that in Fig. 5, on this formula, SPOT toke more time than both LTL3BA and LTLNFBA, and the time consumed by LTL3BA and LTLNFBA is nearly the same.

Table 1. Size of the TGBAs of formula $R(n)$

Parameter	LTL3BA		SPOT		LTLNFBA	
n	States	Transitions	States	Transitions	States	Transitions
1	3	5	3	6	3	5
2	9	21	4	11	9	21
3	27	83	6	23	27	83
4	81	321	9	50	81	321

Table 2 presents the size of the TGBAs of formula $Q(n)$ produced by the three tools. It illustrates that LTLNFBA lists in the middle, and SPOT the best. Also, as shown in Fig. 5, on this formula, LTL3BA toke the least time and LTLNFBA lists in the middle.

In addition, for the following four parametric formulas presented in [24]:

$$\alpha(n) = \Diamond(p \wedge \bigcirc(p \wedge \bigcirc(p \wedge \cdots))) \wedge \Diamond(q \wedge \bigcirc(q \wedge \bigcirc(q \wedge \cdots)))$$
$$(n \text{ occurences of } p \text{ and } q)$$
$$\beta(n) = \Diamond(p_1 \wedge \Diamond(p_2 \wedge \Diamond(\cdots \Diamond p_n)) \wedge \Diamond(q_1 \wedge \Diamond(q_2 \wedge \Diamond(\cdots \Diamond q_n))$$
$$\varphi(n) = \Box\Diamond p_1 \wedge \Box\Diamond p_2 \wedge \cdots \wedge \Box\Diamond p_n$$
$$\psi(n) = \Diamond\Box p_1 \vee \Diamond\Box p_2 \vee \cdots \vee \Diamond\Box p_n$$

Table 2. Size of the TGBAs of formula $Q(n)$

Parameter	LTL3BA		SPOT		LtlNfBa	
n	States	Transitions	States	Transitions	States	Transitions
1	3	4	3	6	3	4
2	9	15	8	27	9	16
3	23	50	18	93	27	64
4	59	168	42	330	81	256
5	144	576	100	1209	243	1024

Table 3. Size of the TGBAs produced by LTL3BA and LtlNfBa on formulas $\alpha(n)$, $\beta(n)$, $\varphi(n)$, and $\psi(n)$

Parameter	$\alpha(n)$		$\beta(n)$		$\varphi(n)$		$\psi(n)$	
n	LTL3BA	LtlNfBa	LTL3BA	LtlNfBa	LTL3BA	LtlNfBa	LTL3BA	LtlNfBa
1	4/9	4/9	4/9	4/9	1/2	1/2	2/3	2/3
2	9/16	9/16	9/36	9/36	1/4	1/4	3/5	3/5
3	16/25	16/25	16/100	16/100	01/8	1/8	4/7	4/7
4	25/36	25/36	25/225	25/225	1/16	1/16	5/9	5/9
...								
7	64/81	64/81	64/1296	64/1296	1/128	1/128	8/15	8/15
...								
10	121/144	121/144	121/4356	121/4356	1/1024	1/1024	12/21	12/21

it is reported in [20] that both LTL3BA and SPOT can compute the automata (TGBA) in minimal form and LTL3BA is 8 times faster than SPOT (v0.7.1).

We run both LTL3BA and LtlNfBa on the four parametric formulas. As shown in Table 3, the size of the TGBAs produced by LTL3BA and LtlNfBa are completely the same and minimal meanwhile. Note that in Table 3, the size of each produced TGBA is expressed in the form of *Amount of States/Amount of Transitions*.

Further, with n ranging from 1 to 20, experimental results in Table 4 show that LtlNfBa runs even faster than LTL3BA. Precisely, on $\alpha(20)$, LTL3BA consumes 0.012000 s whereas LtlNfBa takes nearly no time. The two tools go nearly head-to-head on $\beta(n)$. On $\varphi(n)$, LtlNfBa clealy outperforms LTL3BA: while LTL3BA takes 25.585661 s on $\varphi(20)$, LtlNfBa consumes only 0.612038 s on the same formula. On the last parametric formula $\psi(n)$, both the two tools return results immediately for all $n \leq 20$.

Table 4. Running time of LTL3BA and LTLNFBA on formulas $\alpha(n)$ $\beta(n)$, $\varphi(n)$, and $\psi(n)$

Parameter	$\alpha(n)$		$\beta(n)$		$\varphi(n)$		$\psi(n)$	
n	LTL3BA	LTLNFBA	LTL3BA	LTLNFBA	LTL3BA	LTLNFBA	LTL3BA	LTLNFBA
1	0.000000	0.000000	0.000000	0.000000	0.000000	0.000000	0.000000	0.000000
2	0.000000	0.000000	0.000000	0.000000	0.000000	0.000000	0.000000	0.000000
3	0.000000	0.000000	0.000000	0.000000	0.000000	0.000000	0.000000	0.000000
4	0.000000	0.000000	0.000000	0.000000	0.000000	0.000000	0.000000	0.000000
5	0.000000	0.000000	0.000000	0.000000	0.000000	0.000000	0.000000	0.000000
6	0.000000	0.000000	0.000000	0.000000	0.000000	0.000000	0.000000	0.000000
7	0.000000	0.000000	0.004000	0.004000	0.000000	0.000000	0.000000	0.000000
8	0.000000	0.000000	0.016001	0.008000	0.004000	0.000000	0.000000	0.000000
9	0.000000	0.000000	0.020001	0.012000	0.004000	0.000000	0.000000	0.000000
10	0.000000	0.000000	0.028001	0.024001	0.008000	0.000000	0.000000	0.000000
11	0.000000	0.000000	0.044003	0.036002	0.016001	0.000000	0.000000	0.000000
12	0.000000	0.000000	0.052003	0.064005	0.048003	0.000000	0.000000	0.000000
13	0.000000	0.000000	0.076005	0.068005	0.060004	0.000000	0.000000	0.000000
14	0.000000	0.000000	0.132008	0.100006	0.132008	0.008000	0.000000	0.000000
15	0.004000	0.000000	0.148009	0.144009	0.224014	0.024001	0.000000	0.000000
16	0.004000	0.000000	0.192012	0.204012	0.536033	0.056003	0.000000	0.000000
17	0.004000	0.000000	0.292018	0.268016	1.280081	0.088005	0.000000	0.000000
18	0.004000	0.000000	0.348022	0.352022	3.144197	0.164010	0.000000	0.000000
19	0.008000	0.000000	0.492030	0.468029	10.036627	0.360022	0.000000	0.000000
20	0.012000	0.000000	0.648040	0.620038	26.585661	0.612038	0.000000	0.000000

6   Conclusions

A simple algorithm for constructing Büchi automata from LTL formulas is presented in this paper. With the new algorithm, TGBA of a formula is gradually produced by decomposing the formula to CF-normal form that represents the formula in the current and future forms. We have implemented a translator named LTLNFBA for constructing Büchi automata from LTL formulas by replacing the translating algorithm from LTL formulas to TGBA used in LTL2BA with the new proposed one. Experimental results show that LTLNFBA is competitive with the current leading tools LTL3BA and SPOT.

References

1. Pnueli, A.: The temporal logic of programs. In: Proceedings of the 18th IEEE Symposium on Foundation of Computer Science, pp. 46–57 (1977)
2. Vardi, M.Y., Wolper, P.: Reasoning about infinite computations. Inf. Comput. **115**(1), 1–37 (1994)
3. Wolper, P., Vardi, M.Y., Sistla, A.P.: Reasoning about infinite computation paths. In: Proceedings of the 24th IEEE Symposium on Foundations of Computer Science, Tucson, pp. 185–194 (1983)

4. Gerth, R., Peled, D., Vardi, M.Y., Wolper, P.: Simple on-the-fly automatic verification of linear temporal logic. In: Dembiski, P., Sredniawa, M. (eds.) Protocol Specification, Testing, and Verification, pp. 3–18. Chapman & Hall, London (1995)
5. Clarke, E.M., Grumberg, O., Hamaguchi, K.: Another look at LTL model checking. In: Dill, D.L. (ed.) CAV 1994. LNCS, vol. 818, pp. 415–427. Springer, Heidelberg (1994)
6. Vardi, M.Y.: Nontraditional applications of automata theory. In: Hagiya, M., Mitchell, J.C. (eds.) TACS 1994. LNCS, vol. 789, pp. 575–597. Springer, Heidelberg (1994)
7. Vardi, M.Y.: Automata-theoretic model checking revisited. In: Cook, B., Podelski, A. (eds.) VMCAI 2007. LNCS, vol. 4349, pp. 137–150. Springer, Heidelberg (2007)
8. Daniele, M., Giunchiglia, F., Vardi, M.Y.: Improved automata generation for linear temporal logic. In: Halbwachs, N., Peled, D.A. (eds.) CAV 1999. LNCS, vol. 1633, pp. 249–260. Springer, Heidelberg (1999)
9. Etessami, K., Holzmann, G.J.: Optimizing Büchi automata. In: Palamidessi, C. (ed.) CONCUR 2000. LNCS, vol. 1877, pp. 153–167. Springer, Heidelberg (2000)
10. Fritz, C.: Constructing Büchi automata from linear temporal logic using simulation relations for alternating Büchi automata. In: Ibarra, O.H., Dang, Z. (eds.) CIAA 2003. LNCS, vol. 2759, pp. 35–48. Springer, Heidelberg (2003)
11. Fritz, C.: Concepts of automata construction from LTL. In: Sutcliffe, G., Voronkov, A. (eds.) LPAR 2005. LNCS (LNAI), vol. 3835, pp. 728–742. Springer, Heidelberg (2005)
12. Somenzi, F., Bloem, R.: Efficient Büchi automata from LTL formulae. In: Emerson, E.A., Sistla, A.P. (eds.) CAV 2000. LNCS, vol. 1855, pp. 248–263. Springer, Heidelberg (2000)
13. Thirioux, X.: Simple and efficient translation from LTL formulas to Büchi automata. Electr. Notes Theor. Comput. Sci. **66**(2), 145–159 (2002)
14. Duan, Z., Tian, C., Zhang, L.: A decision procedure for propositional projection temporal logic with infinite models. Acta Informatica **45**(1), 43–78 (2008)
15. Emerson, A.E.: Temporal and modal logic. In: van Leeuwen, J. (ed.) Handbook of Theoretical Computer Science. Formal Methods and Semantics, vol. B, pp. 995–1072 (1990)
16. Duan, Z.: An extended interval temporal logic and a framing technique for temporal logic programming. Ph.D. thesis, University of Newcastle Upon Tyne, May 1996
17. Katoen, J.-P.: Concepts, Algorithms, and Tools for Model Checking. Lecture Notes of the Course Mechanised Validation of Parrel Systems (1999)
18. Gastin, P., Oddoux, D.: Fast LTL to Büchi Automata Translation. In CAV , LNCS 2102, pp. 53–65, Springer-Verlag, 2001. (2001)
19. Babiak, T., Křetínský, M., Řehák, V., Strejček, J.: LTL to Büchi automata translation: fast and more deterministic. In: Flanagan, C., König, B. (eds.) TACAS 2012. LNCS, vol. 7214, pp. 95–109. Springer, Heidelberg (2012)
20. Babiak, T., Kretinsky, M., Rehak, V., Strejcek, J.: LTL to Büchi Automata Translation: Fast and More Deterministic. CoRR, abs/1201.0682 (2012)
21. Duret-Lutz, A., Poitrenaud, D.: SPOT: an extensible model checking library using transition-based generalized Büchi automata. In: MASCOTS 2004, pp. 76–83 (2004)
22. Couvreur, J.-M.: On-the-fly verification of linear temporal logic. In: Wing, J.M., Woodcock, J. (eds.) FM 1999. LNCS, vol. 1708, p. 253. Springer, Heidelberg (1999)
23. Tian, C., Duan, Z.: A note on stutter-invariant PLTL. Inf. Process. Lett. **109**(13), 663–667 (2009)
24. Cichon, J., Czubak, A., Jasinski, A.: Minimal Büchi automata for certain classes of LTL formulas. In: DEPCOS-RELCOMEX 2009, pp. 17–24. IEEE (2009)

PPTL_SPIN: A SPIN Based Model Checker for Propositional Projection Temporal Logic

Xiaoming Zhang, Zhenhua Duan$^{(\boxtimes)}$, and Cong Tian$^{(\boxtimes)}$

ICTT and ISN Laboratory, Xidian University,
Xi'an 710071, People's Republic of China
zhenhua_duan@126.com

Abstract. This paper introduce a tool named PPTL_Spin which supports the verification of temporal properties specified with Propositional Projection Temporal Logic (PPTL). To this end, a translator from PPTL formulas to Büchi automata (PPTL2BA) is implemented and integrated in SPIN. We evaluate efficiency of the translator by parameter formulas and show how PPTL_SPIN works with a case study.

Keywords: Propositional projection temporal logic · Büchi automata · Model checking · SPIN · Verification

1 Introduction

SPIN [7,10] is a famous model checker which uses PROMELA to model the system to be verified and adopts Linear Temporal Logic (LTL) [12] formula to specify the desired property. To check whether the system can satisfy the desired property, both the system model and negation of the LTL formula are transformed to Büchi automata. Then product of the two automata are constructed and emptiness of the product automaton is checked. Subsequently, if no words can be accepted by the product automaton, we can say that the desired property is valid on the system model. Otherwise, each accepting run indicates a counterexample where the system model violates the desired property. However, the expressive power of LTL is limited which is known as star-free regular. Thus, there are a number of regular properties that cannot be verified by SPIN directly.

Propositional Projection Temporal Logic (PPTL) [3,5], whose expressive power is equal to full regular expressions [6], subsumes LTL. It is a useful logic in the specification and verification of concurrent systems. In the past years, an Labeled Normal Form Graph (LNFG) based decision procedure is given for PPTL formulae [1] which is improved in [2,8]. The decision algorithm is actually to find out a model in the LNFG of a formula. Given a PPTL formula P, to check whether or not it is satisfiable, we first try to construct its LNFG, then look for a model in the LNFG of the formula. If a model is found out for P in its LNFG, P is satisfiable, otherwise, it is unsatisfiable.

This research is supported by the NSFC Grant Nos. 61133001, 61322202, 61420106004, 91418201, and 61272117.

S. Liu and Z. Duan (Eds.): SOFL+MSVL 2015, LNCS 9559, pp. 195–205, 2016.
DOI: 10.1007/978-3-319-31220-0_14

Considering the full regular expressive power of PPTL, we are motivated to enhance SPIN with the ability of verifying properties specified with PPTL [4,11]. In this way, full regular properties can be verified by SPIN. This paper introduces the implemented tool named PPTL_Spin which strengthens SPIN with PPTL specifications. To achieve the goal, a translator from PPTL formulas to Büchi automata (PPTL2BA) is implemented and integrated in SPIN. We evaluate efficiency of the translator by parameter formulas and show how PPTL_SPIN works with a case study.

The rest of this paper is organized as follows. In the next section, preliminaries including PPTL, Büchi automata, and SPIN are briefly introduced. Subsequently, Sect. 3 shows the translating tool PPTL2BA and the relative efficiency evaluation results. Section 4 studies how SPIN is enhanced with PPTL and the case study. Finally, in Sect. 5, conclusion and future work are discussed.

2   Preliminaries

This section briefly introduces preliminaries including PPTL, Büchi automata, and SPIN.

2.1   Propositional Projection Temporal Logic

Syntax. Let $Prop$ be a countable set of atomic propositions. The formula P of PPTL is given by the following grammar:

$$P:: = p| \bigcirc P|\neg P|P_1 \vee P_2|(P_1, ..., P_m) \ prj \ P$$

where $p \in Prop$, $P_1, ..., P_m$, P are well-formed PPTL formulas.

Semantics. We define a state s over $Prop$ to be a mapping from $Prop$ to $B = \{true, false\}$, $s : Prop \rightarrow B$. We will use $s[p]$ to denote the valuation of p at state s. An interval σ is a non-empty sequence of states, which can be finite or infinite. The length, $|\sigma|$, of σ is ω if σ is infinite, and the number of states minus 1 if σ is finite. We consider the set N_0 of non-negative integers and ω, $N_\omega = N_0 \cup \{\omega\}$, and extend the comparison operators, $=, <, \leq$, to N_ω by considering $\omega = \omega$, and for all $i \in N_0$, $i < \omega$. Moreover, we define $\preceq$ as $\leq -\{(\omega, \omega)\}$. To simplify definitions, we will denote σ as $< s_0, ..., s_{|\sigma|} >$, where $s_{|\sigma|}$ is undefined if σ is infinite. With such a notation, $\sigma_{(i...j)}(0 \leq i \preceq j \leq |\sigma|)$ denotes the sub-interval $< s_i, ..., s_j >$. The concatenation of a finite σ with another interval (or empty string) σ' is denoted by $\sigma \cdot \sigma'$.

Let $\sigma =< s_0, s_1, ..., s_{|\sigma|} >$ be an interval and $r_1, ..., r_h$ be integers $(h \geq 1)$ such that $0 \leq r_1 \leq r_2 \leq ... \leq r_h \leq |\sigma|$. The *projection* of σ onto $r_1, ..., r_h$ is the interval

$$\sigma \downarrow (r_1, ..., r_h) =< s_{t_1}, s_{t_2}, ..., s_{t_l} >$$

where $t_1, ..., t_l$ are obtained from $r_1, ..., r_h$ by deleting all duplicates. For instance,

$$< s_0, s_1, s_2, s_3, s_4 >\downarrow (0, 0, 2, 2, 2, 3) =< s_0, s_2, s_3 >$$

An interpretation is a quadruple $\mathcal{I} = (\sigma, i, k, j)$, where σ is an interval, i, k integers, and j an integer or ω such that $i \leq k \preceq j \leq |\sigma|$. We use the notation $(\sigma, i, k, j) \models P$ to mean that some formula P is interpreted and satisfied over the subinterval $< s_i, ..., s_j >$ of σ with the current state being s_k. The satisfaction relation ($\models$) is inductively defined as follows:

$I - prop$ $\mathcal{I} \models p$ iff $s_k[p] = true$, for an atomic proposition p.
$I - not$ $\;\;\mathcal{I} \models \neg P$ iff $\mathcal{I} \nvDash P$.
$I - or$ $\;\;\;\mathcal{I} \models P \vee Q$ iff $\mathcal{I} \models P$ or $\mathcal{I} \models Q$.
$I - next$ $\mathcal{I} \models \bigcirc P$ iff $k < j$ and $(\sigma, i, k+1, j) \models P$.
$I - prj$ $\;\;\mathcal{I} \models (P_1, ..., P_m)$ prj Q iff there exist integers $k = r_0 \leq r_1 \leq ... \leq$
$\quad\quad\quad\quad r_m \preceq j$ such that $(\sigma, i, r_0, r_1) \models P_1, (\sigma, r_{l-1}, r_{l-1}, r_l) \models P_l$
$\quad\quad\quad\quad (1 < l \leq m)$ and $(\sigma', 0, 0, |\sigma'|) \models Q$ for one of the following σ' :
$\quad\quad\quad\quad (a) r_m < j$ and $\sigma' = \sigma \downarrow (r_0, ..., r_m) \cdot \sigma_{(r_m+1..j)}$,
$\quad\quad\quad\quad (b) r_m = j$ and $\sigma' = \sigma \downarrow (r_0, ..., r_h)$ for some $0 \leq h \leq m$.

2.2 Büchi Automata

Büchi automata (BA) play a special role in model checking PPTL formulas. To check whether a system satisfies the given property P, we transform $\neg P$ to Labeled Normal Form Graph (LNFG) and then BA via Generalized Büchi Automata (GBA) [9]. Here we give the definitions of GBA and BA.

Definition 1. A generalized Büchi automaton is a five-tuple $G_A = (Q, \Sigma, \Delta, I, T)$ where:

- Q is a finite, non-empty set of states;
- Σ a finite, non-empty alphabet;
- $\Delta \subseteq Q \times \Sigma \times Q$ the transition relation;
- $I \subseteq Q$ a non-empty set of initial states;
- $T = \{T_1, ..., T_r\}$, where $T_j \subseteq \Delta$, the accepting transitions.

An infinite word u over Σ is an infinite sequence $u = u_0 u_1, ...$ where $u_i \in \Sigma$ for each $i \geq 0$. A run ρ of G_A on a word $u = u_0 u_1...$ is an infinite sequence of states in Q, $q_0 q_1...$, such that $q_0 \in I$ and $(q_i, u_i, q_{i+1}) \in \Delta$ holds for all $i \geq 0$. The run ρ is acceptable iff for each $j(1 \leq j \leq r)$, it uses infinitely many transitions in T_j.

Definition 2. A Büchi automaton is a five-tuple $B = (Q, \Sigma, \Delta, I, F)$ where:

- Q is a finite, non-empty set of states;
- Σ a finite, non-empty alphabet;
- $\Delta \subseteq Q \times \Sigma \times Q$ a transition relation;
- $I \subseteq Q$ a non-empty set of initial states;
- $F \subseteq Q$ the set of accepting states.

An infinite word u' over Σ is an infinite sequence $u' = u'_0 u'_1....$. A run ρ' of B on a word $u' = u'_0 u'_1...$ is an infinite sequence of states in Q, $q'_0 q'_1...$, such that $q'_0 \in I$ and $(q'_i, u'_i, q'_{i+1}) \in \Delta$ holds for all $i \in N_0$. The run ρ' is accepting if there exists infinitely many states in F.

2.3 SPIN

SPIN is a general tool for verifying the correctness of distributed software models in a rigorous and mostly automated fashion. SPIN offers a large number of options to speed up the model-checking process and save memory, such as partial order reduction, state compression, bitstate hashing and weak fairness enforcement. In SPIN, the model of the system sys described by PROMELA is transformed into a Büchi automaton A_{sys} in which all states are accepting and the property to be checked is specified in PLTL formula yielding ϕ, negated, and subsequently transformed into a second Büchi automaton $A_{\neg\phi}$; further the product of these two automata represents all possible computations that violate ϕ is constructed; finally, by checking the emptiness of this automaton, it is thus determined whether ϕ is satisfied by the system model sys or not.

3 Transforming PPTL Formulas to Büchi Automata

In this section, we introduce the tool PPTL2BA for transforming PPTL formulas to BA. PPTL2BA is written in C++. For the convenience of demonstration and usage, we use MFC to develop interface of the tool.

3.1 Structure

The structure of the PPTL2BA is depicted in Fig. 1. PPTL2BA takes a PPTL formula given by users. First the formula is parsed and the syntactic tree is built. Then the tool constructs LNFG of the formula and give satisfiability of the input PPTL formula. Finally, based on the LNFG, it gains the equivalent GBA and BA. The tool consists of three modules: parser, constructing LNFG, and transforming LNFG to BA module. In the parser module, atomic propositions and operators contained in the input PPTL formula are identified with the help of Flex and Bison and the syntax tree is generated eventually.

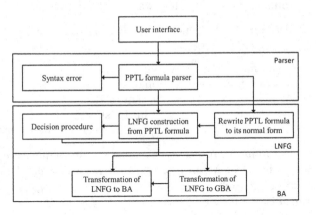

Fig. 1. The structure of the transformation tool

Constructing LNFG Module. This module contains three functions: (1) Rewriting a PPTL formula to normal form; (2) Constructing LNFG; and (3) Deciding whether or not the input PPTL formula is satisfiable. A PPTL formula P is in normal form if P has been rewritten as $P \equiv (P_e \wedge \varepsilon) \vee \bigvee_{i=1}^{r}(P_i \wedge \bigcirc(P_i'))$

where P_e and P_i are state formulae. The algorithms of rewriting PPTL formulae to normal forms are given in [1].

Based on normal form of PPTL formula, LNFG of the formula can be constructed which not only contains nodes and edges but also identifies some nodes with fin labels. Specifically, if the node is a chop formula, fin label is added on the node to denote that the chop formula cannot be repeated infinitely many times. In an LNFG, the initial nodes are denoted by a double circle, ε node by a black dot, and each of other nodes by a single circle. Each edge is denoted by a directed arc connecting two nodes. When LNFG is constructed for a formula P, we can further check the satisfiability of P. If a model is found out for P in its LNFG, P is satisfiable, otherwise, it is unsatisfiable.

Transforming LNFG to BA Module. Two transformations are included in this module: (1) transformation from LNFG to GBA; and (2) transformation from LNFG to BA. As a matter of fact, we can transform an LNFG to a BA directly if the LNFG does not contain any fin labels. However, if the LNFG contains fin labels, we cannot transform it to a BA directly because of the difference between LNFG and BA in accepting conditions. In this case, we need to transform the LNFG to a GBA first, and then to a BA eventually.

The BA output by the transformation tool are in the following form: the initial nodes are denoted by a double circle, ε node by a black dot, and each of other nodes by a single circle. Each edge is denoted by a directed arc connecting two nodes. Also, the accepting nodes are pointed out.

3.2 Example

In the following, we illustrate the BA constructed by PPTL2BA with an example.

Example 1 *Constructing BA of $P \equiv (p \wedge \bigcirc true; q) \wedge \square \bigcirc (p; q)$ by PPTL2BA.*

The BA of formula P constructed by PPTL2BA is shown in Fig. 2. Totally, 7 nodes and 13 edges are contained in the generated BA. Among them, two nodes are accepting.

3.3 Evaluation Results

This section evaluates the efficiency of PPTL2BA. We use PPTL2BA to translate a group of formulas to BA and compare the time consumed as well as sizes of the resulting BA with LTL2BA [9] which is a widely used tool for translating LTL to BA. Note that some PPTL formulas are also LTL formulas. For these formulas, we directly use both PPTL2BA and LTL2BA to translate them to BA. While some formulas are not LTL formulas, we slightly revise them as LTL formulas by replacing chop operators with until operators.

The first group of formulas are $\theta_n = \neg((GF p_1 \wedge ... \wedge GF p_n) \rightarrow G(q \rightarrow Fr))$ where n is a positive integer. Table 1 shows the number of states and transitions

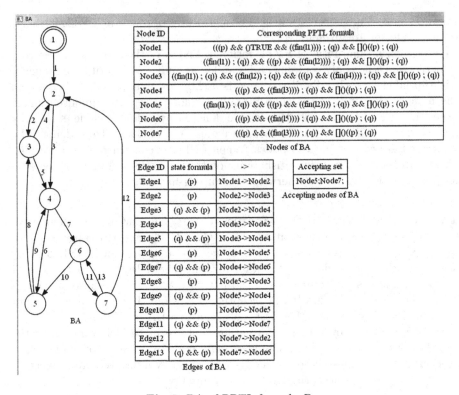

Fig. 2. BA of PPTL formula P

generated by the two tools for θ_n. From Table 1 we can see that the size of BA produced by PPTL2BA are smaller than the ones constructed by LTL2BA.

Another group of formulas are $\varphi'_n = (...(p_1; p_2); ...); p_n$. By replacing chop operators with until operator which can be dealt with LTL2BA, a group of variations are formed: $\varphi_n = (...(p_1 \mathrm{U} p_2) \mathrm{U}...) \mathrm{U} p_n$. The experimental results are shown in Table 2. As we can see, the size of the BA obtained by PPTL2BA are much more smaller than the ones constructed by LTL2BA.

4   PPTL_SPIN and a Case Study

4.1   Structure of PPTL_SPIN

Based on the transformation tool given in the previous section, we develop a translator which further represents a BA as Never Claim which is acceptable by SPIN. This translator is integrated in SPIN so that PPTL specifications are supported in SPIN. The structure of PPTL_SPIN is shown in Fig. 3.

As shown in Fig. 3, a PPTL parser and translator is integrated in the original SPIN that forms the enhanced tool PPTL_SPIN. With the new tool, first we give a model that specified in the verification language PROMELA. Then we can

Table 1. Comparison on formulae θ_n for $2 \le n \le 8$

	Number of states		Number of transitions	
	PPTL2BA	LTL2BA	PPTL2BA	LTL2BA
θ_2	4	4	8	10
θ_3	4	5	8	15
θ_4	4	6	8	21
θ_5	4	7	8	28
θ_6	4	8	8	36
θ_7	4	9	8	45
θ_8	4	10	8	55
Average	4	7	8	30

Table 2. Comparison on the formulae φ'_n/φ_n for $2 \le n \le 8$

	States		Transitions	
	PPTL2BA	LTL2BA	PPTL2BA	LTL2BA
φ'_2/φ_2	5	2	11	3
φ'_3/φ_3	6	6	16	17
φ'_4/φ_4	7	15	22	73
φ'_5/φ_5	8	37	29	311
φ'_6/φ_6	9	89	37	1290
φ'_7/φ_7	10	209	46	5207
φ'_8/φ_8	11	481	56	20548
Average	8	120	31	3921

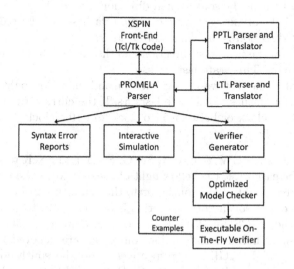

Fig. 3. Structure of PPTL_SPIN

choose PPTL or LTL to express the property. If we choose PPTL to express the property, the PPTL parser and translator is invoked to transform the negation of this formula to a Büchi automaton. Finally we execute the verification. If the result is not valid, a counterexample will be provided.

4.2 Case Study: Verifying Traffic Light Control System with PPTL_SPIN

Traffic Light Control System (TLCS) is common in our daily life. As we all know, the duration of the green lights for the main road should be longer than that of the red lights in the rush hours. Now a simple rule is made for TLCS. We assume there are two modes in the system. Mode 1 represents the rush hours and mode 0 represents the other time. When the current time is between 7 o'clock and 9 o'clock or between 17 o'clock and 19 o'clock, the system is in mode 1.

Specifically, TLCS works as follows:

(1) The system starts at 0 o'clock.
(2) The mode of the system is set to 0. The green light of the east-west direction and the red light of the south-north direction are on. This state lasts for 25 s.
(3) The yellow light of the east-west direction flashes and the red light of the south-north direction is on. This state lasts 5 s.
(4) The red light of the east-west direction and the green light of the south-north direction are on. This state lasts 25 s.
(5) The red light of the east-west direction is on and the yellow light of the south-north direction flashes. This state lasts 5 s. If the current time is between 7 o'clock and 9 o'clock or between 17 o'clock and 19 o'clock, the next step is (6), otherwise the next step is (2).
(6) The mode of the system is set as 1. The green light of the east-west direction and the red light of the south-north direction are on. This state lasts 30 s.
(7) The yellow light of the east-west direction flashes and the red light of the south-north direction is on. This state lasts 5 s.
(8) The red light of the east-west direction and the green light of the south-north direction are on. This state lasts 20 s.
(9) The red light of the east-west direction is on and the yellow light of the south-north direction flashes. This state lasts 5 s. If the current time is between 7 o'clock and 9 o'clock or between 17 o'clock and 19 o'clock, the next step is (6), otherwise the next step is (2).

Here we use EW_G, EW_Y, EW_R, SN_G, SN_Y and SN_R to represent the green light of the east-west, the yellow light of the east-west, the red light of the east-west, the green light of the south-north, the yellow light of the south-north or the red light of the south-north direction is on, respectively.

We model the TLCS by PROMELA as shown in appendix. In the program, the east-west lights in red, yellow and green are denoted by EW_RED, EW_YELLOW, and EW_GREEN respectively, and the south-north lights in red, yellow and green are denoted by SN_RED, SN_YELLOW, and SN_GREEN respectively. We use boolean variable *sign* to denote the mode and int variable t to denote the time. If the current time is between 7 o'clock and 9 o'clock or between 17 o'clock and 19 o'clock, the value of *sign* is true, that is to say it is in mode 1.

First we consider a safety property. At any state, when the green light of the east-west direction is on, the yellow light and the red light of the east-west direction are off. So does the south-north direction. We can specify this property by the PPTL formula:

$$P \equiv \Box((p \rightarrow (q \wedge r)) \wedge (s \rightarrow (t \wedge v)))$$

and we define p, q, r, s, v, t as follows:

#define p EW_GREEN==true
#define q EW_YELLOW==false
#define r EW_RED==false
#define s SN_GREEN==true
#define t SN_YELLOW==false
#define v SN_RED==false

Using the PPTL_SPIN, it can be obtained that the property is valid on the model.

Now we check a periodically repeated property in mode 0. The property is that in every four states the green light of the east-west direction and the red light of the south-north direction are on and the mode is 0. This property cannot be described by an LTL formula. We specify this property by the PPTL formula:

$$P \equiv (p \wedge q \wedge r); (\bigcirc^4 (p \wedge q \wedge r))^*$$

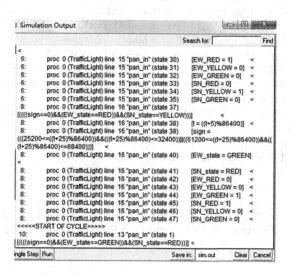

Fig. 4. An error trail that does not satisfy property P

The PROMELA model of TLCS

```
mtype=RED,YELLOW,GREEN
bool EW_RED=false,EW_YELLOW=false,EW_GREEN=true;
bool SN_RED=true,SN_YELLOW=false,SN_GREEN=false;
bool sign=false;
int t=0;
active proctype TrafficLight(){
  byte EW_state=GREEN;
  byte SN_state=RED;
  do
    :: atomic{(sign==false)&&(EW_state==GREEN)&&(SN_state==RED) ->
       t=(t+25)%86400;sign=false;EW_state=YELLOW;SN_state=RED;
       EW_RED=false;EW_YELLOW=true;EW_GREEN=false;SN_RED=true;
       SN_YELLOW=false;SN_GREEN=false;}
    :: atomic{(sign==false)&&(EW_state==YELLOW)&&(SN_state==RED) ->
       t=(t+5)%86400;sign=false;EW_state=RED;SN_state=GREEN;
       EW_RED=true;EW_YELLOW=false;EW_GREEN=false;SN_RED=false;
       SN_YELLOW=false;SN_GREEN=true;}
    :: atomic{(sign==false)&&(EW_state==RED)&&(SN_state==GREEN) ->
       t=(t+25)%86400;sign=false;EW_state=RED;SN_state=YELLOW;
       EW_RED=true;EW_YELLOW=false;EW_GREEN=false;SN_RED=false;
       SN_YELLOW=true;SN_GREEN=false;}
    :: atomic{(sign==false)&&(EW_state==RED)&&(SN_state==YELLOW) ->
       t=(t+5)%86400;sign=(25200<=((t+25)%86400) &&((t+25)%86400)
       <=32400|| 61200<=((t+25)%86400) &&((t+25)%86400)<=68400);
       EW_state=GREEN; SN_state=RED;EW_RED=false;EW_YELLOW=false;
       EW_GREEN=true;SN_RED=true;SN_YELLOW=false;SN_GREEN=false;}
    :: atomic{(sign==true)&&(EW_state==GREEN)&&(SN_state==RED) ->
       t=(t+30)%86400;sign=true;EW_state=YELLOW;SN_state=RED;
       EW_RED=false;EW_YELLOW=true;EW_GREEN=false;SN_RED=true;
       SN_YELLOW=false;SN_GREEN=false;}
    :: atomic{(sign==true)&&(EW_state==YELLOW)&&(SN_state==RED) ->
       t=(t+5)%86400;sign=true; EW_state=RED; SN_state=GREEN;
       EW_RED=true;EW_YELLOW=false;EW_GREEN=false;SN_RED=false;
       SN_YELLOW=false;SN_GREEN=true;}
    :: atomic{(sign==true)&&(EW_state==RED)&&(SN_state==GREEN) ->
       t=(t+20)%86400; sign=true;EW_state=RED; SN_state=YELLOW;
       EW_RED=true;EW_YELLOW=false;EW_GREEN=false;SN_RED=false;
       SN_YELLOW=true;SN_GREEN=false;}
    :: atomic{(sign==true)&&(EW_state==RED)&&(SN_state==YELLOW) ->
       t=(t+5)%86400;sign=(25200<=((t+30)%86400) &&((t+30)%86400)
       <=32400 —— 61200<=((t+30)%86400) &&((t+30)%86400)<=68400);
       EW_state=GREEN; SN_state=RED;EW_RED=false;EW_YELLOW=false;
       EW_GREEN=true;SN_RED=true;SN_YELLOW=false;SN_GREEN=false;}
  od;
}
```

where p, q, and r are defined as follows:

#define p sign==false
#define q EW_GREEN==true
#define r SN_RED==true

With PPTL_SPIN, it is obtained that this property is not valid on the model. Meanwhile, a counterexample which shows how the property is violated is provided as shown in Fig. 4. Intuitively, this property is not satisfied when the TLCS turns to rush when the mode is 1 and sign is true.

5   Conclusion

We present a tool PPTL_SPIN which enhances SPIN with PPTL specification and shows how it works with a case study. Experiment shows that the tool works well in practice. However, the time complexity of constructing LNFGs is high when full regular properties are given. We will reduce the time of constructing BAs and the state space of the system model in the future.

References

1. Duan, Z., Tian, C., Zhang, L.: A decision procedure for propositional projection temporal logic with infinite models. Acta Inform. **45**(1), 43–78 (2008)
2. Duan, Z., Tian, C.: A practical decision procedure for propositional projection temporal logic with infinite models. Theor. Comput. Sci. **554**, 169–190 (2014). doi:10.1016/j.tcs.2014.02.011
3. Duan, Z.: Temporal Logic and Temporal Logic Programming. Science Press, Beijing (2006)
4. Tian, C., Duan, Z.: Model checking propositional projection temporal logic based on SPIN. In: Butler, M., Hinchey, M.G., Larrondo-Petrie, M.M. (eds.) ICFEM 2007. LNCS, vol. 4789, pp. 246–265. Springer, Heidelberg (2007)
5. Duan, Z.: An extended interval temporal logic and a framing technique for temporal logic programming. Ph.D. thesis, University of Newcastle upon Tyne (1996)
6. Tian, C., Duan, Z.: Expressiveness of propositional projection temporal logic. Theor. Comput. Sci. **412**(18), 1729–1744 (2011). doi:10.1016/j.tcs.2010.12.047
7. Clarke, E.M., Grumberg, O., Peled, D.A.: Model Checking. MIT Press, Cambridge (1999)
8. Duan, Z., Tian, C.: An improved decision procedure for propositional projection temporal logic. In: Dong, J.S., Zhu, H. (eds.) ICFEM 2010. LNCS, vol. 6447, pp. 90–105. Springer, Heidelberg (2010)
9. Gastin, P., Oddoux, D.: Fast LTL to Büchi automata translation. CAV 2001. LNCS, vol. 2102, pp. 53–65. Springer, Heidelberg (2001)
10. Holzmann, G.J.: The model checker spin. IEEE Trans. Softw. Eng. **23**(5), 279–295 (1997)
11. Duan, Z., Tian, C., Tian, C., Duan, Z.: Propositional projection temporal logic, Büchi automata and ω-regular expressions. In: Agrawal, M., Du, D.-Z., Duan, Z., Li, A. (eds.) TAMC 2008. LNCS, vol. 4978, pp. 47–58. Springer, Heidelberg (2008)
12. Pnueli, A.: The temporal logic of programs. In: Proceedings of 18th IEEE Symposium Foundations of Computer Science, pp. 46–57 (1977)

Automatic Transformation from SOFL Module Specifications to Program Structures

Xiongwen Luo$^{(\boxtimes)}$ and Shaoying Liu$^{(\boxtimes)}$

Department of Computer and Information Sciences, Hosei University, Tokyo, Japan
Xiongwen.luo.2b@stu.hosei.ac.jp, sliu@hosei.ac.jp

Abstract. The Structured Object-oriented Formal Language (SOFL) method is developed to overcome the disadvantages of existing formal methods and provide effective techniques for writing formal specifications and carrying out verification and testing. Although it has been applied to system modeling and design in practical and research projects, SOFL has not been widely applied to the industrial software development systems because of the lack of efficient tool support. Aiming at improving the existing SOFL supporting tool and solving the problem that the formal specifications cannot be directly executed, this paper firstly analyzes the relationship between the structures of SOFL formal specifications and C# programs, and then discusses how module transformation and data type transformations are implemented. Finally, a testing is performed to ensure the reliability of the implemented software system.

Keywords: SOFL · Specification transformations · Data type · Programs

1 Introduction

Specification-based testing and inspection for programs are two major techniques in the SOFL method [1], but they are facing challenges due to possible inconsistency between SOFL formal specifications and programs in some programming language such as Java or C#. The inconsistency may exist in process signatures, data types, or the structure of the documents. A process in SOFL is an operation transforming input to output, but with multiple input and/or output ports, which differs from an operation in other formal notations, such as VDM [2], Z [3], and B-Method [3]. When a process is implemented in a program, it is usually realized by a method in a class. It is highly possible that the parameters of the method are inconsistent with those of the process in the specification. Further, the data types adopted in SOFL, such as set, sequence, map, composite types, may be easily implemented using similar data types in the programming language, but the associated operators defined on those types may be represented using the different syntax in both the specification and the program. Thus, test cases generated based on the specification may not be directly applicable in executing the program for testing. This sets a big hurdle for a complete automatic testing technique to be established.

To deal with this problem, in this paper we describe a new approach called *signature-preserved transformation*. The essential points of the approach are threefold.

© Springer International Publishing Switzerland 2016
S. Liu and Z. Duan (eds.): SOFL+MSVL 2015, LNCS 9559, pp. 206–218, 2016.
DOI: 10.1007/978-3-319-31220-0_15

Firstly, the signature of each process in the specification is automatically transformed into a method signature that preserves the number of the parameters and their types declared in the process specification. The body of the method is left to the programmer to complete manually based on the pre- and post-conditions of the process specification. Secondly, all of the SOFL data types and all the associated operators are implemented in the programming language in the manner their syntax is almost preserved. Thus, once the package containing the implementation classes of the data types is imported, the same operators with the same syntax in SOFL can be directly used in the program. This will facilitate the application of test cases generated from the specification to the program implementing the specification. Finally, the structure of the entire module structure can be automatically transformed into a class structure in which all of the related constants, type declarations, state variable declarations are properly presented.

The rest of this paper is organized as follows. Section 2 briefly describes the structure of module in SOFL. Section 3 analyzes the principles of transformation. These transformations are process transformation, module structure transformation, and data type transformation. Section 4 discusses the design and implementation of transformation. Section 5 presents the testing of the programming for verifying the validation and reliability of the programs. The related work is given in Sect. 6. Finally, the last section, Sect. 7, concludes the work of this paper, and points out the future research directions.

2   The SOFL Module

In this section, we briefly introduce the structure of a SOFL module in order to help the reader understand our discussions on automatic transformation late in the paper.

A module in SOFL is a textual document defining the semantics of all of the components occurring in an associated condition data flow diagram (CDFD) [3]. The most important part of the module is the process specifications. Each process models a transformation from input data flows to output data flows and its functionality is specified

```
module ModuleName
const ConstantDeclaration;
type TypeDeclaration;
var VariableDeclaration;
inv TypeandStateInvariants;
behav CDFD_no;
InitializationProcess;
process_1;
process_2;
        ...
function_1;
function_2;
        ...
function_m;
end_module
```

Fig. 1. Structure of module

using pre- and post-conditions. All of the data flows are associated with processes in the way they are used as either input or output. Each process can also access or update some data stores where each data store is represented by a variable of some type. For the purpose of constructing the process specifications, necessary constants identifiers and type identifiers may need to be declared, and all of the data store variables must be declared with proper types in the module, as illustrated in Fig. 1. Another important part is function definitions. Functions can be applied in the pre- or post-conditions of some process specifications, but for this purpose, they must be defined either explicitly or implicitly. We omit the details here for the sake of space. The reader who is interested in the details can refer to the SOFL book [3].

3   Principles of Transformation

In this section, we focus on the principles for process transformation, module struc-ture transformation, and data type transformation. From the next section, we will extend our discussion to the implementation of the transformation principles.

3.1   Process Transformation

A process, basically, consists of five parts: process name, input data flow variables, output data flow variables, pre-condition and post-condition. The process presents an action or operation that consumes the input data flows and generates the output data flows. If there are external variables that need to be used in this process, they are stated after the keyword **ext**. A complex process may be decomposed into the lower level CDFD whose associated module is written after the keyword **decom**. The keyword **comment** starts the informal comment section, which is usually written to improve the readability of the formal specifications (Fig. 2).

```
process ProcessName(input) output
ext ExternalVariable
pre PreCondition
post PostCondition
decom LowerLevelModuleName
explicit ExplicitSpecification
comment
end_process
```

Fig. 2. The structure of process

As process is one of the most essential parts in module [4], we firstly transform the process to the programs. The process has two types: one is the single-port process with only one input port and one output port, the other is the multiple-port process with exclusive input or output data flows. When dealing with the transformations of process, we implement these two types in two different forms.

```
process A(x_1: Ti_1, x_2: Ti_2, ..., x_n: Ti_n)
      y_1: To_1, y_2: To_2, ..., y_m:To_m
pre pre_A
post post_A
end_process
```

```
class ModuleName{
To_1 y_1;
To_2 y_2;
...
To_m y_m;
public void A(Ti_1 x_1, Ti_2 x_2, ..., Ti_n x_n){
      if(pre_A) Tran(post_A)
   ...
   }
}
```

Fig. 3. General form of single-port process   **Fig. 4.** Transformation of single-port process

Firstly, the general form of single-port process is presented in the Fig. 3, and transforming this process into method is shown in Fig. 4.

Then, the general form of multiple-port process is presented in the Fig. 5, and transforming this process into method is shown in Fig. 6.

```
process A(x_1: Ti_1| x_2: Ti_2 | ... | x_n: Ti_n)
      y_1: To_1 | y_2: To_2 | ... | y_m:To_m
pre pre_A
post post_A
end_process
```

Fig. 5. General form of multiple-port process

```
class ModuleName{
To_1 y_1;
To_2 y_2;
...
To_m y_m
public To_1 A_y_1(Ti_1 x_1, Ti_2 x_2, ..., Ti_n x_n){
      if(pre_A(x_1))
   {
      Tran(post_A)
   }
}
public To_2 A_y_2(Ti_1 x_1, Ti_2 x_2, ..., Ti_n x_n){
      if(pre_A(x_2))
   {
      Tran(post_A)
   }
}
...
public To_m A_y_m(Ti_1 x_1, Ti_2 x_2, ..., Ti_n x_n){
      if(pre_A(x_n))
   {
      Tran(post_A)
   }
}
}
```

Fig. 6. Transformation of multiple-port process

3.2   Module Transformation

As illustrated in Fig. 1, the beginning of the module is the keyword **module**. *Module-Name* is a unique identifier of module in SOFL specifications. The key words **const**,

type and **var** start the sections for constant declarations, type declarations, and variable declarations respectively. The key word **inv** stands for the type and state invariants, which represents the constraints on the type declarations section and variable declarations section. The *CDFD_no* after the key word **behav** specifies the affiliated CDFD. The last two parts, beginning with keyword **process** and **function**, offers some processes and functions.

Apparently, a module is similar to a class in C# in structure. Therefore, we take the straightforward principle to transform a module into a C# class. Specifically, the ideas of transforming each part of the module are given as follows:

- Transform the constant declaration to the constant in C#, using the keyword **const** prior to the constant variables.
- Transform the type declaration to either a basic type or a class, whose form is in compliance with C# language syntax. However, the data type is written in SOFL language, so that it needs to be implemented by C# language as I discuss later.
- Transform the variable declarations to the instance variables, stored and accessed in the external file, but used in this transformation class.
- Transform the processes to the target methods.
- Transform the functions to the target methods, which are similar to that of processes.

3.3 Data Type Transformation

Data types, an essential part for specifications, provide a notation to define data structures in the SOFL formal specification [5]. Although we can transform a module to a class in the programming language, only completing data type transformations can the results of module transformations be used for final automatic specifications testing. Because the data types in SOFL are not identical with C# language data types both in semantics and syntax [6], we cannot directly execute the results of module transformations. In other words, it attaches no significance to the transformations of module without the data type transformations. Only with the support of data types transformations, results of module transformations can be used for specifications and program testing.

In SOFL language, the data types are divided into two categories: built-in type and user-defined types. The built-in types have fourteen kinds of data types, which are further divided into basic types and compound types. The basic types include *nat0* type, *nat* type, *int* type, *real* type, *bool* type, *char* type, *string* type and *Enumeration* type, while the compound types are: *set* type, *sequence* type, *composite* type, *map* type, *product* type and *union* type. The user-defined types are defined by the specification writers. They are based on the built-in data types, so the transformation guidelines of built-in data types also apply to the transformation of user-defined types.

It is worth noting that transformations from data types in SOFL to the data types in C# language require both semantics preservation and syntactic changes [7]. Firstly, the syntax of variable declaration in SOFL language is not identical with that of variable declaration in C#. The former lets the type appear behind the variable with a colon separating them, while the latter makes the type appear prior to the variable with a space between them. What is more, in the semantics perspective, some of the types are in accordance with that in C#, such as *int* type, *char* type, *string* type, *bool* type and *Enumeration* type. While some of the types are similar to that in C#, for example *nat0* type, *nat* type and *real* type. In addition, some of the types are different from that in C#, for instance, *set* type, *sequence* type, *composite* type, *map* type, *product* type and *union* type.

In general, the choice of the concrete data types in the transformation will affect somehow the algorithms of the implemented program using the data types [8, 9]. Therefore, it is essential to strike a balance between data structures and algorithms. Under this circumstance, we consider that some of the data types do not need to be transformed, as they have already existed in the C# and can be executed directly. While some of the data types need to be implemented by the similar data types available in C#, the transformations of which can be quite straightforward owing to the support of.Net platform with rich data structures and class libraries.

Based on this analysis, we adopt several principles for data type transformation summarized as follows:

- The *int* type, *char* type, *string* type, *bool* type, and *Enumeration* type do not need to be transformed because they have already existed in C# and can be used directly.
- The *nat0* type defines the natural numbers including zero and *nat* type defines the natural numbers, so that these two types can be implemented by *int* type in C#.
- The *real* type represents the real numbers, which can be implemented by *double* type in C#.
- The *set* type is an unordered collection of distinct objects, which is similar to the *HashSet* type in C#, so it is natural to implement it through *HashSet* type.
- The *sequence* type is an ordered collection of objects that allows duplications of objects. Taking this into account, I believe that *List* type in C# is the best choice to implement it.
- The *map* type is a finite set of pairs, the domain and range to the map share the similar meaning with the key and value to the *dictionary* type in C#.
- The *composite* type and *product* type represent a collection of several data items, so the abstract classes are used to implement these two types and their inherent functions.
- The *union* type is a special type associated with several functions. It can be regarded as a collection of variables in different types. We consider that we will transform this type to a class with many fields in C#.

4   Design and Implementation of Transformations

In general, we create three packages to implement the transformations. One is automatic transformation package, and other two are module transformations package and data type transformations package as shown in Fig. 7. In the automatic transformation package, we need to invoke the methods defined in the module transformations package to complete the module transformations. The results of transformations cannot be executed without the support of data type transformations which are completed in data type transformations package.

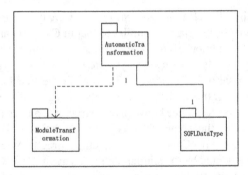

Fig. 7. The structure of transformation framework

The AutomaticTransformation package includes the main class of the transformations, whose *main* method is the entry of the automatic transformations. This package invokes the methods of classes in the ModuleTransformation package and is supported by the classes in the SOFLDataType package.

4.1   Main Program in AutomaticTransformation

The AutomaticTransformation package includes the main program used to complete the automatic transformations. The *main* method in this program is the entry of the automatic transformations and it invokes the methods of classes in the ModuleTransformation package.

In this process, firstly, we enter the path of XML file, and then judge whether the file exists or not. If the XML file exists, we have to enter the output file path and also make a judgement to ensure that the file name is legal. In the next step, we will make a choice to decide whether to start the transformations or not. If we choose to start the transformations, the specifications will be transformed to C# programs. After completing the transformation, the system will terminate.

4.2   Implementation Classes in ModuleTransformation

Figure 8 shows the classes in ModuleTransformation, the details of each class is introduced in the following:

- XmlTool class: The objective of this class is to provide a XML file tool used for extracting the data information of SOFL formal specifications form the XML files. Before executing the transformations process, we should make formal specifications generate the corresponding XML files through the existing SOFL supporting tool, then this class is to parse these XML files to get the data information we need.
- ConstantTransformation class: This class mainly deals with constant declaration in SOFL formal specifications. It contains two methods, one is to get the constant variables and write into the external file, and the other is to judge constant variables types and invoke the former method to write the corresponding constants.
- TypeTransformation class: This class is used to complete the type declaration transformations. Because there are many kinds of different data types, we need to invoke

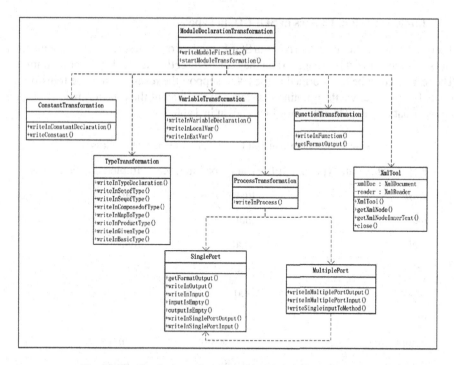

Fig. 8. The implementation classes in ModuleTransformation

different methods to implement the transformations. In other words, each of the compound type transformation uses one method.

- VariableTransformation class: The purpose for this class is to transform the variable declaration section to the programing in C#. Since the variables appearing in this corresponding part are either the local variables or external variables, so we design two methods to implement this process. One is for writing the local variables into target files and the other is for writing the external variables.
- FunctionTransformation class: This class is to handle the transformations from function declaration to programs. Owing to the similar structure with the method in C#, we design a method to write these function declarations into the target files.
- ProcessTransformation class: In this class, a method is defined to judge different cases, and for each case, we invoke the methods of SinglePort class to execute the single-port process transformations and the methods of MultiplePort class to execute the multiple-port process transformations.
- ModuleDeclarationTransformation class: This class is to realize the functions of module transformations by invoking the methods in other classes. It has two methods, one is to write the first line of module and the other is to complete the transformations of other parts in module sequentially.

4.3   Implementation Classes in SOFLDataType

There are fourteen kinds of data types in SOFL, but five of them share the same semantics and syntactic with C# language so that they can be directly executed in the programming. The rests need to be transformed in the C# to support the results of module transformations. In this case, we design nine interfaces to implement the transformations of nine kinds of data types. The relationship is shown in Table 1.

Table 1. Data types in SOFL and their implementation classes

Key word of data type in SOFL	Data type interface	Implementation class
nat0	Inat0	nat0
nat	Inat	nat
real	Ireal	real
set	Iset	set
seq	Iseq	seq
map	Imap	map
composite	Icomposite	composite
product	Iproduct	product
union	Iunion	union

Note that the naming conventions of class in C# is that the first letter of class name is capitalized, but we do not observe this rule because we want to make the name of implementation classes in accordance with the keyword of data type in SOFL, so as to use the implementation classes efficiently and unambiguously. The more details about the design of data type interfaces and the implementations of methods in corresponding classes are presented by the UML class diagram as follows:

We design nine interfaces, which are *Inat0, Inat, Ireal, Iset, Iseq, Imap, Icomposite, Iproduct* and *Iunion*, to implement the transformations of these nine kinds of data types. The methods in each interface are consistent with the operators in the related SOFL data types. Then, the nine classes, which are nat0, nat, real, set<T>, seq<T>, map<T, E>, composite, product and union, are created to implement the corresponding interfaces (Fig. 9).

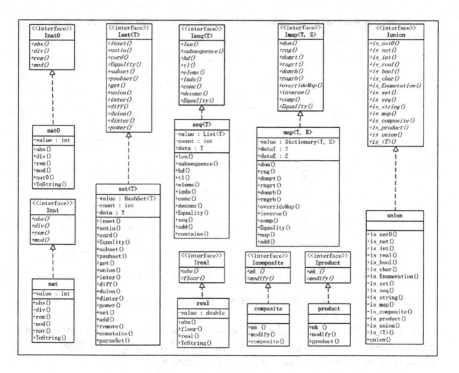

Fig. 9. The implementation classes in SOFLDataType

5   Transformation Results

After the transformation software system is implemented, it is essential to perform a test to detect faults and ensure the validity and robustness of the system. In order to check whether each function in the transformations can be used correctly, we adopt the black-box testing method to test the transformations process. Firstly, unit testing method is used to test each transformation section, and then the integration testing methods are adopted to ensure the success of the entire transformations (Fig. 10).

The testing procedures can also be the guidance of how to use these programs to make the automatic transformation, which are listed as follows:

1. Using the existing SOFL supporting tool to create the formal specifications and draw the related CDFDs [10].

    In the existing SOFL supporting tool, we can use the three-step approach to constructing the formal specifications. The structure of the components in current project is displayed in the upper-left corner. In the center, a CDFD related to the module is drawn. If one item in the CDFD is selected, the attributes of it will be presented in the lower-left corner. The module in detail is written in the right side.

2. Generating the related XML file through the existing SOFL supporting tool.

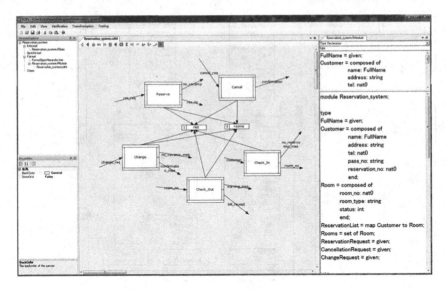

Fig. 10. Snapshot of the SOFL formal specification of a hotel reservation system

In Fig. 11, the names of labels are related to the corresponding keywords in the SOFL formal specifications constructed in step 1. For example, the label "module" is related to the keyword **module** in the specification.

```
 2  □<module name="Reservation_system">
 3  □    <constantDeclaration>
 4       </constantDeclaration>
 5  □    <typeDeclaration>FullName = given;
 6       Customer = composed of
 7                      name: FullName
 8                      address: string
 9                      tel: nat0
10                      pass_no: string
11                      reservation_no: nat0
12                      end;
13       Room = composed of
14                  room_no: nat0
15                  room_type: string
16                  status: int
17                  end;
18       ReservationList = map Customer to Room;
19       Rooms = set of Room;
20       ReservationRequest = given;
21       CancellationRequest = given;
22       ChangeRequest = given;</typeDeclaration>
23  □    <variableDeclaration>rlist:ReservationList;
24       rooms:Rooms;</variableDeclaration>
25  □    <typeAndStateInvariants>
26       </typeAndStateInvariants>
27  □    <moduleDecom>
28       </moduleDecom>
29  □    <processList>
30  □        <process name="Reserve" head="(res_req: ReservationRequest)no_vacancy: string | res_no: nat0">pre.
31       post...</process>
32  □        <process name="Cancel" head="(cancel_req: CancellationRequest)confirmation: string">pre...
33       post...</process>
34  □        <process name="Change" head="(change_req: Change_Request)no_vavancy_mes: string | confirmation_me:
35       post...</process>
```

Fig. 11. XML file of the related SOFL formal specification

3. Using the software system we have developed to parse the XML file and complete the transformation. A result of the transformation is presented in Fig. 12.

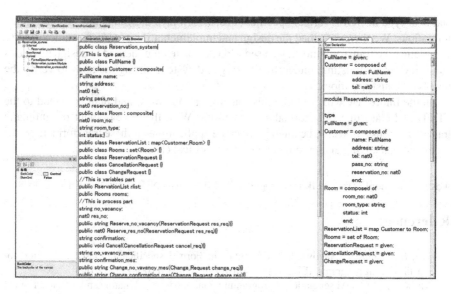

Fig. 12. Results of transformations

In Fig. 12, the module name is related to the class name. The constant declarations in the module are transformed to the constant variables. The type declarations are transformed to either a basic type or a class. The variable declarations are transformed to the instance variables. The process and function are implemented by the target methods.

6   Related Work

There exist some tools to support automatic transformation from other formal notation to programming languages. VDMTools [11] offer the functions of analyzing the system models expressed in the formal language of VDM, which has been applied to developing industrial software systems. The VDM specification can be executed directly through the interpreter inside this tool. ProB [12] is a validation toolset for the B method. In this tool, a model checker and a refinement checker can be used for executing the B specifications to detect various errors. UPPAAL [13] is a verification tool for timed automate. In UPPAAL, there is no textual specification, but user can construct the finite state machine to module the functions of a system, which can be executed in this tool to detect faults.

7   Conclusions and Future Work

In this paper, we discuss the principles and implementation of automatic transformations from SOFL formal specifications to programs. We first analyzed the module structure and data type in SOFL formal specifications, which lays the foundation for the transformations. We then described the design and implementation of transformations. After completing the transformations, we used a black-box testing method to design test cases and carry out unit testing, integration testing and system testing methods to verify the results of transformations.

In the future, we will continue this transformations work and plan to extend to the CDFD and class in SOFL formal specifications. With the development of automatic transformations, we would be interesting in the applications of these transformations for specifications testing and automatic generation of test cases.

Acknowledgment.   This work was supported by JSPS KAKENHI Grant Number 26240008.

References

1. Liu, S., Chen, Y., Nagoya, F., McDermid, J.: Formal specification-based inspection for verification of programs. IEEE Trans. Softw. Eng. **38**(5), 1100–1122 (2012)
2. Mosses, P.D.: VDM semantics of programming language: combinators and monads. Formal Aspects Comput. **23**, 221–238 (2011)
3. Liu, S.: Formal Engineering for Industrial Software Development: Using the SOFL Method. Springer, Heidelberg (2004). ISBN 3-540-20602-7
4. Liu, S.: An approach to applying SOFL for agile process and its application in developing a test support tool. Innovations Syst. Softw. Eng. **6**(1), 137–143 (2009). Springer
5. Zainuddin, F.B., Liu, S.: An approach to low-fidelity prototyping based on SOFL informal specification. In: IEEE APSEC (2012), ISSN: 1530-1362/12
6. Miao, W., Liu, S.: Service-oriented modeling using the SOFL formal engineering method. In: IEEE APSCC (2009), ISBN: 978-1-4244-5336-8/09
7. Liu, S., Xue, X.: Automated software specification and design using the SOFL formal engineering method. In: IEEE WCSE (2009), ISBN: 978-0-7685-3570-8/09
8. Chen, Y., Liu, S., Nagoya, F.: A Framework for SOFL-based Program Review. In: IEEE ICECCS (2005), ISBN: 0-7695-2284-X/05
9. Chen, Y.: A case study of using SOFL to specify a concurrent software system. In: IEEE (2010), ISBN: 978-1-4244-6055-7/10
10. Li, M., Liu, S.: Tool support for rigorous formal specification inspection. In: IEEE CSE 2014 (2014), ISBN: 978-1-4799-7981-3/14
11. Fitzgerald, J., Larsen, P.G., Sahare, S.: VDMTools: advances in support for formal modeling in VDM. ACM SIGPLAN Not. **43**(2), 3–11 (2008)
12. Leuschel, M., Butler, M.: PROB: an automated analysis toolset for the B method. Int. J. Softw. Tools Technol. Transf. **10**, 185–203 (2008)
13. Behrmann, G., David, A., Larsen, K.G.: UPPAAL 4.0. In: IEEE QEST06 (2006), ISBN: 0-7695-2665-9/06

Author Index

Printed in the United States
By Bookmasters